THE PAINTER'S EYE

Henry James, 1906. Photograph by Alice Boughton. Reproduced by permission of the Houghton Library, Harvard University.

The Painter's Eye

NOTES AND ESSAYS ON THE PICTORIAL ARTS BY

HENRY JAMES

SELECTED AND EDITED
WITH AN INTRODUCTION BY
JOHN L. SWEENEY

WITH A FOREWORD BY
SUSAN M. GRIFFIN

THE UNIVERSITY OF WISCONSIN PRESS

The University of Wisconsin Press
114 North Murray Street
Madison, Wisconsin 53715

3 Henrietta Street
London WC2E, 8LU, England

First Wisconsin printing
Originally published in 1956 by Rupert Hart-Davis
Introduction by John L. Sweeney reprinted with the
permission of Grafton Books, A Division of the
Collins Publishing Group, 8 Grafton Street,
London WIX 3LA

Printed in the United States of America

Library of Congress Cataloging-in-Publication Data
James, Henry, 1843–1916.
The painter's eye.
Reprint. Originally published:
London: R. Hart-Davis, 1956.
1. Art, Modern—19th century. I. Sweeney, John L.
II. Title.
N6450.J36   1989   759.05   89-40258
ISBN 0-299-12280-8
ISBN 0-299-12284-0 (pbk.)

CONTENTS

THE PAINTER'S EYE

FOREWORD

When *The Painter's Eye* first appeared in 1956, reviews were almost uniformly laudatory. Yet most of the reviewers were also united in their amusement at the image of Henry James that introduces the collection. Formally dressed and top-hatted, James stands, with gloves and stick in hand, closely inspecting a painting. For the modernist critic of the 1950s, this figure captured James's identity as eminent Victorian and implied the drawbacks of that lofty position. Despite the generally enthusiastic response, nearly all the reviews of *The Painter's Eye* at some point characterized James's essays as, variously, moralistic, elitist, aesthetic, insufficiently technical, inappropriately literary, flawed in judgment (admirative of Burne-Jones, disdainful of the Impressionists), and frivolous in their extra-artistic concern with the personality, psychology, and nationality of both painters and viewers. However, recent reevaluations of Victorian art, rethinkings of modernist notions of artistic purity, and rehistoricizing of James's own work enable us to recognize the acute eye of the professional artist beneath that top hat. While we may not share all of James's judgments on individual painters, we can begin to recover the art critic whose writings Ruskin so valued that he wished James to succeed him as Slade Professor.

Immersed in the nineteenth-century art world in all its variety, James's art criticism shows the influence of critics as diverse as Ruskin and Taine yet confronts on its own terms the practical and theoretical artistic questions of his time: the Whistler-Ruskin controversy; the connections and distinctions between "the sister arts" ("literary" art criticism, "narrative" painting); the possibility of morality and the

perniciousness of moralism in art; the relationships between caricature, journalism, and the political history of a
culture; the relative values of Pre-Raphaelitism, Realism,
and Impressionism. Reviewing official Academy exhibitions, "alternative" shows, and private galleries in France,
England, and America, James charts the nineteenth-century
shift from aristocratic patronage to mass (or at least middle-
class) culture, from the epoch of "lordly" art purchases to
the era of "paying a shilling to an extremely civil person in
a front shop" on Bond Street (137).

The pieces that compose *The Painter's Eye* display at
every point James's pragmatic cognizance of the dynamic
interrelationship of critic, artist, audience, market, and object. Of James's essays on the theatre, Allen Wade asserts:
"In all his criticism it is not merely the play and the acting
that he has in mind, but also the social setting—the state of
affairs, moral and intellectual, which makes it possible for
that particular form of theatrical art, whatever it may be, to
find acceptance." In his art criticism, too, James analyzes the
interplay between the work of art and its societal "setting,"
the ways in which what he calls "the language of painting"
(220) constructs and is constructed by a culture. For James,
analyzing a work of art in context means considering not
only the paintings that physically surround it (French pictures in Boston "form a group interesting in more ways
than one—as to the reciprocal light they shed upon each
other" [43]), but also the gallery in which the picture is
hung, the neighborhood and city in which the gallery is
located (see his discussion of the Wallace collection at Bethnal Green), the natures of the audience that views the painting and the patron who purchases it—even the price paid
for it.

In fact, sometimes a too credulous viewer can see nothing but the price tag. "If a certain number of persons have
been found to agree that such and such an enormous sum
is a proper valuation of a picture, a book, or a song at a

concert, it is very hard not to be rather touched with awe and to see a certain golden *reflet* in the performance," James observes (109). Writing at the moment of the "democratization of all tastes and fashions" (137), the nineteenth-century critic's task is both to take into account and, at times, to counter such valuations. "Art, at the present day, is being steadily and rapidly vulgarized (we do not here use the word in the invidious sense); it appeals to greater numbers of people than formerly, and the gate of communication has had to be widened, perhaps in a rather barbarous fashion" (89). The threat of barbarism, a threat that James feels increasingly with the years, means that in viewing the painting, the critic must not only act as the audience's representative but also play a central role in its aesthetic education. Speaking of the Duke of Montpensier's gift of pictures to the Boston Athenaeum, James argues that while gratitude is appropriate, "it is of still more importance that people in general in this part of the world should not form an untruthful estimate of the works now at the Athenaeum" (86). For James, the life of the critic "is heroic, for it is immensely vicarious. He has to understand for others, to answer for them" ("Criticism" 1891).

The critic is heroic for the artist's sake as well. James finds this dual allegiance in the work of French critics who position themselves as mediators between artist and audience: "They examine pictures . . . with an equal regard to the standpoint of the painter and that of the spectator, whom the painter must always be supposed to address" (35). Himself financially dependent upon the sale of his art, James is acutely aware of the ways that the nationality, education, taste, and experience of an audience can enter into artistic creation. His agreement to write essay-letters for the *New York Tribune*, three of which are collected here, ends because, as he says in response to his publishers's request for shorter and more newsy contributions, "If my letters have been 'too good' I am honestly afraid that they are the

poorest I can do, especially for the money!" (letter to
Whitelaw Reid, August 30, 1876). Despite—or rather because of—such lessons in market economy, James's discus-
sions of painting do not deplore the unavoidable fact that
the artistic object functions in his culture as a commodity.
What they do decry is the smug, Philistine taste of the British consumer. "Reading into the impression produced" by
a picture, discovering "the public involved or implied, the
public addressed and aimed at, wooed, whether won or not,
and on theory at all events to be captured" (255), James
finds that in England the implied audience is "the British
merchant and paterfamilias and his excellently regulated
family" (148). Too many painters are painting "down" to
this group's demand for moralizing lessons "without a
struggle, without a protest" (148). Even the talented Millais
paints Lily Langtrey "as if he meant to make her pass for
the heroine of a serial in a magazine" (169). As this example makes clear, James feels that nineteenth-century
painting has also been corrupted by technological change;
a proliferation of photographic likenesses, magazine illustrations, and advertising images has altered audience expec-
tations, and perhaps even artists' eyes (of Frederick Leighton, James quips, "His texture is too often that of the glaze
on the lid of a prune-box; his drawing too often that of the
figures that smile at us from the covers of these receptacles"
[214–15]). The artist needs to be cognizant of, but not cir-
cumscribed by, the demands of the marketplace.

In describing the negative power of the British audience,
James points to what he sees as an imbalance in the relationships among artist, art object, and audience. James's
criticism, like that of the French, restores the necessary balance, and in doing so proves useful to the artist once again.
What James demonstrates in his position as representative
viewer is that a critical encounter with a painting entails the
imaginative recreation of the artist's act of creation. James
is explicit about the necessity of this critical revision. The

fancy that informs Decamps' painting is "the same faculty which exists in most of us, and which, we should never forget, helps us to enjoy as well as to judge" (74). At its best, Sargent's painting "arouses even in the profane spectator something of the painter's sense, the joy of engaging also, by sympathy, in the solution of the artistic problem" (219).

The writer who in rereading his works for the New York Edition will take "his whole unfolding, his process of production, for a thrilling tale, almost for a wondrous adventure" (Preface to *Roderick Hudson*) finds that the paintings which interest him most are those in which he can discern precisely such a thrilling tale of artistic production. To read a painting in this way is not to respond to "the importunately narrative quality of the usual English picture" (150), to the didactic, the anecdotal, or the allegorical. Rather, it is to recognize a quality that we might call textuality and that James terms, variously, mystery, suggestiveness, imagination, poetry, atmosphere, metaphysics, and perhaps most tellingly, difficulty. As he says in the Preface to *The Wings of the Dove*, "The enjoyment of a work of art, the acceptance of an irresistible illusion, constituting, to my sense, our highest experience of 'luxury,' the luxury is not greatest, by my consequent measure, when the work asks for as little attention as possible. It is greatest, it is delightfully, divinely great, when we feel the surface, like the thick ice of the skater' s pond, bear without cracking the strongest pressure we throw on it." James's repeated contention in *The Painter's Eye* that painting's purpose is the viewer's enjoyment is not a demand for familiar, comfortable, genteel art, any more than his recognition in "The Art of Fiction" (1884) that certain readers will "like" certain subjects represents a call for conventional love stories with happy endings. Instead, James is claiming the pleasurable "luxury" of difficulty as the beholder' s share. The works of Turner, Tintoretto, Michelangelo, and above all, Delacroix represent "a genius in

actual, visible contact—and conflict—with the ever-
reluctant possibilities of the subject in hand" (40) and invite
the viewer's reconstruction of the creative problem-solving
process. Indeed, in what many have recognized as his pre-
scient remarks on Sargent, it is the absence of such fruitful
difficulties that troubles James.

This deep interest in artistic problem-solving explains
James's rejection of what he describes in the Preface to *The
Awkward Age* as "the vanity of the *a priori* test of what an
idée-mère may have to give." His reminder that "the palace
of art has many chambers" runs throughout *The Painter's
Eye* like a refrain. This architectural forerunner of the
many-windowed house of fiction embodies the Jamesian
notion that artists must be granted their *données*. To judge
the imaginative talent of Burne-Jones by realist standards is
"idle; the actual does not gain and the artist does not suffer"
(206). What suffers instead is criticism. James makes it clear
that refusal to accept artistic variety results in critical failure; his own 1876 reaction to the Impressionists demonstrates this point. Unable to recover the artistic problem
that engages Impressionism, James lamely falls back on
"the good old rules which decree that beauty is beauty and
ugliness ugliness" (114). Yet despite this early espousal of
dogma, James retains critical flexibility. In his ability to
reassess Impressionism over the years, James rises to his
own description of the critic: "He knows that the whole
honor of the matter, for him, besides the success in his own
eyes, depends upon his being indefatigably supple" ("Criticism" 1891).

An ardent respect for the individuality of the artist fuels
this tireless critical elasticity. Perhaps the finest essays in
The Painter's Eye are those devoted to a single artist whom
James admires, to Delacroix, Sargent, and Daumier. None-
theless, for James, suppleness is especially important when
the critic is not in sympathy with a particular painter or
painting. For example, his oft-quoted negative remarks on

Winslow Homer are embedded in a careful (and generally unquoted) effort to appreciate Homer's individual talent. James insists that "he is a genuine painter," that there is "something one likes about him," that a given picture is "a very honest, and vivid, and manly piece of work" (96–97). Even in his 1876 criticism of the Impressionists, James is not attempting to limit artistic choice. His remarks are based on his judgment (albeit a mistaken one) that the Impressionists are naïve realists who do not understand that artistic selection is unavoidable. This insistence on the artist's discriminating eye remains a constant in James's criticism, informing even his 1914 critique of the "slice of life" school of literature: "there being no question of a slice upon which the further question of when and how to cut it does not wait, the office of method, the idea of choice and comparison, have occupied the ground from the first" ("The New Novel").

Yet while the individuality of the artist's vision (literal as well as metaphoric) is primary for James, the artist's very genius lies in the ability to see as another. This is especially true in the case of portrait painters, for whom, in an extraordinary passage, James confesses a professional envy: "A spectator trying for a different form of representation (I mean in another craft) could wonder what it would have been for himself—what it would have *not* been, rather—to have felt and imagined, with that intensity, during so long a career, so much definitely distinguished life. It could only have been a great adventure, a sort of vicarious thrill" (245). Not only does James's language here anticipate his self-description in the Prefaces, it demonstrates that the point-of-view technique he perfected is not merely technical but also profoundly social in its conception. The artist, like the critic, proceeds vicariously. In his review of "The Letters of Eugène Delacroix," James's statement that "The wiser the artist, and the finer the genius, the more easy will it be to conceive of other points of view, other ways of look-

ing at things, than one's own" (183) is followed immediately by a reference to "the writer of these lines" (184),
artfully implying that the wise artist is both Delacroix and
his critic, Henry James.

The figure of James as artist can also be traced in his
comment that "Nothing tends more to make an observer
doubt whether human nature be worth his hopes than the
absence, among men engaged in a common undertaking, of
a certain mutual respect" (183). The writings contained in
The Painter's Eye combat that doubt by holding out the hope
of an artistic community. Intertwined in an intimacy that is
at times almost an identity, the Jamesian artist, critic, and
audience together create the work of art. Through his own
enactment of these roles, James analyzes the relations
among them and renders to his readers "a sense of the great
breadth of the province of art, and of its intimate relations
with the rest of men's intellectual life" (35).

The Painter's Eye is reprinted here with John L. Sweeney's
useful introduction which sketches James's interest in the
visual arts over the years, focusing particularly on the ways
in which painting and painters entered his work as subjects.
Corrected versions of Sweeney's original appendices, which
list James's writings on art not contained in the collection,
have also been included. My thanks to Beth Basham, who
aided greatly in the preparation of these materials.

SUSAN M. GRIFFIN

University of Louisville

INTRODUCTION

'The most fundamental and general sign of the novel, from one desperate experiment to another, is its being everywhere an effort at *representation*—this is the beginning and the end of it.

'To the art of the brush the novel must return, I hold, to recover whatever may be still recoverable of its sacrificed honour.'

HENRY JAMES: THE LESSON OF BALZAC.

THE 'painter's eye' which John La Farge discerned in the youthful Henry James was, happily, destined to serve the fine art of representation but not in the painter's medium. Throughout the writer's life, however, it sought and studied the products of the painter's arts. In his attention to these Henry James was an appreciative critic, an amateur, rather than a strict connoisseur, and it was in studious enjoyment that he composed his opinions of pictures. He regarded himself as 'a person whose sole relation to pictures is a disposition to enjoy them', content to rest quite comfortably upon his 'personal impressions'. Occasionally he published his impressions, including some comment on sculpture, and from those publications the present selection is drawn.[1] Its purpose is to provide, for those who are interested in the life and work of Henry James, a convenient means of observing a significant tributary of his talent. This volume includes only those articles which most suggestively indicate the extent of James's experience as an 'attentive spectator' of painting and reflect his persistent concern with the question of representation.

Although it is proper to regard most of the articles reprinted in this volume as 'reviews', one may do so with a difference. James distinguished sternly between 'rough-and-ready reviewing' and 'the art of criticism', identifying the former as 'a periodicity of platitude and irrelevance' and the latter as 'the most

[1] See Appendix A (p. 262) for a list of the articles not included in this volume.

complicated and particular of the arts'. His reviewing intentions shared the breadth of his mind and can be best understood if we consider him in the light in which he saw the serviceable literary critic, 'as the real helper of the artist, a torch-bearing outrider, the interpreter, the brother'. His further phrase, 'armed *capà-pie* in curiosity and sympathy', completes the suggestion of chivalrous purpose; quixotic, if you like, but definitely not donnish.

James was well aware of the sensitive, professional boundaries which may be invoked among the various arts and he realized that the practitioners of painting seldom welcome and less often heed the counsels or comments of the *littérateur*. Nevertheless he proudly faced the fact that he was inveterately a *littérateur* and avowed, in extenuation of trespass, a felt responsibility (a willing but not a 'chilling' one) towards 'the question of art'. His claims for the artistic value of such criticism as he offered were modest indeed but he vigorously defended such criticism as practically beneficial at the intermediary level.

We frankly confess it to be our own belief that even an indifferent picture is generally worth more than a good criticism; but we approve of criticism nevertheless. It may be very superficial, very incompetent, very brutal, very pretentious, very preposterous; it may cause an infinite amount of needless chagrin and gratuitous error; it may even blast careers and break hearts; but we are inclined to think that if it were suppressed at a stroke, the painters of our day would sadly miss it, decide that on the whole it had its merits, and at last draw up a petition to have it resuscitated. It makes them more patrons than it mars; it helps them to reach the public and the public to reach them. It talks a good deal of nonsense, but even its nonsense is a useful force. It keeps the question of art before the world, insists upon its importance, and makes it always in order.

Those lines were written in 1875 when James was thirty-two years old. To-day it would be difficult to question the astuteness and accuracy of the practical argument. The real interest, however, lies in James's emphasis on a question which, for him, was more meaningful than even 'the question of our speech'. But one may fairly wonder whether the novelist had not some supplementary and more specifically personal reasons for exposing himself to the charge of trespass.

We may occasionally, simply for the pleasure in the image, think of Henry James during his London lifetime as a debonair visitor sociably 'bowing among the Titians'. The social aspect of gallery visits, painting-prattle and acquaintance with the handsome spoils of inheritance, was undoubtedly an important part of his communion with painters and painting and patrons. But it went beyond 'bowing'. It furnished hardy returns in background, manner and metaphor which he could and did securely invest in his private enterprises. The language of painting grew into his vocabulary, and the terms of connoisseurship became available to him when he needed a peculiar tone for a special purpose as in the sidelights on Isabel Osmond and Mr Rosier in *The Portrait of a Lady*.

We know what Mr. Rosier thought of her and the terms in which, to Madame Merle, he had expressed his admiration. Like his appreciation of her dear little stepdaughter it was based partly on his eye for decorative character, his instinct for authenticity; but also on a sense for uncatalogued values, for that secret of 'lustre' beyond any recorded losing or rediscovering, which his devotion to brittle wares had still not disqualified him to recognize.

The 'artist-life' persistently fascinated him as a source of plot.

To 'do something about art'—art, that is, as a human complication and a social stumbling-block—must have been for me early a good deal of a nursed intention, the conflict between art and 'the world' striking me thus betimes as one of the half-dozen great primary motives.[1]

As early as 1866 in *The Landscape Painter* and as late as 1911 in *The Outcry* he worked from that 'nursed intention' and between those years he dealt four times intensively with art 'as a human complication'; in his novels *Roderick Hudson* and *The Tragic Muse* and in his tales *The Madonna of the Future* and *The Real Thing*.[2]

His published reviews of exhibitions, however, show us a different side of James. In them we see a diligent, literate journa-

---

[1] Preface to *The Tragic Muse*, New York Edition, 1908.
[2] See Appendix B (p. 265).

list who knew the 'why' of his likes and dislikes, and expressed his opinions without any effort to conceal the fact that he was interested in pictures for their literary as well as for their plastic values. He *read* pictures with an eye for their possible lurking *donnée*.

It seems a great pity that a painter should ever reproduce a thing without suggesting its associations, its human uses, its general sentimental value.

Pictures were for him, as prose was, nothing if not 'representational', and within that broad adjective they were pictorial agencies of communication. He was highly conscious of the difference between the pictorial and the purely decorative, and although he was warmly responsive to the public and private services of the latter he did not consider it pictorial in a representational way. By itself it was a lesser and somewhat inert product of the artistic consciousness, and however well composed and pleasing to the eye it lacked the fully expressive force of a representation. He drew this distinction against Whistler's paintings in the Grosvenor Gallery exhibition of 1878.

Mr. Whistler's productions are pleasant things to have about, so long as one regards them as simple objects—as incidents of furniture or decoration. The spectator's quarrel with them begins when he feels it to be expected of him to regard them as pictures.

For James the main thing, the telling thing, was the presence or absence of his beloved Hydra. 'All art', as Nick Dormer says in *The Tragic Muse*, 'is one'. And he goes on to say:

It's the same great many-headed effort, and any ground that's gained by an individual, any spark that's struck in any province, is of use and of suggestion to all the others. We're all in the same boat.

Dormer was here referring specifically to the plastic arts, but his author was deliberate in phrasing the statement so as to permit it a broader application. The idea of the large art of representation fascinated James as it did Nick Dormer and made him assiduously eager to learn more about it wherever he might. The theatre was, of course, one cherished institution of such learning; the pictorial arts were another.

The latitude of 'any' in the context of Dormer's statement should be noted, for it is significant in relation to the way Henry James looked at the pictures he reviewed. The least *scintilla* of 'suggestion' was of value to him and, in some instances, might earn indulgence and even commendation for work which asserted a thorough range of aesthetic ineptitude. Consider, for example, the terms of mitigation with which he rounds out his estimate of British art in a comment on the Royal Academy for the *Atlantic* of August 1882.

The British artist is apt to be an arrant Philistine, but he is by no means without his good points. He is wanting in science; he is wanting even in art; but he has a great deal of observation and a great deal of feeling.

And in the same article James considers Burne-Jones whom he elsewhere described as an artist of such strong literary predilection that he 'paints, one may almost say, with a pen'.

Amid the hard, loud chatter and clash of so many of his colleagues, the painting of Mr. Burne-Jones is almost alone in having the gravity and deliberation of truly valuable speech. It needs, however, to be looked at good-humouredly and liberally; he offers an entertainment which is for us to take or to leave. It pretends to please us, if we care to be pleased—to touch us in the persuasive, suggestive, allusive, half-satisfying but more mystifying way in which distinguished artists of the imaginative class have always appealed to us.

In his reference to 'distinguished artists of the imaginative class' James may or may not have been thinking of poets (and prose writers 'under the descent of the god') but he was certainly not far from himself in his reference to 'the gravity and deliberation of truly valuable speech'. In any case it is clear that his interest and pleasure in pictures were not annulled, though sensibly diminished, by a lack of plastic excellence.

James's good-humoured and liberal interest in pictures had an early start. The opening passages of his essay on George Du Maurier contain a charming reminiscence of 'a small American child' in New York, 'a silent devotee of *Punch*'.

From about 1850 to 1855 he lived, in imagination, no small part of his time, in the world represented by the pencil of Leech. He pored over the pictures of the people riding in the Row, of the cabmen and the costermongers, of the little pages in buttons, of the bathing-machines at the sea-side, of the small boys in tall hats and Eton jackets, of the gentlemen hunting the fox, of the pretty girls in striped petticoats and coiffures of the shape of the mushroom.[1]

His eye and memory were thus filled with images of a 'world' (his world-to-be as things turned out) long before discriminations had begun to 'bristle'. And even after the bristling had set in James never tired of the observations and types disclosed by competent caricature. They were, for him, fragments of graphic social history and, as such, thoroughly satisfying so long as they included his world. Omission of that world checked his enjoyment and, in his appraisal of Daumier, caused him to temper his admiration with reproach for an artist who could leave out 'the manners of those social groups of whom it may most be said that they *have* manners'. The demand expressed by that little comment tells us much about the way James looked at pictures, what he expected of them in terms of 'subject' and why, for example, he 'detested' Winslow Homer's 'flat-breasted maidens, suggestive of a dish of rural doughnuts and pie'. Above all, it explains why James preferred Gavarni to Daumier and prepares us somewhat for his surprising criticism of the latter.

We feel that Daumier reproduces admirably the particular life that he sees, because it is the very medium in which he moves. He has no wide horizon; the absolute bourgeois hems him in, and he is a bourgeois himself, without poetic ironies, to whom a big cracked mirror has been given.

James's preference was not, of course, based solely on the fact that Gavarni's representations were closer than Daumier's to the social groups that '*have* manners'. Gavarni was peculiarly *persona grata* in the private world of Henry James, being, as Baudelaire noted, a *littérateur*.

Il n'est pas tout à fait un caricaturiste, ni même uniquement un artiste, il est aussi un littérateur. Il effleure, il fait deviner. Le caractère par-

[1] *Partial Portraits*, 1888.

ticulier de son comique est une grande finesse d'observation, qui va
quelquefois jusqu'à la ténuité.[1]

It is to Gavarni that James compares his friend George Du
Maurier in whose gifts for representing modes, manners and
passing fashions he, rather extravagantly, remarked 'a very
Gallic element', noting particularly

his fineness of perception, his remarkable power of specifying types,
his taste, his grace, his lightness, a certain refinement of art.

These charming qualities James did not readily find in purely
British or American art. They were a product of France, strictly
native and, for him, infinitely delightful. It should be remembered in this connexion that the 'silent devotee of *Punch*' was,
at the age of thirteen, translated to Paris and, with his brother
William, visited the Louvre. He recalls his first large exercise in
the appreciation of painting in Chapter XXV of *A Small Boy
and Others.*

It was a comfortable time—when appreciation could go so straight,
could rise, and rise higher, without critical contortions; when we
could, I mean, be both so intelligent and so 'quiet'.

And how vividly and characteristically he recalls the 'suggestion'
transmitted to him, at this time, by Paul Delaroche's picture of
the doomed princes:

Yet Les Enfants d'Edouard thrilled me to a different tune, and I
couldn't doubt that the long-drawn odd face of the elder prince, sad
and sore and sick, with his wide crimped side-locks of fair hair and
his violet legs marked by the Garter and dangling from the bed, was
a reconstitution of far-off history of the subtlest and most 'last word'
modern or psychologic kind. I had never heard of psychology in art or
anywhere else—scarcely anyone then had; but I truly felt the nameless
force at play.

His young companion, the future psychologist, was elsewhere
enchanted, 'repeatedly laying his hand on Delacroix whom he
found always and everywhere interesting'. Henry was deeply
impressed by William's judgement on that occasion.

[1] *Curiosités Esthétiques,* 412.

Four years later the charms of France companionably confronted Henry James in America. Their bearer was John La Farge, the young painter, 'our Franco-American' who so amiably shared his intellectual acquisitions with William and Henry and so perceptively encouraged the latter to turn his 'painter's eye' to writing. La Farge's part in the novelist's development is summarized by Leon Edel in *The Untried Years*:

For Henry James he opened 'more windows than he closed'. The windows he closed were those of the practice of art. He let Henry daub but encouraged him and pushed him to write. He taught him that the 'arts were after all essentially one'.

We can only speculate as to whether the initial force of this lesson in artistic community had been increased by the ready and suggestive example of the painter Fromentin, 'the adorable Fromentin', whose *Dominique* in the *Revue des Deux Mondes* was first revealed to William and Henry by La Farge in those idyllic days of discovery. Here unmistakably was the painter's eye in prose. A landscape appears on a page of *Dominique* as it might appear in a painter's notebook.

Les arbres entièrement dépouillés, j'embrassais mieux l'étendue du parc. Rien ne le grandissait comme un léger brouillard d'hiver qui en bleuissait les profondeurs et trompait sur les vraies distances.

In 1868 when James was twenty-five years old he reviewed P. G. Hamerton's *Contemporary French Painters* for the *North American Review*. This unsigned piece is James's earliest review, thus far identified, on the subject of painting. His comments on Hamerton's discourse are interesting not only because they indicate an early stage in the growth of his own taste but also because they seem to carry a mindful allusion to the superiority of William's judgement years before.

He discourses at greater length upon Horace Vernet, Léopold Robert, and Paul Delaroche, than the character and importance either of their merits or their defects would seem to warrant. The merits of Eugène Delacroix, on the other hand, are such as one does not easily appreciate without the assistance of a good deal of discriminating counsel. . . .

Delacroix is not a painter for whom it is easy to conciliate popular sympathy, nor one, indeed, concerning whose genius it is easy to arrive in one's own mind at a satisfactory conclusion.

Many years later he was to observe in the challenge of Daumier's work 'an element of fascination not attaching to conciliatory talents'. James was sympathetic to 'the "exasperated" charm of extreme difficulty'. He was to become a virtuoso of that element of fascination in his own art.

In 1869 James entered upon a planned and purposeful novitiate in the appreciation of painting—a novitiate *en voyage*—under the sympathetic directorship of Charles Eliot Norton. The first stop in his tour was London and there Norton hospitably introduced him to Ruskin, Rossetti and Morris. He received those introductions calmly but his response to the National Gallery was all fervour and discriminations. 'I admire Raphael, I enjoy Rubens; but I passionately love Titian', he wrote to his brother William. He remained in England through the spring, spent the summer in Switzerland and descended on Italy in the autumn of 1869. Norton had given him experienced and conscientious advice in a letter written from Vevey on 14 August 1869.[1] The novice was told that he must be sure to visit Pavia, Verona, Vicenza, Padua and Brescia. The letter includes one very specific direction which is clearly reflected in James's essays on Venice.

At Venice you will find in the Public Library a copy of Ruskin's *Stones of Venice*—and the list of churches and pictures at the end of the third volume is simply invaluable.

Long after that first visit James set down in *The Wings of the Dove* a mature impression of Venice, a fabric of sounds and sights to which the Venetian masters lent something of their triumph.

Venice glowed and plashed and called and chimed again; the air was like a clap of hands, and the scattered pinks, yellows, blues, sea-greens, were like a hanging-out of vivid stuffs, a laying-down of fine carpets.

From Venice James travelled through Tuscany and entered Florence in early October. There again it was an excitement of

[1] Houghton Library, Cambridge, Mass.

B

pictures—the Uffizi, the Pitti and the churches. On 29 October he arrived in Rome and stayed there until almost the end of December when he began his reluctant journey back to England. In the spring of 1870 he returned to America with an increased knowledge of painters and painting, but it was not until 1872 that he became a professional reporter on the Fine Arts.[1] His letter to Charles Eliot Norton of 4 February 1872[2] tells us how that came about.

Howells is making a very careful and businesslike editor of the *Atlantic*. As proof of his energy—he has induced me to write a monthly report on the Fine Arts in Boston!!

The first of these reports, in the *Atlantic* of January 1872, gave him an opportunity 'to record a personal predilection' and a discrimination.

We can imagine ourselves becoming intensely fond of a Delacroix—never of a Meissonier. Delacroix takes you so frankly into the confidence of his faults, that you scarcely resent them, and by the very fact, indeed, stand in a closer sympathy with him. Like all really great masters—like his great brothers in art, Turner and Tintoretto—he can be described only by seeming paradoxes and contradictions. He is at once the most general and the most specific of painters. His drawing is in the last degree incorrect, and yet he produces unsurpassed effects of design, form, and attitude.

In Florence, during the spring of 1874, James began work on *Roderick Hudson*, his 'first attempt at a novel'. His hero's patient helper, Rowland Mallet, is described in terms worth noting at this point.

He was extremely fond of all the arts and had an almost passionate enjoyment of pictures. He had seen a great many and judged them sagaciously.

James remained in Europe until September 1874. A final dutiful attempt 'to live at home' proved unsuccessful. In the autumn of 1875 he returned to Europe and, with ampler subjects at hand, continued to write reports on the world of art. By the end of that

[1] See Appendix C (p. 266).
[2] Houghton Library, Cambridge, Mass.

year he had, through the *Nation* and the *New York Tribune*, a somewhat broader field of publication at his command.

In 1876 James reviewed Fromentin's *Les Maîtres d'Autrefois* for the *Nation*. The article is appreciative, critical, explicit and, here and there, interestingly petulant. James evidently responded keenly to the situation which this *critique* involved: a novelist reviewing the work of an art-critic, an art-critic reviewing the work of a novelist, the painter's eye, in different strengths, on each side. He meets the situation with a graceful opening but by the time he reaches the second paragraph he has marked his targets.

We repeat that his whole volume is extremely interesting, but it strikes us as curious rather than valuable. We have always had a decided mistrust of literary criticism of works of plastic art; and those tendencies which have suggested this feeling are exhibited by M. Fromentin in their most extreme form. He would deny, we suppose, that his criticism is literary and assert that it is purely pictorial—the work of a painter judging painters. This, however, is only half true. M. Fromentin is too ingenious and elaborate a writer not to have taken a great deal of pleasure in the literary form that he gives to his thoughts; and when once the literary form takes the bit into its teeth, as it does very often with M. Fromentin, the effect, at least, of over-subtlety and web-spinning is certain to be produced.

And further on in the same paragraph the second fault is noted.

He enters too much, in our opinion, into the technical side, and he expects of his readers to care much more than should be expected even of a very ardent art-lover for the mysteries of the process by which the picture was made. There is a certain sort of talk which should be confined to manuals and note-books and studio records; there is something impertinent in pretending to work it into literary form—especially into the very elegant and rather self-conscious literary form of which M. Fromentin is master.

Whether we accept or reject these strictures the essay is an engaging one, skilfully composed, and informative. More clearly and thoroughly than any other piece in this volume it states James's view of what art criticism should not attempt and indicates what it should be. It should be the voice of the amateur who knows that pictures 'are meant above all things to be enjoyed'. The painter's voice, if it must be heard, should be in a minor key; the writer's voice restrained. If the art-critic be too 'ingenious and elaborate' a writer not to take a great deal of pleasure in the literary form that he gives to his thoughts, then let him draw the curb rein firmly. Fromentin's regard for Rubens was, no doubt, another source of James's dissatisfaction with *Les Maîtres d'Autrefois*.

> M. Fromentin indulges in more emotion on the subject of Rubens than we have ever found ourselves able to do, and his whole dissertation is a good example of the vanity of much of the criticism in the super-subtle style.

It is instructive, at this point, to recall the flourish with which James loosed his literary bridle in a traveller's comment on Rubens two years before; in 'Florentine Notes' of 1874:

> Was Rubens lawfully married to Nature, or did he merely keep up the most unregulated of flirtations? Three or four of his great carnal cataracts ornament the walls of the Pitti. If the union was really solemnized it must be said that the ménage was at best a stormy one. He is a strangely irresponsible jumble of the true and the false. He paints a full flesh surface that radiates and palpitates with illusion, and into the midst of it he thrusts a mouth, a nose, an eye, which you would call your latest-born a blockhead for perpetrating.

This passage was omitted from 'Florentine Notes' when the essay was reprinted in *Italian Hours* in 1909 but it is probable that James, with his constitutional fondness for precise and delicately detailed 'illusion', never became reconciled to the 'carnal cataracts' of Rubens. In his comments on Delacroix's 'The Death of Sardanapalus' he draws a comparison with Rubens which makes one wonder what words he would have written about the final phase of Renoir's work.

> One of the women, half-naked and tumbling over helpless on her face against the couch of her lord, with her hands bound behind her, and her golden hair shaken out with her lamentations, seems, in her young

transparent rosiness, like the work of a more delicate and more spiritual Rubens.

James's independence of the critical seers (especially the literary ones), when it was a question of what *he* wanted to see, is sharply marked in his condemnation of Ruskin's doctrinaire rigidities and rudeness of tone. In 1877 *Mornings in Florence* stirred James to unusual feats of irony and invective. These little books 'seemed invidious and insane' and their author a 'light *littérateur*'. Then, after three pages of thrusts, comes the *coup de grâce* from the knight-errant of 'illusion' and 'ease' in the enjoyment of art.

One may read a great many pages of Mr. Ruskin without getting a hint of this delightful truth; a hint of the not unimportant fact that art, after all, is made for us, and not we for art. This idea of the value of a work of art being the amount of entertainment it yields is conspicuous by its absence. And as for Mr. Ruskin's world of art being a place where we may take life easily, woe to the luckless mortal who enters it with any such disposition. Instead of a garden of delight, he finds a sort of assize court, in perpetual session. Instead of a place in which human responsibilities are lightened and suspended, he finds a region governed by a kind of Draconic legislation.[1]

To savour fully the flavour of independence in that passage we should recall the terms in which Ruskin's respect for James was conveyed to the younger man in a letter written by Charles Eliot Norton from London on 23 March 1873.[2]

Ruskin has been spending a great part of the day with me in one of his sweetest moods. I read to him what you say of Tintoret, which had greatly pleased me when I first read it yesterday in the *Nation* of March 6th.[3] It would have been pleasant to you to see the cordial admiration he felt for your work and to hear his warm expressions of the good it did him, to find such sympathies and such appreciations, and to know that you were to be added to the little list of those who really and intelligently and earnestly care for the same things that

---

[1] 'Recent Florence', *Atlantic Monthly*, May 1878. This passage, somewhat revised, appears also in *Portraits of Places*, 1883, and in *Italian Hours*, 1909.

[2] Houghton Library, Cambridge, Mass.

[3] Reprinted in 'From Venice to Strassburg', *Transatlantic Sketches*, 1875.

touched him most deeply and influenced his life most powerfully. You may be pleased from your heart to have given not merely pleasure, but stimulus, to a man of genius very solitary, and with few friends who care for what he cares for.

James never entirely dismissed Ruskin's insights and there is more than a little evidence of the 'illustrious teacher's' influence in his descriptive reporting of pictures. Surely, too, he must have heartily embraced the literary good sense of Ruskin's note on Frith's 'Sophia Western' in the Royal Academy exhibition of 1875.

But what is the use of painting from Fielding at all? Of all our classic authors, it is he who demands the reader's attention most strictly; and what modern reader ever attends to anything?[1]

James would have agreed with Ruskin on the point of attention —he insisted on 'attention of perusal'—but he would have been permissive about 'the use of painting Fielding at all'. He distinguished reasonably and sensibly between the independent image and the image 'grafted' on the text.

One welcomes illustration, in other words, with pride and joy; but also with the emphatic view that, might one's 'literary jealousy' be duly deferred to, it would quite stand off and on its own feet and thus, as a separate and independent subject of publication, carrying its text in its spirit, just as that text correspondingly carries the plastic possibility, become a still more glorious tribute.[2]

But, if 'the painter's eye' had persisted creatively in James, might he not have been tempted to illustrate his own text; to cultivate two gardens on one plot? Surely that arrangement would have afforded no cause for 'jealousy' of any sort. His uneasiness about Du Maurier's illustrations for *Trilby* is indicative if not conclusive.

Every one, every thing, is beautiful for Mr. Du Maurier. We have only to look, to see it proved, at the admirable, lovable little pictorial notes to his text. I will not profess for a moment that the effect of these notes is not insidious and corrupting, or that with such a perpetual nudging

[1] *Notes on some of the Principal Pictures exhibited in the Rooms of the Royal Academy 1875* by John Ruskin, 1875, p. 23.
[2] Preface to *The Golden Bowl*, New York Edition, 1909.

of the critical elbow one can judge the text with adequate presence of mind. There is an unprecedented confusion, in which the line seems to pass into the phrase and the phrase into the line—in which the 'letter-press', in particular, borrows from the illustrations illicit advantages and learns impertinent short-cuts; though this, indeed, is by no means inveterate, the written presentation of the tall heroine, for instance, being, to my sense, decidedly preferable to the drawn.[1]

Quite apart from the question of 'jealousy', the duty of responsible prose remains to haunt 'the lover of literature'.

Anything that relieves responsible prose of the duty of being, while placed before us, good enough, interesting enough and, if the question be of picture, pictorial enough, above all *in itself*, does it the worst of services, and may well inspire in the lover of literature certain lively questions as to the future of that institution.[2]

James's collaboration with the American artist Joseph Pennell is interesting in connexion with the question of illustration. In his preface to the edition of *A Little Tour in France*, which appeared in 1900 'with illustrations by Joseph Pennell', James is almost apologetic as he describes his own contributions which he characterizes as 'notes'. They are 'pictorial' but, he seems to be saying, their images are not quite full-fledged.

They are impressions, immediate, easy, and consciously limited; if the written word may ever play the part of brush or pencil, they are sketches on 'drawing-paper' and nothing more.

They were, in short, not intended to be 'pictorial enough' in themselves. They were originally planned for a 'picture-book', but 'the series of illustrations to which it had been their policy to cling for countenance and company failed them, after all, at the last moment' and they went forth 'to live their little life without assistance' in 1884. Sixteen years later they were reprinted and granted, as James phrased it, 'in an association with Mr. Pennell's admirable drawings, the benefit they have always lacked'. Here, therefore, was prose which the author had consciously 'limited'

[1] *Harper's Weekly*, 14 April 1894.
[2] Preface to *The Golden Bowl.*

in order to accommodate companion images by another hand. The 'muffled majesty of authorship' might rest easy under these circumstances. Pennell in *The Adventures of an Illustrator* says of his work with James: 'I visited every one of the places he mentions, on a bicycle, doing every drawing on the spot'. Places! Portraits of places! May it not have been through his experiences with Pennell that James conceived the idea of 'the aspect of things or the combination of objects that might, by a latent virtue in it, speak for its connexion with something in the book, and yet at the same time speak enough for its odd or interesting self'? In 1906 Alvin Langdon Coburn, a young American photographer, went from London to the Continent 'armed with a detailed document from James explaining exactly what he wanted me to photograph'.[1] More portraits of places, but this time to accompany human portraiture in profoundly 'responsible' prose.

James satisfactorily solved the problem of illustrations for the New York Edition of his *Novels and Tales* by commissioning Coburn to furnish a series of atmospheric photographs which the novelist appreciatively described as 'decorative "illustrations" '. These photographs, he said, put forth no 'illustrative claims'. They were

expressions of no particular thing in the text, but only of the type or idea of this or that thing. They were to remain at the most small pictures of our 'set' stage with the actors left out.[2]

James, more than any other writer of his time and place, was conscious of fashion in dress and must certainly have been aware of the 'dating' conferred by illustrations which display the styles of a season.

Photographically-illustrated books were by no means a novelty in 1906. The first of them, *The Pencil of Nature* by W. Fox Talbot, was published in 1844, and Julia Cameron's

[1] 'Illustrating Henry James by Photography', a B.B.C. Third Programme Talk by Alvin Langdon Coburn, 17 July 1953.
[2] Preface to *The Golden Bowl*.

illustrated edition of *Idylls of the King* with a frontispiece photograph of Tennyson had appeared in 1875. James's decision to have photographic illustrations was therefore not without precedent. It is interesting nevertheless because it indicates that the quality of Coburn's work was something of a revelation to him and enabled him to see in photography something more agreeable than 'that hideous inexpressiveness of the mechanical document' which he had remarked in 1877. James was, throughout his life, learning how to see and appreciate, and his concern with learning was always at its highest pitch when the subject or object which engaged him also engaged the question of art.

The years in which James published art reviews are roughly those from 1868 to 1882 with a brief resumption in 1897. The gap is regrettable because it was between 1882 and 1897 that his sense of artistic experiment was sharpened and developed by his own exercises. A milestone in his learning process is emphatically marked in '*The Art of Fiction*' (1884).[1]

Art lives upon discussion, upon experiment, upon curiosity, upon variety of attempt, upon the exchange of views and the comparison of standpoints.

In 1877 (and again in 1878) he had given the conventional response to Whistler's pictures with only slightly more benignity than the other London reviewers bestowed on the American painter.

I will not speak of Mr. Whistler's 'Nocturnes in Black and Gold' and in 'Blue and Silver', of his 'Arrangements,' 'Harmonies', and 'Impressions', because I frankly confess they do not amuse me. The mildest judgement I have heard pronounced upon them is that they are like 'ghosts of Velasquezes'; with the harshest I will not darken my pages. It may be a narrow point of view, but to be interesting it seems to me that a picture should have some relation to life as well as to painting. Mr. Whistler's experiments have no relation whatever to life; they have only a relation to painting.

In his review of the Grosvenor Gallery in 1882 James is less

[1] Reprinted in *Partial Portraits*, 1888, and in *The Art of Fiction*. ed. Morris Roberts, 1 8.

astringent in his estimate of Whistler's 'experiments'. This time he finds them 'extremely amusing' but the entertainment he acknowledges is of the broad and comic sort. He compassionates the artist for once having given the measure of his talent, 'and a very high measure it was', in the portrait of his mother. It was 'such a masterpiece of tone, of feeling, of the power to render life, that the fruits of his brush offered to the public more lately have seemed in comparison very crude'. To one of these latter, however, he pays some shadowy tribute, and to the painter awards a semi-complimentary play on words:

Mr. Whistler is a votary of 'tone'; his manner of painting is to breathe upon the canvas. It is not too much to say that he has, to a certain point, the creative afflatus. His little black and red lady is charming; she looks like someone, as I have said, and if she is a shadow she is the shadow of a graceful personage.

Fifteen years later James's comment on Whistler's 'exquisite image' of Henry Irving as Philip II (the 'Arrangement in Black No. 3', which was one of the 'ghosts' he had viewed at the Grosvenor Exhibition in 1877) shows an enlargement of receptivity and vision:

To pause before such a work is in fact to be held to the spot by just the highest operation of the charm one has sought there—the charm of a certain degree of melancholy meditation.

It is clear from his tone (it expresses no shock of recognition) that James had come to more comfortable terms with the pictorial as well as the decorative talents of Whistler before he wrote those lines. His interest in portraiture, the drama and Henry Irving had, probably, much to do with his feeling response to this particular canvas. At all events the 'arrangement' which, among others, once seemed to him to have 'no relation whatever to life', now disclosed for him a lifelike if not lively suggestion, 'the charm of a certain degree of melancholy meditation'.

A more striking revision seems to have modified James's initial attitude towards Impressionism. In 1876 he attended the exhibition of Impressionists at Durand-Ruel's—a notable early showing of their work—and saw paintings by Renoir, Monet, Sisley, Pissarro and Morisot, but apparently considered none of the artists worth naming in his despatch to the *New York Tribune*. 'This little band', as he calls them,

is on all grounds less interesting than the group out of which Millais and Holman Hunt rose into fame. None of its members show signs of possessing first-rate talent, and indeed the 'Impressionist' doctrines strike me as incompatible, in an artist's mind, with the existence of first-rate talent.

It was dislike at first sight. The Impressionists raised for him a 'moral' question of subject and treatment which blurred his view of their technical experiment and pictorial accomplishment.

But the divergence in method between the English Pre-Raphaelites and this little group is especially striking, and very characteristic of the moral differences of the French and English races. When the English realists 'went in', as the phrase is, for hard truth and stern fact, an irresistible instinct of righteousness caused them to try and purchase forgiveness for their infidelity to the old more or less moral proprieties and conventionalities, by an exquisite, patient, virtuous manipulation —by being above all things laborious. But the Impressionists, who, I think, are more consistent, abjure virtue altogether, and declare that a subject which has been crudely chosen shall be loosely treated. They send detail to the dogs and concentrate themselves on general expression.

It would be unreasonable to criticise James's lack of enthusiasm for work which had been so sharply attacked by experienced and eminent painters and critics, among whom was Fromentin. In an instalment of *Les Maîtres d'Autrefois* in the *Revue des Deux Mondes* of 15 February 1876 Fromentin named no names but his *critique* was clearly aimed at the Impressionists.[1]

Le *plein air*, la lumière diffuse, le *vrai soleil*, prennent aujourd'hui, dans la peinture at dans toutes les peintures, une importance qu'on ne leur avait jamais reconnue, et que, disons-le franchement, ils ne méritent point d'avoir.

[1] Duranty replied to Fromentin in his pamphlet *La Nouvelle Peinture*, 1876.

It is remarkable, however, that James, who was as a rule scrupulous about identifying individual artists regardless of his opinion of their work, reviewed the Impressionists as anonymous members of a group. His scorn for them was evidently deeply felt and it is reasonable to assume that he had found 'the adorable Fromentin' persuasive or, at the very least, corroborative on this occasion. Two years later James still slightly aches from his encounter with this little band of French 'cynics'. He is reminded of them by Whistler:

His manner is very much that of the French 'Impressionists', and, like them, he suggests the rejoinder that a picture is not an impression but an expression—just as a poem or a piece of music is.

We have no conclusive evidence that James eventually 'embraced' the Impressionists. We have, however, some convincing hints that he learned in later years to appreciate them and to utilize their 'suggestion'.

In *The Ambassadors*, published in 1903, it is a painting, or rather the memory of a painting, that sets the stage for the final crisis. Lambert Strether's sentimental journey beyond the *banlieue* (this time he hasn't missed the train!) begins as a pictorial remembrance of things past. He recollects a small landscape which 'had charmed him, long years before, at a Boston dealer's' and which he had failed to acquire although its price was ridiculously low. His recollection is a sidelong glance at missed opportunity, a symbolic variation on the theme of his advice to little Bilham:

Live all you can; it's a mistake not to. It doesn't so much matter what you do in particular, so long as you have your life. If you haven't had that what *have* you had?

In a few hours on that remarkable day in the country Strether lives imaginatively within the 'oblong gilt frame' of his lost landscape. His musing establishes a significant contrast between the 'inner-shrine' of the Tremont Street art shop and the open air which he is at last possessing. The lost landscape was by

Lambinet,[1] a Romantic painter who died in 1877, but the land-scape in which Strether finds himself reflects the ascendancy of Impressionism.

Meanwhile at all events it was enough that they did affect one—so far as the village aspect was concerned—as whiteness, crookedness and blueness set in coppery green; there being positively, for that matter, an outer wall of the White Horse that was painted the most improbable shade.

As the dramatic moment in the chapter approaches, the touch and treatment of Impressionism compose the scene, and Strether is *en plein air*, or nearly so, at last.

The valley on the further side was all copper-green level and glazed pearly sky, a sky hatched across with screens of trimmed trees, which looked flat, like espaliers; and though the rest of the village straggled away in the near quarter the view had an emptiness that made one of the boats suggestive. Such a river set one afloat almost before one could take up the oars—the idle play of which would be moreover the aid to the full impression.

A more specific acknowledgement of the Impressionists appears in the course of James's essay 'New England: An Autumn Impression' (1905). The immediate subject is 'a great new house',[2]

in which an array of modern 'impressionistic' pictures, mainly French, wondrous examples of Manet, of Degas, of Claude Monet, of Whistler, of other rare recent hands, treated us to the momentary effect of a large slippery sweet inserted, without a warning, between the compressed lips of half-conscious inanition. One hadn't quite known one was starved, but the morsel went down by the mere authority of the thing

---

[1] 'William Hunt . . . had prolonged his studies in Paris under the inspiration of Couture and Edouard Frère; masters in a group completed by three or four of the so finely interesting landscapists of that and the directly previous age, Troyon, Rousseau, Daubigny, even Lambinet and others, and which summed up for the American collector and in the New York and Boston markets the idea of the modern in the masterly.' *A Small Boy and Others*, 1913, Ch. XXV.

[2] Hill-Stead near Farmington, Connecticut, was built in 1901 by Mr Alfred Atmore Pope. The house is now Hill-Stead Museum. The essay was reprinted in *The American Scene*, 1907.

consummately *prepared*. Nothing else had been, in all the circle, prepared to anything like the same extent; and though the consequent taste, as a mixture with the other tastes, was of the queerest, no proof of the sovereign power of art could have been, for the moment, sharper. It happened to be that particular art—it might as well, no doubt, have been another; it made everything else shrivel and fade: it was like the sudden trill of a nightingale, lord of the hushed evening.

And in the same essay 'impressionism' becomes a very felicitous element in his own method of expression.

Cape Cod, on this showing, was exactly a pendent, pictured Japanese screen or banner; a delightful little triumph of 'impressionism', which, during my short visit at least, never departed, under any provocation, from its type.

The relative ease with which James learned to accommodate and enjoy new developments in nineteenth-century painting becomes more striking if we remember how deeply conventional he was. Indeed if we forget this we miss one important aspect of his genius. His own creative adventure was conservatively based on social convention. With his art he succeeded in spreading this narrow foundation into an interesting and enduring breadth. His sense of the future was constantly as alert as his sense of the past, but the past was always with him. In a memorable sentence written a few years before his death he remarked the changes which new realizations in painting had wrought in the pictorial scene during his lifetime.

Oh the cold grey luminaries hung about in odd corners and back passages, and that we have known shining and warm![1]

Friendship played a large and generous part in Henry James's relation to the pictorial arts. The generosity was of course on two sides. James learned a great deal from his painter friends about their mystery. He, in turn, was characteristically extravagant in commendation whenever he had an opportunity to write about them. Indeed his one collection of essays on the

[1] *Notes of a Son and Brother*, 1914, Ch. IV.

pictorial arts *Picture and Text*,[1] which was published only in New York, is more an act of friendship than a book. Apart from the articles on Daumier and Sargent and the oddly-appended dialogue called 'After the Play', *Picture and Text* is quite evidently an amiable compliance on James's part—a little garland of advertisement for his friends Abbey, Boughton, Reinhart, Millet and Parsons and for the publishers who employed them as illustrators. In his essay on Sargent, however, some of his comments seem prophetically critical when one recalls how thoroughly the painter's career bore out James's misgivings about its future. Dazzled by Sargent's brilliant technical skill, 'the attentive spectator' is led 'to ask unanswerable questions' about 'a career which is not yet half unfolded'.

He finds himself murmuring, 'Yes, but what is left?' and even wondering whether it be an advantage to an artist to obtain early in life such possession of his means that the struggle with them, discipline, *tâtonnement*, cease to exist for him. May not this breed an irresponsibility of cleverness, a wantonness, an irreverence—what is vulgarly termed a 'larkiness'—on the part of the youthful genius who has, as it were, all his fortune in his pocket? Such are the possibly superfluous broodings of those who are critical even in their warmest admirations and who sometimes suspect that it may be better for an artist to have a certain part of his property invested in unsolved difficulties.

Such perception and writing merit grateful admiration, and make one regret that James wrote so little about the pictorial arts after 1882. The accurate answer is the most consoling one for the beneficiaries of his genius. His responsibilities lay elsewhere during 'the middle years' and he held himself 'altogether to a higher account'.

JOHN L. SWEENEY

---

[1] Harper and Brothers, New York, 1893.

ACKNOWLEDGEMENTS

I wish to express my gratitude to Mr and Mrs William James for their kind permission to reprint the notes and essays in this volume and for their gracious response to my interest in its subject, to Mr Le Roy Phillips whose *Bibliography of the Writings of Henry James* served as my primary guide among the periodicals, and to Professor Leon Edel who encouraged me in this undertaking and generously gave me the benefit of his knowledge and insight whenever I turned to him.

I am deeply appreciative of the help I have received from M. Jean Adhémar, Mr Donald Brien, Mr Alvin Langdon Coburn, Mr W. G. Constable, Miss Elizabeth Drew, Mr Albert Ten Eyck Gardner, Mr John Gere, Professor William A. Jackson, Professor John Kelleher, Professor Harry Levin, the late F. O. Matthiessen, Mr David McKibbin, Professor Samuel Morse, Professor Kenneth Murdock, Mr Peter Murray, Mr Simon Nowell-Smith, Mr Joseph Trapp, and Mr Alfred Yockney.

I would also like to acknowledge assistance given me by the Houghton Library and Fogg Museum Library of Harvard University, the Frick Art Reference Library, the British Museum, the Victoria and Albert Museum Library, and the Witt Library of the Courtauld Institute.

To the late Allan Wade I acknowledge a debt of affectionate gratitude for countless advisory kindnesses. To Mr Rupert Hart-Davis I am grateful for good counsel and great forbearance.

And, finally, I thank my wife for her constant help.

J. L. S.

NOTE ON THE TEXT

Except for the pieces which were reprinted in *Picture and Text*, it seems unlikely that James saw or corrected proofs of any of these articles and that each periodical followed its own house rules of styling. Except for the correction of a few obvious misprints, the original texts have been followed, but the names of books and newspapers have been uniformly printed in italics, the titles of pictures in roman type enclosed within quotation marks, and the spelling of a few proper names (such as Van Dyck) has been standardized. All the pieces are printed in full, except where otherwise indicated in the Table of Contents.

AN ENGLISH CRITIC OF
FRENCH PAINTING
1868

THE profession of art-critic, so largely and successfully exercised in France, has found in England but a single eminent representative. It is true, indeed, that Mr. Ruskin has invested the character with a breadth and vigour which may be thought to have furnished, without emulation on the part of other writers, sufficient stress of commentary on the recent achievements of English art—at the same time that, on the other hand, this remarkable man has of late years shown a growing tendency to merge the function of art-critic in that of critic of life or of things in general. It is nevertheless true, that, as Mr. Ruskin is in the highest degree a devotee of art, he applies to the contemplation of manners and politics very much the same process of reflection and interpretation as in his earlier works he had acquired the habit of applying to the study of painting and architecture. He has been unable to abandon the aesthetic standpoint. Let him treat of what subjects he pleases, therefore, he will always remain before all things an art-critic. He has achieved a very manifest and a very extended influence over the mind and feelings of his own generation and that succeeding it; and those forms of intellectual labour, or of intellectual play, are not few in number, of which one may say without hesitation, borrowing for a moment a French idiom and French words, that Ruskin has *passé par là*. We have not the space to go over the ground of our recent literature, and enumerate those fading or flourishing tracts which, in one way or another, communicate with that section of the great central region which Mr. Ruskin has brought under cultivation. Sometimes the connecting path is very sinuous, very tortuous, very much inclined to lose itself in its course, and to disavow all acquaintance with its parent soil; sometimes it is a mere thread of scanty vegetation, overshadowed by the rank growth of adjacent fields; but with perseverance we can generally trace it back to its starting-point, on the margin of *Modern Painters.* Mr. Ruskin has had passionate admirers; he has had disciples of the more rational kind; he has been made an object of study by persons whose adherence to his principles and whose admiration for his powers, under certain applications, have been equalled only by their dissent and distaste in the presence of others; and he has had, finally, like all writers of an uncompromising originality of genius, his full share of bitter antagonists. Persons belonging to either of these two latter classes bear testimony to his influence, of course, quite as much as persons belonging to the two former. Passionate reactionists are the servants of the message of a man of genius to society, as indisputably as passionate adherents. But descending to particulars, we may say, that, although Mr. Ruskin has in a very large degree affected writers and painters, he has yet not in any appreciable degree quickened the formation of a school of critics—premising that we use the word 'school' in the sense of a group of writers devoted to the study of art according to their own individual lights, and as distinguished from students of literature, and not in the sense of a group of writers devoted to the promulgation of Mr. Ruskin's own views, or those of anyone else.

There are a great many pictures painted annually in England, and even, for that matter, in America; and there is in either country a great deal of criticism annually written about these pictures, in newspapers and magazines. No portion of such criticism, however, possesses sufficient substance or force to make it worth anyone's while to wish to see it preserved in volumes, where it can be referred to and pondered. More than this, there are, to our knowledge, actually very few books in our language, belonging in form to literature, in which the principles of painting, or certain specific pictures, are intelligently discussed.

There is a small number of collections of lectures by presidents of the Royal Academy, the best of which are Reynolds's; there is Leslie's *Handbook;* there are the various compilations of Mrs. Jameson; and there is the translation of Vasari, and the recent valuable *History of Italian Art* by Crowe and Cavalcaselle. For the needs of serious students, these make a very small library, and such students for the most part betake themselves, sooner or later, to the perusal of the best French critics, such as Stendhal, Gustave Planche, Vitet, and in these latter days Taine. They find in these writers, not, of course, everything, but they find a great deal, and they acquire more especially a sense of the great breadth of the province of art, and of its intimate relations with the rest of men's intellectual life. The writers just mentioned deal with painters and paintings as literary critics deal with authors and books. They neither talk pure sentiment (or rather, impure sentiment), like foolish amateurs, nor do they confine their observations to what the French call the *technique* of art. They examine pictures (or such, at least, is their theory) with an equal regard to the standpoint of the painter and that of the spectator, whom the painter must always be supposed to address —with an equal regard, in other words, to the material used and to the use made of it. As writers who really know how to write, however, will always of necessity belong rather to the class of spectators than to that of painters, it may be conceded that the profit of their criticism will accrue rather to those who look at pictures than to those who make them.

Painters always have a great distrust of those who write about pictures. They have a strong sense of the difference between the literary point of view and the pictorial, and they inveterately suspect critics of confounding them. This suspicion may easily be carried too far. Painters, as a general thing, are much less able to take the literary point of view, when it is needed, than writers are to take the pictorial; and yet, we repeat, the suspicion is natural and not unhealthy. It is no more than just, that, before sitting down to discourse upon works of art, a writer should be required to prove his familiarity with the essential conditions of the production of such works, and that, before criticizing the way in which objects are painted, he should give evidence of his knowledge of the difference between the manner in which they strike the senses of persons of whom it is impossible to conceive as being tempted to reproduce them and the manner in which they strike the senses of persons in whom to see them and to wish to reproduce them are almost one and the same act. With an accomplished sense of this profound difference, and with that proportion of insight into the workings of the painter's genius and temperament which would naturally accompany it, it is not unreasonable to believe that a critic in whom the faculty of literary expression is sufficiently developed may do very good service to the cause of art—service similar to that which is constantly performed for the cause of letters. It is not unreasonable to suppose that such a writer as the late Gustave Planche, for instance, with all his faults, did a great deal of valuable work on behalf of the French school of painters. He often annoyed them, misconceived them, and converted them into enemies; but he also made many things clear to them which were dark, many things simple which were confused, and many persons interested in their work who had been otherwise indifferent. Writers of less intensity of conviction and of will have done similar service in their own way and their own degree; and on the whole, therefore, we regret that in England there has not been, as in France, a group of honest and intelligent mediators between painters and the public. Some painters, we know, scorn the idea of 'mediators', and claim to place themselves in direct communication with the great mass of observers. But we strongly suspect, that, as a body, they would be the worse for the suppression of the class of interpreters. When critics attack a bad picture which the public shows signs of liking, then they are voted an insufferable nuisance; but their good offices are very welcome, when they serve to help the public to the appreciation of a good picture which it is too stupid to understand. It is certain that painters need to be interpreted and expounded, and that as a general thing they are themselves incompetent to the task. That they are sensible of the need is indicated by the issue of the volume of *Entretiens*, by M. Thomas Couture. That they are incompetent to supply the need is equally evident from the very infelicitous character of that performance.

The three principal art-critics now writing in England—the only three, we believe, who from time to time lay aside the anonymous, and republish their contributions to the newspapers—are Mr. W. M. Rossetti, Mr. F. T. Palgrave, and Mr. P. G. Hamerton, the author of the volume whose title is prefixed to this notice. Mr. Hamerton is distinguished from the two former gentlemen by the circumstance that he began life as a painter, and that in all that he has written he has stood close to the painter's point of view. Whether he continues to paint we know not, but such reputation as he enjoys has been obtained chiefly by his writings. We imagine him to belong to that class of artists of whom he speaks in the volume before us, who, in the course of their practical work, take to much reading, and so are gradually won over to writing, and give up painting altogether. Mr. Hamerton is at any rate a very pleasant writer. He took the public very much into his confidence in the history of his *Painter's Camp*, in Scotland and France; but the public has liked him none the less for it. There is a certain intelligent frankness and freedom in his style which conciliates the reader's esteem, and converts the author for the time into a sort of personal companion. He uses professional terms without pedantry, and he practises with great neatness the common literary arts. His taste is excellent, he has plenty of common sense, he is tolerant of differences of opinion and of theory, and in dealing with aesthetic matters he never ceases to be clear and precise. The work before us is an essay upon the manner of some twenty French painters, representatives of the latest tendencies and achievements of French art, and it is illustrated by photographs from their works or from engravings of them. Mr. Hamerton's observations are somewhat desultory, and he makes no attempt to deduce from his inquiry a view of the probable future stages of French art—in which, on the whole, he is decidedly wise.

The reader with a taste for inductions of this kind will form his own conclusions on Mr. Hamerton's data. He will find these data very interesting, and strongly calculated to impress him with a sense of the vast amount of intellectual force which, during the last thirty years, has been directed in France into the channel of art.

Mr. Hamerton begins his essay with a little talk about David —the first, in time, of modern French painters, and certainly one of the most richly endowed. David leads him to the classical movement, and the classical movement to Ingres. Of the classical tendency—the classical 'idea'—Mr. Hamerton gives a very fair and succinct account, but we may question the fairness of his estimate of Ingres. The latter has been made the object of the most extravagant and fulsome adulation; but one may admire him greatly and yet keep within the bounds of justice. Nothing is more probable, however, than that those theories of art of which his collective works are such a distinguished embodiment are growing daily to afford less satisfaction and to obtain less sympathy. It is natural, indeed, to believe that the classical tendency will never become extinct, inasmuch as men of the classical temperament will constantly arise to keep it alive. But men of this temperament will exact more of their genius than Ingres and his disciples ever brought themselves to do. Mr. Hamerton indicates how it is that these artists can only in a restricted sense be considered as *painters*, and how at the same time the disciples of the opposite school have gradually effected a considerable extension of the term 'painting'. The school of Ingres in art has a decided affinity with the school of M. Victor Cousin in philosophy and history, and we know that the recent fortunes of the latter school have not been brilliant. There was something essentially arbitrary in the style of painting practised by Ingres. He looked at natural objects in a partial, incomplete manner. He recognized in Nature only one class of objects worthy of study—the naked human figure; and in art only one method of reproduction—drawing. To satisfy the requirements of the character now represented by the term 'painter', it is necessary to look at Nature in the most impartial and comprehensive manner, to see objects in their integrity, and to reject nothing. It is constantly found more difficult to distinguish between drawing and painting. It is believed that Nature herself makes no such distinction, and that it is folly to educate an artist exclusively as a draughtsman. Mr. Hamerton describes the effect of the classical theory upon the works of Ingres and his followers—how their pictures are nothing but coloured drawings, their stuffs and draperies unreal, the faces of their figures inanimate, and their landscapes without character.

As Ingres represents the comparative permanence of the tendency inaugurated by David, Mr. Hamerton mentions Géricault as the best of the early representatives of the reactionary or romantic movement. We have no need to linger upon him. Everyone who has been through the Louvre remembers his immense 'Raft of the Medusa', and retains a strong impression that the picture possesses not only vastness of size, but real power of conception.

Among the contemporary classicists, Mr. Hamerton mentions Froment, Hamon, and Ary Scheffer, of whose too familiar 'Dante and Beatrice' he gives still another photograph. As foremost in the opposite camp, of course, he names Eugène Delacroix; but of this (to our mind) by far the most interesting of French painters he gives but little account and no examples. As a general thing, one may say that Mr. Hamerton rather prefers the easier portion of his task. He discourses at greater length upon Horace Vernet, Léopold Robert, and Paul Delaroche, than the character and importance either of their merits or their defects would seem to warrant. The merits of Eugène Delacroix, on the other hand, are such as one does not easily appreciate without the assistance of a good deal of discriminating counsel. It may very well be admitted, however, that Delacroix is not a painter for whom it is easy to conciliate popular sympathy, nor one, indeed, concerning whose genius it is easy to arrive in one's own mind at a satisfactory conclusion. So many of his merits have the look of faults, and so many of his faults the look of merits, that one can hardly admire him without fearing that one's taste is getting vitiated, nor disapprove him without fearing that one's judgement is getting superficial and unjust. He remains, therefore, for this reason, as well as for several others, one of the most interesting and moving of painters; and it is not too much to say of him that one derives from his works something of that impression of a genius in actual, visible contact—and conflict—with the ever-reluctant possibilities of the subject in hand, which, when we look at the works of Michael Angelo, tempers our exultation at the magnitude of the achievement with a melancholy regret for all that was not achieved. We are sorry, that, in place of one of the less valuable works which Mr. Hamerton has caused to be represented in his pages, he has not inserted a copy of the excellent lithograph of Delacroix's 'Dante et Virgile', assuredly one of the very finest of modern pictures.

Of Couture Mr. Hamerton says nothing. A discreet publisher would very probably have vetoed the admission of the photograph of his famous 'Romans of the Decline', had such a photograph been obtainable. Couture's masterpiece[1] is interesting, in a survey of the recent development of French art, as an example of a 'classical' subject, as one may call it—that is, a group of figures with their nakedness relieved by fragments of antique drapery—treated in a manner the reverse of classical. It is hard to conceive anything less like David or Ingres; and although it is by no means a marvellous picture, we cannot but prefer it to such examples as we know of Ingres's work. You feel that the painter has ignored none of the difficulties of his theme, and has striven hard to transfer it to canvas without the loss of reality. The picture is as much a *painting* as the 'Apotheosis of Homer' (say) by Ingres is little of one; and yet, curiously, thanks to this same uncompromising grasp towards plastic completeness, the figures are marked by an immobility and fixedness as much aside from Nature as the coldness and the 'attitudes' of those produced in the opposite school.

---

[1] 'I could never, in the long aftertime, face his masterpiece and all its old meanings and marvels without a rush of memories and a stir of ghosts.'
A Small Boy and Others, Ch. XXV.

Apropos of Horace Vernet and military painters, Mr. Hamerton introduces us to Protais, an artist little known to Americans, but who deserves to become well known, on the evidence of the excellent work of which Mr. Hamerton gives a copy. 'Before the Attack' is the title of the picture: a column of chasseurs halting beneath the slope of a hill in the gray dusk of morning and eagerly awaiting the signal to advance. Everything is admirably rendered—the cold dawn, the half-scared, half-alert expression of the younger soldiers, and the comparative indifference of the elder. It is plain that M. Protais knows his subject. We have seen it already pointed out, that, in speaking of him as the first French painter of military scenes who has attempted to subordinate the character of the general movement to the interest awakened by the particular figures, Mr. Hamerton is guilty of injustice to the admirable Raffet, whose wonderfully forcible designs may really be pronounced a valuable contribution to the military history of the First Empire. We never look at them ourselves, at least, without being profoundly thrilled and moved.

Of Rosa Bonheur Mr. Hamerton speaks with excellent discrimination; but she is so well known to Americans that we need not linger over his remarks. Of Troyon—also quite well known in this country—he has a very exalted opinion. The well-known lithograph, a 'Morning Effect', which Mr. Hamerton reproduces as a specimen of Troyon, is certainly a charming picture. We may add, that, while on the subject of Troyon, this author makes some useful remarks upon what he calls *tonality* in painting—a phenomenon of which Troyon was extremely, perhaps excessively, fond—remarks which will doubtless help many readers to understand excellences and to tolerate apparent eccentricities in pictures on which without some such enlightenment they would be likely to pass false judgement.

Of Décamps Mr. Hamerton speaks sympathetically; but we are not sure that we should not have gone farther. His paintings contain an immense fund of reality, hampered by much weakness, and yet unmistakable. He seems to have constantly attempted, without cleverness, subjects of the kind traditionally consecrated to cleverness. Apropos to cleverness, we may say that Mr. Hamerton gives a photograph from Gérôme, along with some tolerably stinted praise. The photograph is 'The Prisoner'—a poor Egyptian captive pinioned in a boat and rowed along the Nile, while a man at the stern twitches a guitar under his nose, or rather just over it, for he is lying on his back, and another at the bow sits grimly smoking the pipe of indifference. This work strikes us as no better than the average of Gérôme's pictures, which is placing a decided restriction upon it—at the same time that, if we add that it is not a bit worse, we give it strong praise. Mr. Hamerton speaks of Gérôme's *heartlessness* in terms in which most observers will agree with him. His pictures are for art very much what the novels of M. Gustave Flaubert are for literature, only decidedly inferior. The question of heartlessness brings Mr. Hamerton to Meissonier, whom he calls heartless too, but without duly setting forth all that he is besides.

The author closes his essay with a photograph from Frère, and another from Toulmouche—of whom it may be said, that the former paints charming pictures of young girls in the cabins of peasants, and the latter charming pictures of young girls in Paris drawing-rooms. But Frère imparts to his figures all the pathos of peasant life, and Toulmouche all the want of pathos which belongs to fashionable life.

We have already expressed our opinion that the one really great modern painter of France is conspicuous by his absence from this volume. Other admirable artists are absent, concerning whom, by the way, Mr. Hamerton promises at some future time to write, and others indeed are well represented. But not one of these, as we turn over the volume, seems to us to possess the rare distinction of an exquisite genius. We have no wish, however, to speak of them without respect. Such men fill the intervals between genius and genius, and combine to offer an immense tribute to the immeasurable power of culture.

FRENCH PICTURES IN BOSTON

1872

THERE HAS lately been on exhibition in Boston, at the rooms of Messrs. Doll and Richards,[1] a small but remarkable collection of French pictures. These paintings, we believe, are privately owned in Boston; and united thus in a charming room they afford a pleasant suggestion and premonition of the artistic taste and wealth scattered, potentially at least, through our supposedly sordid American community. Several of the first names of the French school are represented—Delacroix, Decamps, Troyon, Rousseau, Jules Duprez, Daubigny, Diaz. They form a group interesting in more ways than one—as to the reciprocal light they shed upon each other as members of a school, and as to their opportune and almost pathetic testimony just now to the admirable aesthetic gifts of the French mind.

None of them are more eloquent in this latter sense than the great Troyon—the edge of a wood, seen on a dampish day in September. A cluster of magnificent forest oaks occupies the middle and left of the picture, rich with the waning maturity of summer, with their sturdy foliage just beginning to rust and drop, leaf by leaf, into the rank river-grass, streaked with lingering flowers, at their feet. The trees are a magnificent study—or rather not a study, but a perfect achievement. They stand there solid and mighty, without the smallest loss of their hugeness and dignity. It is noteworthy too, that, vast and elaborate as they are, they are far from filling and crowding the picture; they are only part of the great landscape beyond and beside them; they seem

---

[1] These 'rooms' were at 145 Tremont Street from 1871 until 1880. Perhaps James had them in his memory when he described the 'sky-lighted inner shrine of Tremont Street' where Strether saw the Lambinet landscape.

really, as we may say, to irradiate atmosphere and space. The tone of colour in this work is extremely subdued, yet consummately sustained—sober and brilliant at once; a powerful harmony of gray and gray-green, relieved with quiet russet and brown. The colour plays along this narrow scale with a kind of rich melancholy, such as perfectly befits the drama of lusty summer just conscious of the touch of autumn. The especial ground of interest in the picture is its happy grasp of the medium between the hard definiteness of some of our recent English and American ultra-realists in landscape, and that exaggerated makeshift breadth and tendency to rough generalization which marks so many French landscapists, and of which the large Daubigny, in this same collection, is so striking an example.

Its smaller companion, although of a more familiar and commonplace cast, is still very charming. It represents half a dozen cows, driven through a field by a young girl on a late summer day. The happy, crooked, scattered movement of the cattle; the sweet midsummer whisper which seems to lurk in the meadow-side copse; the rare and natural luminosity, without *recherche*, without a hint of that cunning *morbidezza* which marks the corresponding portion of the small Decamps near by, in the tender sky, dappled at cool intervals—make of the work a genuine pastoral. It is, perhaps, as a whole, a little blank and thin; but it is indefinably *honnête*. It reminds us of one of George Sand's rural novels—*François le Champi* or the *Petite Fadette*.

By so much as Troyon is a diffuse painter is Théodore Rousseau, who is here represented by two extremely characteristic works, a concentrated one. The dogged soberness of his manner strikes us as the last word of the distinctively French treatment of landscape. We know of no painter who depends less on extraneous effects and suggestions, on the graceful byplay of a Diaz, or the almost literary allusiveness of a Decamps. His sole effort seems to be to enter more and more into his subject. Sometimes, we think, he gets lost in it, as in the overwrought interconfusion of the trees and ground in the smaller of these two pictures. It wears, nevertheless, an admirable expression of size and space, of condensed light and fresh air. The sky, in spite of a thick, over-glazed look, is full of a natural cloud-filtered radiance. The picture, altogether, has more nature than grace. Its larger companion, however, is a thoroughly noble and perfect work. A broad low plain at dusk, with a small stone farm-house and its wall to the right, and, to the left, in mid-distance, a light screen of thin young trees, form the lower portion; over this is erected as true a sunset as ever was painted. The field of sky is immense and the distribution of cloud most elaborate; but the composition is admirably free from that cheapness of effect which attends upon the common sunset of art. It is not an American sunset, with its lucid and untempered splendour of orange and scarlet, but the sinking of a serious old-world day, which sings its death-song in a muffled key. The tone of the clouds is gray, that of the light a deep grave crimson; and this crimson and gray, this conflicting cold and warmth, play against each other in the vast realm of evening with tremendous effect. It is all admirably true; you seem, as you look, to be plodding heavy-footed across the field and stumbling here and there in the false light which is neither night nor day. The struggle and mixture of the dusk and glow in all the little ruts and furrows of the field is perfectly rendered. If we were asked for an example in painting of that much-discussed virtue 'sincerity', we should indicate this work as a capital instance.

In just the same measure we should indicate the beautiful Decamps hard by as a signal instance of factitious art. Decamps won his spurs years ago as one of the first of the modern realists, and we fancy that we might trace in his successive works a vivid reflection of the private history of the movement he represents. Poor realism! we can fancy the puzzled sadness with which she beholds herself imaged in this little canvas of Decamps. We can imagine her crying out with the old woman in the nursery song, who in her sleep was curtailed of her petticoats, 'Lord, have mercy! this is none of I.' Decamps represents that gifted class of artists—they exist in literature, in music, in the drama, as well as in the plastic arts—whose mission is the pursuit of effect, without direct reference to truth. Decamps was superbly endowed for this pursuit; the effect he sought he seldom missed. He has certainly not missed it in this little picture of 'The Centurion'. A more subtle piece of painting we have seldom beheld—a work in which skill and science and experience offer a more effective substitute for the simplicity of genuine inspiration, for that quality which is so strongly embodied in that least clever of fine pictures, the small Delacroix which hangs near it. It is in this respect a striking example of its class. In refinement of taste, in delicacy of invention, in a nice calculation of effect, it is incomparably fine; and up to a certain point it grows and grows upon the mind; but it lacks the frank good faith of the best masters. The nominal subject of the work is the incident related in the first gospel, of the centurion who comes to Jesus at Capernaum to demand that his servant be healed, and who finds that, inasmuch as he believed, in the self-same hour it was done. There is something that provokes a smile in the attempt of a painter like Decamps to treat a Scriptural subject—a painter who represents the opposite pole of art from even the most sceptical of the great pietistic masters. But in truth, he has shown his good taste by touching the theme as lightly as possible, and making it the mere pretext for a bit of picturesqueness. The face of Christ is not even painted; faces were evidently Decamps's weak point. It is as a fantastic composition that the picture must be judged. We know not what warrant the author has for his conception of the colossal architecture of Capernaum; but, after all, what better warrant need one have in such a case than such a penetrating imagination? The little group of figures occupies the middle of the scene, dipped, as it were, in a wash of cool purple shadow; out of this rise mighty, into a glow of afternoon light, the walls and towers and ramparts and battlements of some visionary city of the antique world. The great success of the picture is in its hint of this pagan vastness (you see the heavy smoke from a perfumed altar rising in the distance) and in the golden luminosity with which the scene is suffused. It seems to us to bear about the same relation to probable fact as some first-rate descriptive titbit of Edgar Poe or Charles Baudelaire; where-as, if we were to seek for a literary correlative for that sadly imperfect Delacroix near by, we should find it in some fragment of Shelley. Our Decamps, in its somewhat arbitrary and am-biguous air of grandeur and lustre, might have been painted by a kind of unimpassioned Turner. Say what we will, it is only a supremely vivid fancy that could have conceived those dizzy and mellow-toned walls and towers and distilled that narrow strip of morbidly tender sky. The predominance of the picturesque in painting is very possibly the token of a decaying system; but this surely is the picturesque at its best; and when we think of all the antecedent failures, all the efforts and gropings, the refined aesthetic experience implied by just such a success, the interest of the work is doubled.

It is still further increased when we compare the picture with the neighbouring Delacroix. We have left this work to the last, because it is the most difficult to characterize fairly—because, indeed, we find it hard even to fix our impression of it. It is a signal example of the author's strength and weakness, of the qualities which charm and those which irritate. These are so grotesquely combined in his genius that it is nearly impossible to separate them and open a distinct account with each. We may even say that he pleases, in certain cases, by virtue of his errors—by reason, at least, of a certain generous fallibility which is the penalty of his generous imagination. Delacroix, more than any painter we know, must be judged by the total impression. This, at least as a final one, is often very slow to come; but it may, we think, generally be resumed in some such conclusion as this—that here is a painter whose imaginative impulse begins where that of most painters ends. It is not that, as a rule, he selects grotesque or exceptional subjects; but that he sees them in a ray of that light that never was on land or sea—which is simply the light of the mind. This conceded, we must admit that the light of Delacroix's mind produced some very singular optical effects. Some of the painter's eccentricities of manner in the present work are so flagrant that any child can point them out. The scene represents a dozen men in Eastern dress, gathered about a campfire, before which one of them stands, with outstretched hand, delivering himself, apparently, of a story or a chant. The fire round which the Arabs are gathered emits no light; as a fire it is quite unpainted; the faces and limbs of the men themselves are so many apologies for the things they represent; the horses tethered in the background are indicated by the very simplest design that will decently serve. Yet in spite of these salient faults, the picture is singularly forcible and true. The *sentiment* of the attitudes, the accidents, the 'form and presence' of the scene, throb there with such a vital warmth, that we can imagine ourselves seeking and enjoying it, in its permanent human significance, long after the hundred literal merits of certain other painters of mark have come to seem stale and soulless. We can imagine ourselves becoming intensely fond of a Delacroix— never of a Meissonier. Delacroix takes you so frankly into the confidence of his faults, that you scarcely resent them, and by the very fact, indeed, stand in a closer sympathy with him. Like all really great masters—like his great brothers in art, Turner and Tintoretto—he can be described only by seeming paradoxes and contradictions. He is at once the most general and the most specific of painters. His drawing is in the last degree incorrect, and yet he produces unsurpassed effects of design, form, and attitude. As with Tintoretto, you fancy him one of the slightest of colourists, till you begin to conceive he is one of the greatest. His great merit, to our mind, is that, more than any of his modern rivals save Turner, he has an eye for that which, for want of a better name, we may call the *mystery* of a scene, and that under his treatment its general expression and its salient details are fused into the harmony of poetry itself. But we stop short; Delacroix must not be written about; he must be seen and felt. In speaking of him thus, we pretend merely to record a personal predilection.

Of the small Diaz and the Jules Duprez there is nothing especial to be said. Diaz is as usual a charming trifler, and Jules

Duprez a very worthy rival of Rousseau. We should have liked, with more space, to devote a few words to three or four American pictures lately visible in the same rooms. The most important of these is a large landscape by Mr. John La Farge, the view of a deep seaward-facing gorge, seen from above, at Newport. This is in every way a remarkable picture, full of the most refined intentions and the most beautiful results, of light and atmosphere and of the very poetry of the situation. We have rarely seen a work in which the painter seems to have stored away such a permanent fund of luminosity. There are parts of the picture which might have been painted by a less sceptical Decamps. A portrait of a little girl, in the most charmingly quaint dress of black velvet and lace and pearls, by Mr. R. C. Porter, demands also very explicit recognition. In complexion and costume, and in the masterly treatment she has received, Mr. Porter's bewitching little model reminds us of some swarthy Infanta of Velasquez. This work, at least, is a purely American product, the author's opportunities for study having been such only as our own country affords. The firmness and richness and confidence of the painter's execution, the excellent modelling of the face and neck, the hint of a sort of easy and spontaneous enjoyment of his materials, indicate that the artist has the real temperament of the painter. Mr. Porter has, in this and other cases, done so well that he may be considered to have pledged and committed himself. His admirers, in future, will be expectant and exacting. We must note, in conclusion, a small picture by Vedder—a little pictorial lyric, as we have heard it called, on the theme of faded stuffs. A young woman, dressed in a charming bedimmed old silken gown, stands before an antique escritoire, in relief against a *passé* hanging of tapestry, opening a box of jewels. The tone of the picture is suffused by a hint of that elegant and melancholy hue which is known, we believe, by the name of ashes-of-roses. A certain flatness and semi-decorative monotony of touch is very discreetly apportioned, and operates as an additional charm.

PICTURES BY WILLIAM MORRIS HUNT, GÉRÔME AND OTHERS

1872

THE exhibition of the works of Mr. William Hunt,[1] at Doll and Richards, struck us as not fairly representative of the painter. It contained, indeed, one of his most ambitious, but not most successful pictures, the 'Hamlet'; but, in general, the works present suggested invidious comparisons with various absent companions, which those who have seen them associate with the artist's best powers—the 'Girl at the Fountain', the 'Belated Kid', the portrait of Chief Justice Shaw, and various charming portraits of women. A critic who should judge Mr. Hunt on the evidence of this collection would, we think, distinctly underestimate him; though, on further information, he would be compelled to regret that the artist should tend increasingly, as it seems, to identify himself with his inferior manner. The trouble is that, while his talent is pre-eminently delicate, his method has taken a turn toward coarseness, so that in the case of a number of these recent pictures, the spectator was vexed by a sense that they deserved to have been better. Delicate talents cannot afford to be reckless, and Mr. Hunt is interesting, in every case, just in proportion as he has been careful. The thoroughly agreeable works of last month's exhibition were neither the 'Hamlet', nor

[1] 'At the risk perhaps of appearing to make my own scant adventure the pivot of that early Newport phase I find my reference to William Hunt and his truly fertilising action on our common life much conditioned by the fact that, since W. J., for the first six months or so after our return, daily and devotedly haunted his studio, I myself did no less, for a shorter stretch, under the irresistible contagion.'

Notes of a Son and Brother (1914), Ch. IV.

the 'Boy and the Butterfly', nor the portrait of Bishop Williams, but half a dozen small canvases, chiefly landscapes, of the most charming quality. We may instance especially the two companion-pieces, representing respectively a bit of French garden and a couple of quaint French houses. Into each of these the very *genius loci* has been cunningly infused. Why should the artist who painted that admirable patch of sky in the latter picture have been content with the sky which forms the background to the young girl in white? It must be confessed, however, that in spite of her sky, this young lady stands up in the open air with no small reality and grace.

Messrs. Williams and Everett have exhibited an excellent Gérôme; none other than the well-known 'Combat de Coqs'. Though small and of simple elements, this picture is a capital example of the master, and presents in remarkably convenient shape the substance of his talent—that indefinable *hardness* which is the soul of his work. The present picture is equally hard in subject and in treatment, in feeling and in taste. A young man, entirely naked, is stooping upon one knee, and stirring two bristling game-cocks to battle. A young woman, also naked— more than naked, as one somehow feels Gérôme's figures to be —reclines beside him and looks lazily on. The room and the accessories are as smartly antique as Gérôme alone could have made them. The picture is of course painted with incomparable precision and skill; but the unloveliness of the subject is singularly intensified by the artist's sentimental sterility. There is a total lack of what we may call moral atmosphere, of sentimental redundancy or emotional by-play. The horrid little game in the centre, the brassy nudity of the youth, the peculiarly sensible carnality of the young woman, the happy combination of moral and physical shamelessness, spiced with the most triumphant cleverness, conduce to an impression from which no element of interest is absent, save the good old-fashioned sense of being pleased.

THE METROPOLITAN MUSEUM'S
'1871 PURCHASE'
1872

THE collection of pictures forming the germ of what it is so agreeable to have the *Revue des Deux Mondes* talking of currently as the *Musée de New York*, has recently been lodged in a handsome and convenient gallery, masked by one of the residential brown-stone fronts of the Fifth Avenue. These pictures, one hundred and seventy-five in number, are, as we may remind our readers, with some dozen exceptions, of the Dutch and Flemish schools. They consist for the most part of the substance of two private collections, purchased in Paris and Brussels respectively, in the summer of 1870.[1] Their authenticity has in each case been attested by proper evidence and by the judgement of experts, and in possessing them the Metropolitan Museum of Art has an enviably solid foundation for future acquisition and development. It is not indeed to be termed a brilliant collection, for it contains no first-rate example of a first-rate genius; but it may claim within its limits a unity and continuity which cannot fail to make it a source of profit to students debarred from European opportunities. If it has no gems of the first magnitude, it has few specimens that are decidedly valueless. We shall by no means attempt a full enumeration of its contents, but we shall make a few remarks on the more important works—a task rendered more easy by the altogether exemplary and artistic Catalogue.

In a corner of the gallery are ranged half a dozen indifferent examples of archaic masters, which will be hardly more than

[1] For details of this transaction see *A History of the Metropolitan Museum of Art* by Winifred E. Howe, New York, 1913.

glanced at as an overture to the main spectacle. The visitor will turn with little delay to the Rubens; he will turn from it perhaps with some disappointment. The picture has a fair share of the Rubens mass and breadth, but it lacks the Rubens lustre—the glowing relief which we demand as the token of a consummate Rubens. The subject is a 'Return from Egypt', and contains four figures—Mary and Joseph leading the Child between them, and the Deity watching them benignantly from the clouds. It is brown and dull in tone, and the figures have not the full-blooded aspect of most of the Rubens progeny; but like all emanations, however slight, of a great talent, it improves vastly on acquaintance and puts forth a dozen reminders of its distinguished kinship. The real success of the picture is in the free and sweeping contour of Mary, and in her extremely handsome head, the outline and relief of which, with her hair and its falling drapery, seems to us vividly characteristic of the master. Rubens alone, too, could have made his Virgin so gracefully huge and preserved the air of mild maternity in such massive bulk. His Mary is a gentle giantess. The picture altogether, though inadequate as an example, is a powerful and delightful reminder. The great Flemish master is represented by a second piece, of large dimensions but limited interest—a couple of lions chasing an antelope. His lions are of the same mock-heroic order as the pictorial charger of that period, but they bound forward with a fine ferocious glare and spring. The name next in importance to that of Rubens is that of Van Dyck, who contributes two imperfect, but interesting works, of which more anon. Jacob Jordaens, a smaller name, is represented by a work of larger substance than either of these. His 'Visit of Saint John to the Infant Jesus' falls little short of being a masterpiece; it would have needed only to be pitched a note or so higher in the scale of the ideal to challenge comparison with Rubens at his best. But these high notes, we take it, Jordaens never struck, and he remains simply one of the first of the secondary masters. He has been happily called 'a plebeian Rubens'; which possibly signifies that, if he was a duller and narrower genius, he had a stronger grasp of

much of the more immediate detail of nature. What he lacks on
the side of Rubens he shows a tendency to recover on the side
of Rembrandt. He seems oppressed and sobered by that sense of
reality which sat so lightly on the buoyant spirit of his master.
The present composition represents the infant Jesus—a tall,
lusty, ugly baby, with his feet planted on a terrestrial globe and
trampling a serpent, leaning with a sort of sturdy shyness against
his mother's side, looking in childish surprise—with an air even
of timid envy of his toy—at the little Saint John who rides
toward him on a lamb. The Virgin is a sweet-faced young woman
whom the painter evidently meant to make pretty within the
limits of Flemish probability, and the child has an odd look of
having just waked up the least bit cross from a nap. Above these
figures are distributed Joseph and the parents of John, looking on
with homely tenderness, the pious concentration of which is
deepened by the sombre vertical light in which the group is
steeped. The Joseph, as we take him to be, leaning his grave and
furrowed face on his big brown hand, is a triumph of expression
and of execution. A plebeian genius, we repeat with emphasis.
We doubt that there has ever been a more spontaneous reflection
of the hard-handed lowliness of the *entourage* of Christ. A work
classified by its dimensions, if not quite by its merit, with this
finely sober Jordaens, is the large and brilliant Gaspard de Crayer
which hangs in the place of honour in the gallery. This 'Diogenes
and Alexander' figured for some time in the collection of the
Empress Josephine at Malmaison. It is a pleasing, almost a charming composition; for although it is an attempt at the heroic-
historical, it is treated with a frank good faith which keeps it
within the range of one's immediate sympathies. The frank
boyish surprise of Alexander, with his steel-clad chest and his
comely head, is very happy and natural, and recalls, at a distance,
the superb modern physiognomy of the generous youth who
stands for the hero in Paul Veronese's great 'Alexander' in
London. Crayer was not a Paul Veronese, but he was a rich
and agreeable colourist, and he diffused through his work an
indefinable geniality which reproduces, in an infinitely lower key,

the opulent serenity of Rubens. This picture, with its slight vulgarity and want of mystery, of tone, is perhaps the 'loudest' piece of colouring in the gallery. We ought not to omit mention of the little page who holds Alexander's red cloak and peers from behind at the recumbent Diogenes. His head has charming vivacity and relief, and is almost a compensation for that of the dappled Bucephalus who prances officially in the rear. An immense 'Jason' by Van Diepenbeck, a pupil of Rubens, is rather a vacant production.

These three fine works share their supremacy with half a dozen strong portraits, to which, as sources of instruction, we feel tempted to offer an even more emphatic welcome. The 'Miss de Christyn' of Van Dyck stands first among them, and is perhaps the most delicate of the stronger pictures. This portrait is, oddly, the more interesting for being hardly more than a third-rate specimen of the master; for it seems that, if we are to have first-rate names, we are, yet awhile, to have them with abatements. The abatement here is a poverty of colouring, possibly aggravated by time, which the Catalogue but imperfectly disguises under the designation of 'extreme delicacy in the tones'. This delicacy the picture possesses, but the spectator unfamiliar with Van Dyck may judge of what it lacks by turning to the smaller example, the 'Saint Martha interceding for the Cessation of the Plague at Tarascon', and noting the lovely flesh-glow of the tumbling cherubs who uplift the pretty postulant into the blue, and who form, with the warm purple of her robe, the main success of the picture. The subject of the portrait perhaps is half its merit—a pale, plain-faced, bright-eyed young gentlewoman carrying her ruff and fan with peculiar distinction. The physiognomy is excessively, almost morbidly, refined, and the painter has touched it with proportionate acuteness. Close beside this elegant work hangs a masterpiece of inelegant vigour, 'Hille Bobbe of Haarlem', by Franz Hals—a broadly grinning street-wench dashed upon the canvas by a brush superbly confident of saving science in the midst of its hit-or-miss rapidity. The picture is in hardly more than two or three gradations of brown, but it is

instinct with energy and a certain gross truth. The face is a
miracle of ugliness; but it is noticeable how little of fantasy, of
imaginative irony, there is in the painter's touch. It needed a
Dutch Franz Hals—sturdy artist as he was—to attribute to
woman such hideousness as a plain matter of course.

Two portraits of equal vigour and of greater delicacy are a
'Burgomaster' by Van der Helst, and a 'Gentleman'—a perfect
gentleman—by Aadrian de Vries. In the former picture the
subject and the artist are rarely well matched, and the result is a
work of the most harmonious completeness—the perfect prose
of portraiture. We doubt that the mouth and chin of small local
authority were ever more inexorably fixed in their pursy identity
than these comfortable attributes of this most respectable Dutchman. It seems almost hyperbolical to talk of Van der Helst as an
artist; genuine painter as he was, his process is not so much the
common, leisurely, critical return upon reality and truth as a
bonded and indissoluble union with it; so that in all his un-
mitigated verity you detect no faintest throb of invention blossoming into style and straggling across the line which separates
a fine likeness from a fine portrait. But it sounds like arrant
frivolity to breathe a word of disparagement against this richly
literal genius, and we can easily fancy that, if Nature were to
give her voice, and appoint once for all her painter-in-ordinary,
she would lay a kindly hand on the sturdy shoulder of Van der
Helst, and say, 'One must choose for the long run: this man I
can *trust.*' And yet the really beautiful de Vries proves that a
little style spoils nothing. Just a little, this portrait contains; but
that little is of the best quality, as may be inferred from the fact
that this painter's works were habitually made to pass by the
dealers for productions of Rembrandt, to the great curtailment
of the author's proper fame. Rembrandt, of whom the Museum
contains no specimen, need not have disowned this mellow and
vigorous head. It is taking rather a harsh tone, in general, to
refer our young painters off-hand to the prime masters, and to
expect in their labours a direct and undiluted reflection of Rembrandt and Titian; but here is an artist modest enough to be

approached as a peer, and yet of substantial attributes as a teacher. The unpretending firmness of this work gives it a value rarely possessed by clever modern portraits, and sets us wondering once more what mystic and forgotten influence it was that governed the art of portraiture during the happy span of years in which this master and his precursors flourished, and kept success a solemn rule and usage. We are inclined to think that our modern degenerescence—we assume it to be incontestable —is less a loss of skill than a defect of original vision. We know more about human character, and we have less respect for human faces. We take more liberties with those that are offered us; we analyse and theorise and rub off the bloom of their mystery, and when we attempt to reproduce them, are obliged to resolve a swarm of fine conflicting impressions back into the unity and gravity of fact. A painter like this quietly wise de Vries (and *a fortiori* a painter like Van Dyck or like Titian) seems to have received and retained a single massive yet flexible impression, which was part and parcel, somehow, of a certain natural deference for his subject. There is little in the remaining works of this order, however, that we need despair of equalling. An exceptionally large Terburg (a likeness of the painter) has lost in interest what it has gained in magnitude. The famous white satin dress of Terburg, however, is represented with almost equal brilliancy in a charming Netscher. The head of a 'Lady', by Lely, is fairly pleasing and unwontedly decent and *collet-monté;* and a 'Duchess of Mazarin', by Nicholas Maas, is worth comparing with the 'Miss de Christyn' for an illustration of the difference between factitious and sincere elegance. This portrait, with the Lely in a less degree, has a poverty and impurity of colouring which almost denotes moral turpitude in the painter. The unlovely cadaverous tones of the Nicholas Maas are, for that matter, in perfect harmony with the sinister flimsiness of his Duchess. Portraiture is once more strongly exemplified in the one important Italian work in the collection, a Paris Bordone; a fine-eyed, sweet-mouthed lad in armour, with a scarf of genuine Venetian purple. This is a noble piece of colouring, and stands

out in agreeably vivid Venetianism. The picture gains by juxtaposition. We know what it is to have turned with a sort of moral
relief, in the galleries of Italy, to some small stray specimen of
Dutch patience and conscience, and we have now a chance to
repair our discourtesy and do homage to Italian 'style'. An
Italian master, whatever his individual worth, possesses this grace
as a matter of course; with the Dutch painters and the smaller
Flemings it is a happy accident. With how little genuine strength
it may occasionally be allied, may be seen in the three small
specimens of that tardy fruit of the Venetian efflorescence, G.
B. Tiepolo. Sincerity, and even sense, with this florid master of
breezy drapery and fastidious *pose*, is on its last legs; but he
retains the instinct of brilliant and elegant arrangement. He offers
a desperately faint but not unmusical echo from the azure-
hearted ceilings of Paul Veronese. Elegance for elegance, however, we prefer that of the small Sassoferrato, the usual Sanc-
tissima Virgo, breathless with adoration, with her usual hard
high polish of creamy white and chilly blue. We confess to a
sneaking relish for a good Sassoferrato. It may have but a pinch
of sentiment, but it is certain to be a pretty piece of work. The
artist had nothing to offer but 'finish', but he offers this in elegant profusion. The French school is adequately represented
only by a small Greuze, which, however, is indubitably French
in manner—a finished sketch for the head of one of the daughters
in the well-known 'Malédiction Paternelle'. It represents a rustic
minois chiffonné, as the French say, in tears and dishevelment,
and includes the usual gaping kerchief which marks the master
and the time. It is at once solid and charming; with a charm owing
partly to the skilful clearness of those whitish-gray tones which
mark the dawn of the sober colouring of modern French art.
The great name of Velasquez is attached to a composition characteristic only in its rugged breadth of touch—a map of mighty
Spanish pomegranates, grapes, and figs, blocked into shape by
a masterly brush, upon that gloomy ground-tone which we
associate with the Spanish genius in general, and which, in the
works of this, with Cervantes, as we suppose, its greatest

representative, oppresses and troubles the spectator's soul. This
picture may be said to express the roughly imaginative view of
fruit; for a most brilliantly literal treatment of the same subject
the observer may turn with profit to a noble piece by Franz
Snyders, the great Flemish animal-painter. The comparatively
modern Spaniard, Goya, contributes a little 'Jewess of Tangier'
—a sketch, by a cunning hand, of a doll-like damsel, bundled
up in stiff brocade and hung about with jewels. The picture is
slight but salient. The remaining strangers in the gallery demand
little notice, and consist chiefly of an indifferent Sir Joshua
Reynolds and several questionable specimens of Albani, the
painter of allegorical infancy.

The chief strength of the collection resides in a number of
those works which we especially associate with the Dutch school
—*genre* subjects, rustic groups, and landscapes. In this line
figure several excellent specimens of eminent names—a superb
Teniers, a good example of each of the Van Ostades, a fine Jan
Steen, three capital Solomon Ruysdaels, a lovely Berghem, an
interesting Hobbema. The little Teniers—the 'Lendemain des
Noces'—is not only a masterpiece of its kind, but may almost
be termed the gem of the Museum. It presents, in remarkable
purity, every merit which we commonly attribute to those vivid
portrayals of rustic conviviality which Louis XIV dismissed
with a 'Take away those *magots*—those little monsters': elaborate
finish, humour tempered by grace, charm of colour, and mingled
minuteness and amplitude of design. It swarms with figures, of
indescribable vivacity and variety, and glows with an undimmed
clearness of tone which promises a long enjoyment of its perfections. May it speak to our children's children with the same
silvery accent, and help them to live for an hour, in this alien
modern world, the life of old bucolic Flanders! To drink and to
dance, to dance and to drink again, was for the imagination of
Teniers the great formula of human life; and his little *bons-
hommes*—picked out in the tenderest tints of gray and blue,
russet and yellow—lift their elbows and lock their hands and
shake their heels with a rich hilarity which makes each

miniature clown of them, whether in jacket or in kerchief, seem a
distinct and complete creation. They are assembled here in a
great audible swarm before a meadow-side tavern, at a couple
of tables spread beneath the trees, and in scattered groups and
couples of dancers in the foreground. Genuine boors as they
are, however, and full of rustic breadth and roundness, they yet
have a touch of grace and *finesse* which separates them widely
from the grotesque creations of the two other noted interpreters
of similar scenes here present, Jan Steen and Isaac Van Ostade.
They pay a certain tribute to elegance. The painter is very far
from partaking of the *naïveté* of his figures; he is a humourist,
and he observes them from without; and while he pulls the
strings which set them dancing, he keeps an eye on the spectator, and cunningly modulates and qualifies his realism. It is an
audacious thing to say, doubtless, but we cannot help thinking
that Louis XIV took a narrower view of the matter than befitted
his exalted position, when he pronounced the artist capable of
producing the little man in the scarlet cap to the right of the
present picture a mere painter of *magots*. Teniers has taken the
measure of this sturdy reveller, as he falls into step with arms
akimbo and eyes askance, with an acuteness which has the advantage of not being blunted by contempt. Isaac Van Ostade,
however, with his 'Fiddler at the Cottage Door', treats us to
magots with a vengeance. Never was human hideousness embalmed in a richer medium than the precious atmosphere of
this composition. In its luminous centre is seen the front of a
hovel, before which a decrepit fiddler is scraping his instrument
for the delectation of a horrible crone who leans over the low
half-door, and of several children who come sniffing round him
with the motion of so many blind puppies. To the right, in the
dark brown foreground, overarched with an equal duskiness,
three or four drinkers are gathered round a barrel. The poor
little peasants, fixed in this mellow *impasto* as helplessly as flies
in amber, with their huge pendulous noses and their groping
and bungling gestures, seem stultified with facial deformity. It
is impossible to conceive a more unprotestingly sordid view of

humanity; and it takes its final stamp from the pitiless ugliness of the innocent children. We can only repeat of this singular genius what we had occasion to say of Franz Hals; that it is a marvel to see the artistic faculty so vigorous, and yet so limited; dealing so freely with the pictorial idea, and yet so servile to base fact. Teniers, beside him, is a Veronese of low life. A work of much greater charm, indeed of the greatest, is the little picture by Aadrian Van Ostade, elder brother and master of Isaac. In this delicious cabinet-piece sits a 'Smoker', filling his pipe amid a wealth of mellow shadows. His figure is full of homely truth and finish, but the only bit of detail is a door vaguely opening in the brown gloom behind, to admit a person whom you hardly discern. This work, a veritable gem, is almost misplaced in a general collection. It ought to hang on the library wall of the most fastidious of amateurs, and be shown solemnly to a chosen friend, who holds his breath for fear of tarnishing its lucid bloom. Of Jan Steen, noted for his vigour and his crudity, there are two strong specimens. One of these, a Dutch 'Kermesse', with the usual boors footing it before the usual tavern, is chiefly remarkable for the figure of a buoyant wench, with flying cap-strings, tossing her head to the music, and shaking her skirts with admirable spirit and glee; the other, No. 127, a finer piece of painting, offers as frank a treatment of a coarse subject as often finds its way upon canvas. Mainly noteworthy are the strong handling of the mass of tumbled bedclothes which occupies the foreground, and the broad realisation of the face, such as it is, of the Dutch Molly Seagrim, who figures as heroine in the episode. Never was a certain redeeming grace more brutally dispensed with. This is more than an ugly picture; it is an offensive act. It makes one think more meanly of the human imagination.

The three noble little Solomon Ruysdaels may at once close our enumeration of the important group-pieces and open the list of the landscapes. There are pictures in the collection of a far more exquisite touch than these, but none of a franker and more wholesome veracity; none that help the spectator so effectively to feel the breath of the level and broad-skied landscape of

Holland. 'A Kermesse', the largest of these three subjects, represents a crowd of country folks collected under a wintry
morning sky before a little tavern, beside a broad frozen stream.
The festival is apparently not yet under way, for there is little
movement in the crowd and certainly no great outlay of invention; yet consisting simply of these stolid little mannikins—well-
wadded burghers, mounted on sturdy nags with buxom wives
and sweethearts *en croupe*, and of a roughly brushed effect of
clear winter light, the picture has an indefinable fascination. The
scene is specialised, as it were, by a dozen coarsely happy touches;
it seems timed, to an hour. The huge cold sky, with its diffused
light, its streaks of pale blue, and the chill-stiffened drag and
stretch of its thin clouds, are admirably rendered, and with a
want of what we may call the coquetry of the brush and
palette, which leaves us wondering that any degree of illusion
should result from such bald simplicity of means. The painter's
means, however, were of course not so simple as they look. The
same solid singleness of effect gives his little 'Marine' a peculiar
charm. A sloop tumbles across a bay; and the toss of the boat,
the pulse of the water, the whistle of the breeze, the moist gray
light, seem to generate a kind of saline aroma. Never was landscape painted in such prosaic good faith. We should perhaps
have given precedence to the great 'Italian Landscape', by
Cornelis Huysmans—a work of infinite gravity and amplitude,
and fit to hang in the council chamber of a prince. It looks as if
it had been lifted straight from the walls of the Doria Gallery
at Rome, so full is it of all romantic Italian tradition and allusion.
Forests, rivers, crags and vales, castles and temples, shepherds
and flocks—everything finds a place in it and only adds to its
academic spaciousness and serenity. Such a work as this is to a
clever modern landscape what a fine piece of descriptive blank-
verse of antique rhythm and savour is to a knowing lyric in a
magazine. We know nothing of Cornelis Huysmans; but he too
was a painter, and he could handle an immense *donnée* in truly
heroic style. He has handled a smaller one most charmingly in a
picture with the same title (No. 12), to whose absurdly azure

cliff, rising in the lovely, bosky distance, we confess to having altogether lost our heart. These works are full to overflowing of style and tone; they would form an inexhaustible fund for our own artistic neophytes to draw upon—sons of an age which has somehow lost the secret of dignity. The small Hobbema, representing a road through a wood, is pleasing but not brilliant. Hobbema ranks in the Dutch landscape school second only to Jacob Ruysdael, but we doubt if he is ever strictly brilliant. A discreet and chastened grasp of local verisimilitude is his peculiar characteristic. This is achieved in the present case with a notably small expenditure of colour. It is a very sober view of nature, though not without a hint of poetry. The little subject is somehow sad—sad as some sunless hour of the world's youth. A picture in which poetry is to our sense very much more than hinted at is the veritable pearl of a Nicholas Berghem entitled 'Rest'. We strongly suspect that we over-estimate this charming little piece, for we confess that, though it is composed of elements more slender, possibly, than any of its companions, none of these have given us a more unmixed and tranquil pleasure. Surely, if human repose were ever to lose its precarious footing in our Western world, the idea would be tenderly embalmed in this delicious fragment of a pastoral. A bare-legged shepherd, leaning on his staff under a sketchy tree, his wife on the ground nursing her baby, and a couple of meagre sheep, blinking at the noonday light, form the sum of its attractions; but it lives, it smiles, it glows through the chill of time. Its sentiment is hardly more than a graceful trick; but the trick, performed for the hundredth time, still draws tears from the eyes. A picture which has yielded us an almost equal degree of contemplative pleasure, and a far more solid piece of work, is the marvellous representation by Jan Van der Heyden of a 'Quay in Leyden'. We doubt whether 'touch' has ever achieved a more signal victory than in this compact pictorial sonnet, as we may call it, to the homely charms of brick-work. A narrow canal divides the picture; on each side of it rise a row of plain high-gabled dwellings. On the left, in the shade, stretches a footway, along which a woman in a ruff and hoop leads a little girl; opposite, the tall red houses dip their feet into the sluggish moat. A sort of antique, palpable stillness seems to pervade the scene; the perspective is so delicate and perfect that you fancy the very genius of geometry having retired thither from the academic hum near by, to revolve a proposition. The poetic strain resides in a ruddy golden exhalation from the plumbed and measured surfaces of brick, and in the infinite patience of the handiwork. The picture tells more of Dutch conscience than all its neighbours together. Each individual brick is laid with a sort of mathematical tenderness, squared and nicked and enriched with its proper particle of damp from the canal; and yet in this aggregation of minute touches, space and unity and harmony are cunningly preserved. A tree stands blooming on the edge of the canal, to the elaborate delicacy of whose foliage a microscope alone could do justice. It contains, we confess, more art than nature, and more fine hair-strokes than verdure. Enthusiasm seems almost profane over this exhibition of the very piety of high finish; but scrupulosity has no business to be so charming. The collection contains a very pretty show of examples of this precious refinement of touch. A couple of exquisite Velvet Breughels, with a brace of David Vinckleboons, and a small J. L. DeMarne, a later Flemish master (the latter, 'A Gust of Wind', is especially noticeable for the skill with which movement has been combined with fastidious over-finish), represent the supreme of the finical, the sublime of the microscopic. Their air of brittle loveliness suggests that the only proper service for them in the plebeian crush of this world would be to adorn the teacups and chimney-vases of some such exalted personage as that princess of anecdote who conceived cake to be the natural diet of the proletariat during the high bread-rates. It should be distinctly noted, however, that in all these little pictures a large sentiment of landscape survives this excessive condensation. In none of them is there any chance for breadth of colour; but the two Breughels have in their degree an amount of 'style' not unworthy of the great Cornelis Huysmans. Their miniature skies and hills and woods are quite in the grand manner. An equally forcible claim to distinction in this line is made by two elegant works by feminine hands; large and brilliant flower-pieces, signed respectively Rachel Ruysch and Margaret Haverman. They exhibit a magnificent elaboration of detail, an almost masculine grasp of the resources of high finish; but they offer, too, but the mechanical view of the subject. The poetry, the atmosphere, the metaphysics, as we may say, of flowers, have been better expressed by certain modern talents who, compared with these clever Dutch ladies, are sad bunglers with the brush, but who have at least read Keats and Shelley. We have it at heart to subjoin mention, in another sense—in the way of a 'moral'—of two small examples of that forlorn straggler in the march of Venetian art, Francesco Guardi. A Tiepolo of landscape we may call this gentleman. A comparison of his cold, colourless, sceptical reflections of Venetian splendour with the glowing fidelity and sincerity of such a picture as the 'Quay in Leyden' is really a theme for the philosopher. It vividly suggests that painfully frequent phenomenon in mental history, the demoralising influence of lavish opportunity. The Italian, born amid lovely circumstance, and debauched, as it were, by the very grace of his daily visions, dispenses with effort and insight, and trusts to mere artifice and manner—and a very light manner at that. He has some shallow faith that the charm of his subjects will save him. The Dutchman, familiar with a meaner and duskier range of effect, feels that, unless he is faithful, he is nothing. He must confer a charm as well as borrow one; he must bring his grist to the mill and grind it with his own strength; and his little picture, therefore, lives and speaks and tells of perfection; while those of Guardi are as torpid and silent as decay. We can, perhaps, not close our review more aptly than with the wholesome text that half the battle in art is won in the artist's conscience, that there are no easy triumphs, and that genuine charm is one of the deepest things in the world. We have neglected mention of many still noteworthy pictures; but we may pay them the compliment of saying that they, for the most part, preach some such sermon as this in good round terms.

If we have seemed to exaggerate the merit of their salient com-panions, our excuse is in our sense of this wholesome moral eloquence. We confess we should be sorry to forget that not an humble masterpiece of them all has anything that one may call imagination. But this makes us none the less willing to hold them up as examples. Imagination is not a quality to recommend; we bow low to it when we meet it, but we are wary of intro-ducing it into well-regulated intellects. We prefer to assume that our generous young art students possess it, and content ourselves with directing them to the charming little academy in the Fifth Avenue for lessons in observation and execution.[1]

[1] In 1872 the Metropolitan Museum was in the Dodsworth Building, formerly Allen Dodsworth's Dancing Academy, at 681 Fifth Avenue between 53rd and 54th Streets.

In his essay on New York in *The American Scene* (1907) James reflected on the evolution of this museum which by then had removed to its present site in Central Park: 'The thought of the acres of canvas and the tons of marble to be turned out into the cold world as the penalty of old error and the warrant for a clean slate ought to have drawn tears from the eyes. But these impending incidents affected me, in fact, on the spot, as quite radiant demonstrations. The Museum, in short, was going to be great, and in the geniality of the life to come such sacrifices, though resembling those of the funeral-pile of Sardanapalus, dwindled to nothing.'

THE WALLACE COLLECTION
IN BETHNAL GREEN
1873

BETHNAL GREEN is mainly known to Americans who remember their nursery ballad books as the residence of a certain Blind Beggar's daughter, the details of whose history indeed we confess ourselves to have forgotten. Known by its beggars in the era of primitive poetry, the region has beggary still for its sign and token. Its wretchedness has been so great that, till within a few months past, there may well have been a question whether a blind beggar was not rather a lucky person, and his imperfect consciousness a matter of congratulation. But now there is a premium on good eyesight, for Bethnal Green discerns itself through the thick local atmosphere the unillumined possessor of a Museum and a gallery of pictures—treasures which all well-dressed London is flocking eastward to behold. Half in charity and (virtually) half in irony, a beautiful art-collection has been planted in the midst of this darkness and squalor—an experimental lever for the 'elevation of the masses'. The journey to Bethnal Green is a long one, and leads you through an endless labyrinth of ever murkier and dingier alleys and slums, and the Museum, whether intentionally or not, is capitally placed for helping you to feel the characteristic charm of art—its being an infinite relief and refuge from the pressing miseries of life. That the haggard paupers of Bethnal Green have measured, as yet, its consolatory vastness, we should hesitate to affirm; for though art is an asylum, it is a sort of moated stronghold, hardly approachable save by some slender bridge-work of primary culture, such as the Bethnal Green mind is little practised in. There are non-paying days at the Museum, as well as days with a sixpenny fee, and on the occasion of our visit the sixpence had excluded the local population, so that we are obliged to repeat from hearsay a graceful legend that the masses, when admitted, exhibit, as one man, a discrimination of which Mr. Ruskin himself might be proud, and observe and admire on the very soundest principles. In the way of plain fact we may say that the building, as it stands, is the first of a projected series of District Museums, to be formed successively of various fragments of the temporary structure at South Kensington, as this great collection is more solidly enclosed; that it was erected toward the close of last year, and opened with great pomp by the Prince of Wales in the following June; and that it immediately derived its present great interest from the munificence of Sir Richard Wallace—heir of that eccentric *amateur* the late Marquess of Hertford—who offered the Museum the temporary use of his various art-treasures, and had them transported and installed at his own expense. It is with the Marquess of Hertford's pictures that we are concerned;[1] the collection otherwise consisting of a small Animal Products Department, which we leave to more competent hands, and (rather grimly, under the circumstances) of a group of FOOD SPECIMENS, neatly encased and labelled—interesting from a scientific, but slightly irritating from a Bethnal Green, that is, a hungry point of view.

Sir Richard Wallace has become eminent, we believe, from his large charities to the poor of Paris during the tribulations of the siege and the Commune, and the observer at Bethnal Green may almost wonder whether a portion at least of his benevolence may not have come to him by bequest, with Lord Hertford's pictures. The most striking characteristic of the collection, after its variety and magnificence, is its genial, easy, unexclusive taste—the good-nature of well-bred opulence. It pretends as little as possible to be instructive or consistent, to illustrate schools or to establish principles; that a picture pleased him was enough; he evidently

---

[1] These pictures now form a part of the Wallace Collection in Hertford House, Manchester Square, London.

regarded art-patronage as an amusement rather than a responsibility. The collection, for instance, is rich in Berghems; a painter for whom you haven't a word to say but that you like him, and that, right or wrong, the pretty trick which is his sole stock-in-trade amuses you. We remember, apropos of Berghem, expressing in these pages a rather emphatic relish for the very favourable little specimen in the possession of the New York Museum. The painter was then new to us; he has since become familiar, and we have at last grown to think of him as one of that large class of artists who are not quite good enough—to put it discreetly—to be the better for being always the same. The Bethnal Green catalogue opens with Sir Joshua Reynolds and Gainsborough, and it mentions no more delightful works than the three or four first-rate examples of these deeply English painters. There is something, to our perception, so meagre and ineffective in the English pictorial effort in general, that when it asserts itself, as in these cases, with real force and grace, it stirs in the sensitive beholder a response so sympathetic as to be almost painful. The merit is not at all school-merit, and you take very much the same sort of affectionate interest in it as you do in the success of a superior *amateur*. Nothing could well be more English, from the name inclusive, than Gainsborough's 'Miss Boothby'; a little rosy-cheeked girl, in a quaint mob-cap and a prodigious mantilla, surveying adult posterity from as divinely childish a pair of hazel eyes as ever was painted. The portrait, though sketchy as to everything but the face, is rich with the morality of all the English nurseries, since English nurseries were. Of Reynolds there are a dozen specimens; most of them interesting, but all inferior to the justly famous 'Nelly O'Brien'—a picture in which you hardly know whether you most admire the work or the subject.

In a certain easy, broad felicity it is almost a match for the finest Italian portraits, and indeed one may say that what Titian's 'Bella Donna' at Florence is in the Italian manner, this charming portrait is in the English. Here, truly, is an English beauty, and an English beauty at her best—but comparisons are odious.

Otherwise we should not scruple to say that *character* plays up into the English face with a vivacity unmatched in that of Titian's heroine—character, if we are not too fanciful, as sweet and true as the mild richness of colour, into which the painter's inspiration has overflowed. As she sits there smiling in wholesome archness, a toast at old-time heavy suppers we may be sure, his model seems to us the immortal image of a perfect temper. She melted many hearts, we conjecture, but she broke none; though a downright beauty, she was not a cruel one, and on her path through life she stirred more hope than despair. All this we read in the full ripe countenance she presents to us, slightly flattened and suffused by the shadow in which she sits. Her arms are folded in her lap; she bends forward and looks up, smiling, from her book. She wears a charming blue hat, which deepens the shadow across her face (out of which her smile gleams all the more cheerfully); a black lace shawl envelops her shoulders, and exposes her charming throat adorned with a single string of pearls; her petticoat is of a faded cherry colour, further subdued by a kind of gauze overskirt, and her dress is of blue satin striped with white. The whole costume is most simply, yet most delightfully, picturesque, and we respectfully recommend it as a model to be followed literally by any fair reader at loss what to wear at a masquerade. Sir Joshua's treatment of it shows him to have been within his narrow limits an instinctive colourist. His watery English sunlight compels the broken tones of silk and satin into a delicious silvery harmony; and hanging there in its crepuscular London atmosphere, the picture has a hardly less distinct individuality of colouring than that to which, as you stand before the Veroneses of the Ducal Palace, the reflected light of the Venetian lagoon seems to make so magical an answer. The painter's touch in the flesh-portions is less forcible; the arms and hands are sketchy, and rigidly viewed, the face and bosom lack relief; but expression is there, and warmth and a sort of delightful unity which makes faults venial. The picture misses greatness, doubtless; but it is one of the supremely *happy* feats of art. If as much can be said for another Sir Joshua, equally noted, the 'Strawberry Girl' (from the collection of Samuel Rogers), it must be said with a certain reserve. This is a charming sketch of a charming child, executed in hardly more than a few shades of brown with that broad, tender relish of infantine dimples in which the painter was unsurpassed; but that it is a little more fondly mannered than critically real, such a trio of neighbours as the uncompromising little Spanish Infants of Velasquez (to whom a child had the same sort of firm, immitigable outline as an adult) helps us materially to perceive. Velasquez's children are the children of history; Sir Joshua's, of poetry, or at least of rhymed lullaby-literature: and the two sorts of representation are as far asunder as Wordsworth and Cervantes. An irresistible little ballad-heroine is this Strawberry Maiden of Sir Joshua's: her pitifully frightened innocent eyes make her the very model of that figure so familiar to our childish imagination—the Little Girl Devoured by a Wolf. There are various other Reynoldses in the collection, but they rarely approach the high level of the two we have spoken of. Oftenest, and especially in the case of the portraits of women, their principal charm is the air of fresh-coloured domestic virtue in the sitter. They offer a vivid reflection of this phase of English character. Sir Thomas Lawrence's 'Lady Blessington' in no degree casts them into the shade. The lady's extremely agreeable face is no more that of a model English countess than the artist's clever hand is that of a first-rate painter.

Except in a couple of capital little Wilkies, four small Turners, and a charming series of Boningtons, English talent figures further with but moderate brilliancy. Turner, however, is a host in himself, and the four little finished water-colours which represent him here are almost a full measure of his genius. That genius, indeed, manifests, proportionately, more of its peculiar magic within the narrow compass of a ten-inch square of paper than on the broad field of an unrestricted canvas. Magic is the only word for his rendering of space, light, and atmosphere; and when you turn from the inscrutable illusion of his touch in these

matters, the triumphs of his cleverest neighbours—those of
Copley Fielding, for instance—seem but a vain *placage* of dead
paint. He never painted a distance out of which it seems a longer
journey back to your catalogue again than the receding undul-
ations of rain-washed moor in the little picture entitled 'Grouse-
Shooting'. It is hard to imagine anything more masterly than
the sustained delicacy of the gradations which indicate the shift-
ing mixture of sun and mist. When Art can say so much in so
light a whisper, she has certainly obtained absolute command of
her organ. The foreground here is as fine as the distance; half a
dozen white boulders gleam through the heather beside a black
pool with the most naturally picturesque effect. The companion
to this piece, 'Richmond, Yorkshire', reverses the miracle, and
proves that the painter could paint slumbering yellow light at
least as skilfully as drifting dusk. The way in which the luminous
haze invests and caresses the castle-crowned woody slope which
forms the background of this composition is something for the
connoisseur to analyse, if he can, but for the uninitiated mind
simply to wonder at. Opie's famous reply to the youth who
asked him with what he mixed his colours, 'With *brains*, sir!' is
but partly true of Turner, whose pigments seemed dissolved in
the unconscious fluid of a faculty more spontaneous even than
thought—something closely akin to deep-welling spiritual
emotion. Imagination is the common name for it, and to an
excess of imagination Turner's later eccentricities are reasonably
enough attributed; but what strikes us in works of the period to
which these belong is their marvellous moderation. The painter's
touch is as measured as the beat of a musical phrase, and indeed
to find a proper analogy for this rare exhibition of sustained
and, as we may say, *retained* power, we must resort to a sister-
art and recall the impression of a great singer holding a fine-
drawn note and dealing it out with measurable exactness. If
Turner is grave, Bonington is emphatically gay, and among
elegant painters there is perhaps none save Watteau (here
admirably represented) who is so rarely trivial. Bonington had
hitherto been hardly more than a name to us, but we feel that

he has been amply introduced by his delightful series of water-colours (some thirty in number) at Bethnal Green.

Bonington died young; these charming works and many more he executed before his twenty-eighth year. They are full of talent and full of the brightness and vigour of youth; but we doubt whether they contain the germs of a materially larger performance. The question, however, is almost unkind; it is enough that while Bonington lived he was happy, and that his signature is the pledge of something exquisite. His works, we believe, have an enormous market value, and this generous array of them gives much of its lordly air to the present collection. He was a colourist, and of the French sort rather than the English. His use of water-colour is turbid and heavy, as it is apt to be in France, where he spent most of his life; but he draws from it the richest and most surprising effects. He packs these into small and often sombre *vignettes*, where they assert themselves with delicious breadth and variety. 'Inattention'—an ancient duenna droning aloud from some heavy tome to a lady lounging, not fancy-free, in a marvellous satin petticoat of silver-gray, among the mellow shadows of an ancient room; the 'Old Man and Child'—a venerable senator in a crimson cap, bending over a little girl whose radiant head and tender profile are incisively picked out against his dusky beard and velvet dress: these are typical Boningtons—bits of colour and costume lovingly depicted for their own picturesque sake, and that of that gently fanciful shade of romantic suggestion which so much that has come and gone in the same line, during these forty years, has crowded out of our active conception. The painter strikes this note with an art that draws true melody; his taste, his eye, as the French say, are unsurpassable. No wonder your aesthetic voluptuary will have his Bonington at any price!

Bonington brings us to the French School, which contributes largely, both in its earlier and its later stages. As we see it here, its most salient modern representative is unquestionably Decamps, of whom there are more than thirty specimens. We have already had occasion to speak of Decamps in these pages; if not with qualified praise, at least with a certain qualified enjoyment. But it is the critic's own fault if he doesn't enjoy Decamps at Bethnal Green; such skill, such invention, such force, such apprehension of colour, such immeasurable vivacity, are their own justification; and if the critic finds the sense of protest uppermost, he need only let out a reef in his creed. His protest, in so far as he makes it, will rest on his impression of what for want of a polite word he will call the painter's *insincerity*. The term is worse than impolite: it is illogical. There are things, and there is the intellectual reflex of things. This was the field of Decamps, and he reaped a richer harvest there than any of his rivals. He painted, not the thing regarded, but the thing remembered, imagined, desired—in some degree or other intellectualized. His prime warrant was his fancy, and he flattered—inordinately, perhaps—that varying degree of the same faculty which exists in most of us, and which, we should never forget, helps us to enjoy as well as to judge.

Decamps made a speciality of Eastern subjects, which he treated with admirable inventiveness and warmth of fancy—with how much, you may estimate by comparing his manner, as you have here two or three opportunities of doing, with the cold literalness of Gérôme. Decamps paints movement to perfection; the animated gorgeousness of his famous 'Arabs Fording a Stream' (a most powerful piece of water-colour) is a capital proof. Gérôme, like Meissonier, paints at best a sort of elaborate immobility. The picturesqueness—we might almost say the grotesqueness—of the East no one has rendered like Decamps; it is impossible to impart to a subject more forcibly that fanciful turn which makes it a picture, even at the cost of a certain happy compromise with reality. In colour, Decamps practised this compromise largely, but seldom otherwise than happily; generally, indeed, with delightful success. We speak here more especially of his oil pictures. His water-colours, though full of ingenious manipulation, are comparatively thick and dull in tone. Several of these (notably the 'Court of Justice in Turkey' and the 'Turkish Boys let out of School') are masterpieces of humorous vivacity; and one, at least, the 'Fording of the Stream', with its splendid dusky harmonies of silver and blue, its glittering sunset, and the splash and swing and clatter of its stately cavaliers, has a delicate brilliancy which possibly could not have been attained in oils. A noticeable point in Decamps, and the sign surely of a vigorous artistic temperament, is that he treats quite indifferently the simplest and the most complex subjects. Indeed he imparted to the simplest themes a curious complexity of interest. Here is a piece of minute dimensions, entitled, for want of a better name, 'The Astronomer'—a little ancient man in a skull-cap and slippers, sitting in profile at a table, beyond which an almost blank white wall receives a bar of sleeping sunlight. This meagre spectacle borrows from the artist's touch the most fascinating, the most puzzling interest. Decamps preserves his full value in the neighbourhood of Delaroche and Horace Vernet, who contribute a number of small performances, most of them early works. 'Touch' had small magic with either of these painters; pitifully small with the former, we may almost say, in view of his respectable and generous aims. He was the idol of our youth, and we wonder we can judge him so coldly. But, in truth, Delaroche is fatally cold himself. His 'Last Illness of Mazarin' and his 'Richelieu and Cinq Mars' (small pieces and meant to be exquisite) exhibit a singular union of vigorous pictorial arrangement and flatness and vulgarity of execution. His clever sunset-bathed 'Repose in Egypt' (a much later picture) shows that he eventually only *seemed*, on the whole, to have materially enriched his touch. Various other contemporary French painters figure in the Museum; none at all considerably save Meissonier, whose diminutive masterpieces form a brilliant group. They have, as usual, infinite finish, taste, and research, and that inexorable certainty of hand and eye which probably has never been surpassed. The great marvel in them is the way in which, in the midst of this perfect revel of execution, human expression keenly holds its own. It is the *manliest* finish conceivable. Meissonier's figures often sacrifice the look of action, but never a certain concentrated dramatic distinctiveness.

We hardly know why we have lingered so long on these clear, but, after all, relatively charmless moderns, while the various Dutch and Spanish treasures of the collection are awaiting honourable mention. The truth is that Velasquez and Murillo, Ruysdael, Terburg, and their fellows have been so long before the world that their praises have been sung in every possible key, and their venerable errors are a secret from no one. Before glancing at them again we must not omit to pay a passing compliment to Watteau, surely the sweetest French genius who ever handled a brush. He is represented at Bethnal Green on a scale sufficient to enable you to say with all confidence that, the more you see him, the more you like him. Though monotonous in subject, he is always spontaneous; his perpetual grace is never a trick, but always a fresh inspiration. And how fine it is, this grace of composition, baptized and made famous by his name! What elegance and innocence combined, what a union of the light and the tenderly appealing! It almost brings tears to one's eyes to think that a scheme of life so delicious and so distinctly conceivable by a beautiful mind on behalf of the dull average of conjecture, should be on the whole, as things go, so extremely impracticable: a scheme of lounging through endless summer days in grassy glades in a company always select, between ladies who should never lift their fans to hide a yawn, and gentlemen who should never give them a pretext for doing so (even with their guitars), and in a condition of temper personally, in which satisfaction should never be satiety. Watteau was a genuine poet; he has an irresistible air of believing in these visionary picnics. His clear good faith marks the infinite distance, in art, between the light and the trivial; for the light is but a branch of the serious. Watteau's hand is serious in spite of its lightness, and firm with all its grace. His landscape is thin and sketchy, but his figures delightfully true and expressive; gentle folks all, but moving in a sphere unshaken by revolutions. Some of the attitudes of the women are inimitably natural and elegant. Watteau, indeed, marks the high-water point of natural elegance. With the turn of the tide, with Lancret, Nattier, Boucher, and Fragonard

—masters all of them of prettiness, and all here in force—affectation, mannerism, and levity begin. Time has dealt hardly with Watteau's colouring, which has thickened and faded to a painfully sallow hue. But oddly enough, the dusky tone of his pictures deepens their dramatic charm and gives a certain poignancy to their unreality. His piping chevaliers and whispering countesses loom out of the clouded canvas like fancied twilight ghosts in the garden of a haunted palace.

In the Dutch painters, Sir Richard Wallace's gallery is extraordinarily rich, and many a State collection might envy its completeness. It has, for instance, no less than five excellent Hobbemas—a painter whose works have of late years, we believe, brought the highest of 'fancy prices'. Ruysdaels, too, Cuyps and Potters, Tenierses and Ostades, Terburgs and Metsus—the whole illustrious company is there, with all its characteristic perfections. Upon these we have no space to dilate; we can only say that we enjoyed them keenly. We never fail to derive a deep satisfaction from these delectable realists—the satisfaction produced by the sight of a perfect accord between the aim and the result. In a certain sense, no pictures are richer than the Dutch; the whole subject is grasped by the treatment; all that there is of the work is enclosed within the frame. Essentially finite doubtless: but the infinite is unsubstantial fare, and in the finite alone is *rest*. M. Ary Scheffer (to whom we owe a hundred apologies for not mentioning him more punctually) has attempted the infinite in his famous 'Francesca da Rimini'; he sends us over with a rush to Gerard Douw. There is no great master of 'style' to gainsay us here; the two small Titians being of slender value. The eleven Rembrandts are, for the most part, powerful examples of the artist's abuse of *chiaroscuro*; of the absolute obscure we might indeed almost say, for in some of them the lights are few and far between. Two or three of the portraits, however, are very frank and simple, and one extremely small picture, 'The Good Samaritan', is a gem. If the little figures were ten feet high, they couldn't be more impressive. There is a splendid array of Murillos, though perhaps the term would be extravagant if applied to them individually. Four or five out of the eleven represent Murillo at his best—his ease, his grace, his dusky harmonies, his beggars and saints, his agreeable Spanish savour; but even these merits fail to make him seriously interesting. His drawing, though often happy, is uncomfortably loose, and his intentions, somehow, fatally vague. Velasquez proudly outranks 'him. *His* intentions were distinct enough and his execution seldom betrayed them.

THE DUKE OF MONTPENSIER'S
PICTURES IN BOSTON
1874

IF WE ARE to believe some of the newspapers, Boston has witnessed during the past month an artistic event of unprecedented magnitude. The Duke of Montpensier's pictures have arrived, been placed on exhibition, visited by great numbers of people, and by this time, we suppose, judged according to their merits. Roughly considered, the coming of these works was certainly something of an event, for the importation of authentic old masters by the dozen is as yet, for the American public, an unfamiliar fashion.

It is a question, however, whether the general magnitude of the event is not a good deal curtailed by particular considerations, and whether the Duke of Montpensier's generosity has been on the whole very profitable to the cause of the fine arts. Our readers have probably not forgotten the circumstances under which this generosity was exercised. The Duke of Montpensier, reflecting presumably on the volcanic condition, as we may call it, of Spanish soil, and wishing to put his property on a safer footing, had sent his best pictures to Gibraltar, with the expectation that they might be conveyed to London for exhibition. The authorities in London declined his offer, but as we of this country in such matters are not proud, we proffered a claim to the rejected entertainment.

The Duke of Montpensier made his own terms (very handsome ones by the way), and his paintings are now installed in the Boston Athenaeum.[1] We know not what, between Carlists and

[1]For an account of the Boston Athenaeum as 'an active patron of art' before the establishment of the Boston Museum of Fine Arts, see *The Athenaeum Gallery 1827-1873* by Mabel Munson Swan (1940).

Republicans, might have befallen them at Seville, but we can answer for it that in their present refuge they are supremely safe from the breath of injury. On the day on which we visited them (it was one of the first), we were struck by the almost reverential demeanour of the spectators. The gentlemen were all uncovered, several were going about on tiptoe, and the room was pervaded by a kind of submissive hush. A person near us proclaimed with religious unction that this was indeed a treat. The pictures are hung with a more than Old-World allowance of light and space. The gem of the collection, the Murillo, has a magnificent margin of maroon-coloured wall, and the work next in value, the head by Velasquez, may be examined in commodious isolation. We confess that, after a glance at the pictures, our attention wandered to some of the indirect characteristics of the scene. We seemed to find in it a mild but irresistible pathos—and we were reminded once more that we are a singularly good-natured people. We take what is given us, and we submit, with inexhaustible docility, to being treated as children and simple persons. We are vast, rich, and mighty, but where certain ideas are concerned we sit as helpless in the presence of Old-World tradition, dim and ghostly though it may be, as Hercules at the feet of Omphale. This is so true that it implies almost a want of integrity in those who, intellectually, have charge of us to give us anything but the best. Our good-nature places us at their mercy, and they should in fairness sow none but chosen seed in such very grateful soil.

The Duke of Montpensier's pictures are some thirty in number, and with three or four exceptions they belong to the Spanish school. If they possess collectively a greater merit than individually, it is that they give one an approximate measure of a distinct department of painting. It happens unfortunately that the Spanish school is of all schools the least valuable; but it is very well nevertheless to make an approach to definite historical notions. Of the only two Spanish names of the first rank the collection contains four specimens. One of these, Murillo's 'Virgin of the Swaddling Clothes', is a most agreeable and satisfactory example of the master, and a picture certainly worth a journey to see. We have seen, out of Spain, several better Murillos, but we have also seen a great many worse. The picture in Boston has been awkwardly repainted in places, and the consequence is a spotty deadness of colour, here and there; but much the larger portion is intact, and full of the mild, mellow harmony characteristic of the painter. Few painters strike us as being so little proper subjects of criticism, for few in proportion to their talent are so modest, so unpretending, so purely natural. Murillo has an indefinable, self-taught air which always reminds us of a painter superior to him in refinement of genius, but marked by this same personal naturalness of manner—we mean Correggio. We should be inclined to cite these artists together as the best examples of unacademical art, for if genius in each of them made its way unguided and unhelped, it was saved by a happy inward rule from fatal eccentricities. Correggio, indeed, made up in a measure for inheriting no mannerism, by founding one; but Correggio passed his life in almost complete ignorance of the aesthetic movement of his time. Murillo had better opportunities, though he never went to Italy. He came up, however, from Seville to Madrid, which was almost as good, for he found there Titians enough to form in themselves an Academy. But he returned early to Seville, and spent the rest of his life in the happy condition of an artist largely using his talent, but never forcing it.

There is in Murillo an almost excessive want of tension—an undue humbleness of inspiration. It increases one's kindness for him, but in the manner of an inaggressive weakness in a dear friend. He reminds us a trifle of a person with some slight physical infirmity—a lisp or a stoop—which at any time might have been corrected by a little resolution. The leading characteristic of the Spanish school is its downright realism; and Murillo, though he has more lightness and grace than any of the company, abides as closely as any of them by the testimony of his senses. He is as little of an intellectual painter as the brutal Ribera himself, and this not because he is harsh, but because he is so sincerely tender. One feels that his tenderness is never theory—

though it may in a great measure have become habit; it is all immediate sentiment. For this reason he seems to us a better Catholic in painting than any other artist subsequent to the fourteenth century. There are painters whose works adapt themselves more strikingly to the formal and ceremonial side of religion, but there are none whose Virgins and infants and saints are more suggestive of the piety that has passed into daily life, and sits down at the board, and goes out into the streets with the believer.

Murillo believes as women do, with never a dream of doubt; and the fact that his Virgins are hard-handed peasant women makes his inspiration seem more sacred, rather than less so. He had to make no effort of the fancy to believe that the Queen of Heaven was originally a poor girl; he had always been told so, and when he came to paint her, his idea of the celestial mildness embodied itself naturally in the sweet, tired face, the half-smoothed hair, and the unbuttoned bodice of some sunburnt daughter of the Andalusian soil. These reflections are not amiss as one stands before the Virgin at the Athenaeum. She sits with her baby in her lap, lying flat at his chubby length, while she binds him about with strips of linen. On the table near her is a linen bandage, and a couple of angelic choristers stand on either side. These boyish angels are charming, especially the one that plays the violin, against which he lays his cheek, as he looks down at the infant, with inimitable friendliness. The other, somewhat older, is drawing the bow across a violoncello; and, winged and haloed as they are, they are no nearer to being angels than a couple of innocent lads borrowed from a neighbour. The face of the Virgin, as well as that of the child, has apparently escaped retouching, and there is something charming in both of them. The Virgin is none the less lovely for being a trifle plain, and if she looks a little weary and serious, one may be sure that now and then she has a beautiful, simple smile. The baby's head, with its big, blue eyes and its little helpless, backward fall, is delightfully painted; there are few divine infants in the range of sacred art on whom divinity sits so easily. This is a better specimen of

Murillo's other gifts than of his colour, but even of his colour it offers an agreeable intimation. We find in him the mildest, quietest sort of pleasure that colour gives. He never approaches splendour, and he rarely reaches pure brilliancy; but he works delightful harmonies of subdued and not especially various tones. His pictures have an air of being painted in the shade, as under a Spanish sun they well might be, and one may fancy that his cheerful duskiness was a natural reaction against the garishness of surrounding nature.

It is a fact that there is a marked duskiness in all Spanish colouring, and that when one hears of a typical Spanish picture one imagines something very sombre both in tone and in subject. Velasquez was certainly a great colourist, but we mean nothing invidious when we say that he was a cold one. In the Doria Palace in Rome is a superb portrait, by this artist, of the Pope Innocent Tenth, clad all in red. His face is red, his cap is red, his gown is red, the chair in which he sits is red, and, if we are not mistaken, the wall behind him is red. The tones are superb in their way, but they don't glow, and one retires with as distinct a memory of the few spots of cool gray white in the picture as of all this pontifical crimson. The small head of Velasquez at the Athenaeum is not an Innocent Tenth, but it is an admirable sketch, and in itself, we should say, offers a liberal education to a young American portrait painter. It is the head of a very young man, said to be the painter's own, and the head simply, for the chin almost rests on the frame. It is impossible to imagine a greater *maestría* of brush, or a better example of the way in which a genius of the calibre of Velasquez has all his powers in hand at any moment, and never needs to step backwards to take his jump. A sketch by an artist as complete as Velasquez is not materially less valuable than a finished picture, for the simple reason that he is constitutionally incapable of painting small, and that all his force passes into it, limited only by outward accident. About Velasquez there are innumerable things to be said, and no artist is more tempting as a text for discussion of the familiar grounds of difference between the realists and the idealists. He ought properly, it seems to us, to be the very apple of a pugnacious idealist's eye, for certainly on no sturdier *cheval de bataille* could the combat possibly be waged. The idealists may treat themselves to the luxury of surrendering him bodily to the foe, in order to snatch him back again in the midst of the latter's exultation. To painters who advocate pure imitation, nothing more and nothing less, he seems at a superficial glance a tower of strength for their cause, and they flatter themselves that he has absolutely no comfort for the other faction, who dream of conferring on the subject an added grace, begotten in their own minds. Velasquez certainly is mighty in imitation, but to those who do him full justice it seems that imitation is not the limit of his power, and that his men and women have a style which belongs to his conception of them quite as much as to their real appearance. Of course there is style and style. That which looks out upon us from the canvases of Velasquez is a noble gravity and solidity; added to his magnificent handling it makes him one of the most powerful of painters. The little head we speak of is an invaluable reminder of the merit of being deep in one's own line; for if Velasquez is a dramatic painter, he is before all things a painter and a painter only, a painter who stands or falls by the stroke of his brush.

These observations are strictly pertinent only if applied to the head at the Athenaeum; the other two small sketches (portraits of Philip IV and the Duke of Olivarez) seem to us of very questionable authenticity. The larger portraits were painted and may be seen in all their magnificence at Madrid; but these little sketches strike us much less as Velasquez reported by himself than as Velasquez repeated by a thinner brush. If they are copies, however, they are interesting copies.

Next in interest are four immense pictures by that profoundly Spanish genius, Francisco Zurbaran. We are not sure that the interest of these works is proportionate to the space they cover, but they nevertheless afford a good deal of simple entertainment. They contain a large amount of genial, honest, and masculine painting, and if a Zurbaran is not a Paul Veronese, one must remember that in the palace of art there are many chambers. The trouble is that if one has seen the colonnades and brocades, the sweeping contours and silver tones, of the great Venetian decorator, one's eyes have been dazzled forever, and the shadow of mediocrity seems to rest upon such dusky Adorations and Presentations as these. Another Adoration and an Annunciation complete the group. Zurbaran is not a colourist, though he is a clever master of light and shade. His tones, moreover, have faded and darkened capriciously, and the quality now chiefly enjoyable is the striking verity and homeliness of many of his types. They are full of nature and *bonhomie*, and have an especial truthfulness of gesture. Excellent are the shepherds and peasants in the first Adoration, excellent the movement of the half-pleased, half-frightened infant to whom the pompous old magus is kneeling. In the way in which he makes a hard opposition of lights and darks the vehicle of a sort of masculine directness, Zurbaran reminds us singularly of Copley. There are passages in each of these four works which, if shown us without the context, we should have unhesitatingly attributed to Copley.

We have mentioned the only pictures which deserve individual notice, and speaking frankly and without human respect, we may add that the less said about the others the better. There is a Ribera of absolutely no value save as a disagreeable curiosity —a Cato of Utica tearing out his entrails. Happy thought! as Mr. Burnand would say. Artists nowadays complain of being at loss for subjects, but it seems as if the perplexity had begun in Ribera's time. This Neapolitan Cato is after all but half in earnest, and looks simply as if he had excoriated himself in the pursuit of a parasitic insect common at Naples. Ribera at his best is never agreeable, though he was handsomely endowed with the painter's temperament, and it is rather an unkindly trick of fortune to confront the aspiring New England mind thus rudely with Ribera at his worst.

Of the remaining Spanish pictures, one only, a small Pietà by the early master Morales, is of measurable importance. It has a certain dry, hard power, both of intention and of treatment.

There is a Juan Valdes Leal, several Herreras, elder and younger, a Ribalta, and—Heaven save the mark—a Boccanegra. There is a so-called Sebastian del Piombo, a Salvator Rosa, a couple of Bassanos, a Snyders, a François Granet, and two or three modern trifles. These pictures are all poor specimens of indifferent painters. Our remark implies no reproach to Sebastian del Piombo, for the canvas bearing his name on a scroll in the corner is but a ghastly simulacrum of his manner. Trusting to our memory we should say it was a copy of a replica of an impressive Sebastian in the Naples Museum. Its companions are the sort of ware that forms the rough padding of large European collections and is generally consigned to the friendly twilight of corridors and staircases. The exhibition has been supplemented by an oddly promiscuous group of pictures borrowed from native amateurs. Imagine side by side a colossal cartoon by Kaulbach, a Hannibal Caracci, a Cristoforo Allori and a Cima da Conegliano! These are all very creditable specimens of the masters. The Kaulbach is an 'Era of the Reformation' (it has of course to be at the least an 'era'), and it contains an incredible amount of science and skill. As for the charms of companionableness, that, of course, is another matter, and for this purpose we prefer the lovely little Cima. But the Luther in the cartoon, standing up on his pedestal and holding aloft the Scriptures, is an admirable plastic figure.

We have ventured, we may say in conclusion, while speaking of the Duke of Montpensier's pictures to close our eyes to the adage that a gift horse should absolutely not be looked at in the mouth. We are the Duke of Montpensier's debtors, and we cordially acknowledge it. This obligation is weighty, but it is of still more importance that people in general in this part of the world should not form an untruthful estimate of the works now at the Athenaeum. Immaturity and provincialism are incontestable facts, but people should never freely assent to being treated as children and provincials. We do not in the least regret the acceptance of the Duke of Montpensier's loan; there are too many reasons for being happy in it. It is chiefly the first step that costs, and we may now claim that, formally, at least, the spell of our disjunction from Europe in the enjoyment of collections has been broken. It has been proved that there is no reason in the essence of things why a room full of old masters should not be walked into from an American street and appear to proper advantage in spite of what in harmonious phrase we suppose we should call its location. There is something we like, moreover, in our sending out at a venture for half a million of dollars' worth of pictorial entertainment; we may say that if the Duke of Montpensier's liberality was princely, our response to it was, in detail, imperial. A kindly welcome therefore to the Ribaltas and Herreras, so long as we take them easily. We wish simply to protest against the assumption that we are greatly privileged in beholding them. We are simple as yet, in our appreciation of the arts, but we are not so simple as that comes to.

ON SOME PICTURES
LATELY EXHIBITED
1875

THE standing quarrel between the painters and the *littérateurs* will probably never be healed. Writers will continue to criticize pictures from the literary point of view, and painters will continue to denounce their criticisms from the free-spoken atmosphere of the studio. Each party will, in a manner, to our sense, be in the right. If it is very proper that the critics should watch the painters, it is equally proper that the painters should watch the critics. We frankly confess it to be our own belief that even an indifferent picture is generally worth more than a good criticism; but we approve of criticism nevertheless. It may be very superficial, very incompetent, very brutal, very pretentious, very preposterous; it may cause an infinite amount of needless chagrin and gratuitous error; it may even blast careers and break hearts; but we are inclined to think that if it were suppressed at a stroke, the painters of our day would sadly miss it, decide that on the whole it had its merits, and at last draw up a petition to have it resuscitated. It makes them more patrons than it mars; it helps them to reach the public and the public to reach them. It talks a good deal of nonsense, but even its nonsense is a useful force. It keeps the question of art before the world, insists upon its importance, and makes it always in order. Many a picture has been bought, not because its purchaser either understood it or relished it—being incapable, let us say, of either of these subtle emotions—but because, for good or for ill, it had been made the subject of a certain amount of clever writing 'in the papers'. It may be said that not only does the painter have to live by his pictures, but in many cases the critic has to as well, and it is therefore in the latter gentleman's interest to foster the idea that pictures are indispensable things.

Of course what most painters urge is not that criticism is *per se* offensive, but that the criticism of the uninitiated, of those who mix things up, who judge sentimentally, fantastically, from the outside, by literary standards, is the impertinent and injurious thing. Painters, we think, complain of this so-called 'literary' criticism more than any other artists—more than musicians, actors, or architects. There is probably more unmeaning verbiage, in the guise of criticism, poured forth upon music than upon all the other arts combined, and yet the melodious brotherhood take their injury, apparently, in a tolerably philosophic fashion. They seem to feel that it is about as broad as it is long, and that as they profit on the one side by the errors of the public, there is a rough reason in their losing, or even suffering, on the other. People in general had rather not take music at all than take it hard. The case is very much the same with the visitors of the galleries and studios. If they always had to show chapter and verse for their impressions and judgements, they would soon declare that the play is not worth the candle, that art is meant for one's entertainment; that a picture is a thing to take or to leave. 'If one didn't look at you imaginatively', they say in many a case, 'if one didn't lend you something of one's own, pray where would you be?' Art, at the present day, is being steadily and rapidly vulgarized (we do not here use the word in the invidious sense); it appeals to greater numbers of people than formerly, and the gate of communication has had to be widened, perhaps in a rather barbarous fashion. The day may come round again when we shall all judge pictures as unerringly as the burghers of Florence in 1500; though it will hardly do so, we fear, before we have, like the Florentines, a native Michael Angelo or an indigenous Andrea del Sarto to exercise our wits upon. Meanwhile, as we are expected to exhibit a certain sensibility to the innumerable productions of our own period, it will not be amiss to excuse us for sometimes attempting to motive our impressions, as the French say, upon considerations not exclusively pictorial. Some of the most brilliant painters of our day, indeed, are themselves more literary than their most erratic critics; we have invented, side by side, the arts of picturesque writing and of erudite painting. When Fortuny painted a picture and Théophile Gautier wrote an account of it, it was hard to say which was the painter and which the writer. Two such diverse painters as Gérôme and Corot, though they may sometimes have complained of the public disposition to *interpret* them, to make them prove something, to refine upon their meaning, yet would have thriven but ill if they had not had this same fanciful, bookish, ingenious, dilettante public to appeal to. The latest phase of the French school—that little group of Gallicized Spaniards of which Fortuny and Zamacois were the most brilliant ornaments—is founded upon a literary taste, upon a smattering of culture, upon a vague, light diffusion of the historic sense. We may say the same of the cleverest English painters of the day, several of whom are so exquisite—Mr. Burne-Jones, Mr. Rossetti, Mr. Leighton. Mr. Burne-Jones paints, we may almost say, with a pen; there is something extremely rare and interesting in his combination of two distinct lines of culture, each in such a high and special degree. These gentlemen's pictures always seem as if, to be complete, they needed to have a learned sonnet, of an explanatory sort, affixed to the frame; and if, in the absence of the sonnet, the critical observer ventures to improvise one, as effective as his learning will allow, and to be pleased or displeased according as the picture corresponds to it, there is a certain justification for his temerity. If some of the clever painters of our day are literary, we do not mean that they are all so; it would be in our power to point out several exceptions; but the generalization is correct enough to warrant us in saying further, that when the average of ability is highest the critic is allowed the widest range in his commentary. Few people, we suppose, will deny that the cleverest painters and the most vivacious critics are to be found together at the present hour in Paris, where their mutual feuds and imprecations and heart-burnings are often a tolerably unprofitable spectacle. Yet, on the whole, we imagine the French plastic artist who is conscious of talent finds it sufficiently easy to regard his literary *confrère*, if not as a positive blessing, at least as a necessary evil.

We have uttered these few reflections rather because we had had them for some time in mind than because they are in especial harmony with our impressions of the exhibition just closing at the Academy of Design.[1] We do not claim the distinction of needing them as a weapon either of defence or of offence. Few of the painters represented at the Academy did much in the way of winning from us an expenditure of fancy and ingenuity. The most striking pictures in the exhibition were perhaps those of Mr. Homer; and this artist certainly can rarely have had occasion to complain of being judged with too much subtlety. Before Mr. Homer's little barefoot urchins and little girls in calico sun-bonnets, straddling beneath a cloudless sky upon the national rail fence, the whole effort of the critic is instinctively to contract himself, to double himself up, as it were, so that he can creep into the problem and examine it humbly and patiently, if a trifle wonderingly. Mr. Homer's pictures, in other words, imply no explanatory sonnets; the artist turns his back squarely and frankly upon literature. In this he may be said to be typical of the general body of his fellow artists. There were the painters who, like Mr. Edgar Ward and Mr. Thayer, desire to be simply and nakedly pictorial, and very fairly succeed; and there were the others who, like Mr. H. P. Gray, with the 'Birth of our Flag', and Mr. Eastman Johnson, with 'Milton Dictating to his Daughters', desire to be complex, suggestive, literary, and very decidedly fail. There is one artist—a complex and suggestive one if there ever was—we mean Mr. John La Farge—whose pictures are always a challenge to the imagination and the culture of the critic. When Mr. La Farge gives himself a largely suggestive subject to handle, he is certain to let it carry him very far; and if there is an occasional disparity between the effort and the total achieve-

[1] In 1875 the Academy building was at Fourth Avenue and Twenty-third Street, New York.

ment, one's sense of it is lost in those delicate minor intimations, that subtle, intellectual detail, in which the artist's genius is so abundant. In his contribution to the present exhibition, however, the disparity of which we speak is perhaps exceptionally marked. Mr. La Farge's 'Cupid and Psyche' is a work of an even over-wrought suggestiveness; but the fugitive, recondite element in the artist's fancy has, to our sense, been unduly reflected in the execution—in something tormented, as the French say, some-thing which fails to explain itself, in the tone of the work, and, in places, in the drawing. What we here say of the Academy we may extend to the annual Water-Colour Exhibition, which almost immediately preceded it. The Water-Colour Exhibition was, relatively speaking, a brighter show than that made by the Academicians; but the best pictures there (contributed by native artists at least) were the simplest—those which attempted least. There too Mr. Homer was in force; and in his little raw aquarelles, as well as in several specimens of the infinitely finer and more intellectual, but still narrow and single-toned work of Miss Fidelia Bridges, we found perhaps, among the American performances, our best entertainment. The most interesting things, however, were not American. These consisted of some four elaborately finished pictures by Mrs. Spartali Stillman, who works in England, under the shadow of Messrs. Burne-Jones and Rossetti; and some dozen sketchier performances, of a very different order of merit, with an Italian signature, and the in-variable 'Roma' scrawled in the corner. In Mrs. Stillman's pictures there is something very exquisite, in spite of a certain lingering amateurishness in the execution. This lady is a really profound colourist; but the principal charm of her work is the intellectual charm—that thing which, when it exists, always seems more precious than other merits, and indeed makes us say that it is the only thing in a work of art which is deeply valuable. Imagination, intellectual elevation, cannot be studied, purchased, acquired; whereas everything else can; even, in a degree, the colourist's faculty. Mrs. Stillman has inherited the traditions and the temper of the original Pre-Raphaelites, about whom we hear nowadays so much less than we used; but she has come into her heritage in virtue of natural relationship. She is a spontaneous, sincere, naïve Pre-Raphaelite.

In the little band of Roman water-colourists whose productions have lately been thrown in such profusion upon the market, there is certainly little enough intellectual elevation; and yet there are several good reasons for enjoying their pictures. At the same moment that the Water-Colour Exhibition was going on, a number of these were also placed on view by Messrs. Goupil. We remember that when we first glanced at them, on going in, we turned away from them with a certain impatience and disgust; then, after half an hour's wandering, and contemplation of their companions, we again gave them our attention, and found we liked them decidedly better. Everything is relative in this world, and in a dull company one may find one's self smiling at a mild joke. These little Roman studies of ugly women in fantastic arrangements of the costume of the last century, of grotesque comedy figures, in attitudes more or less trivial and licentious, painted with a coarse, brilliant, liquid brush, executed with extreme rapidity, baptized as you please, and dedicated to the public which cultivates a taste for old china of the debased periods, have at least a certain play, a certain deviltry, a certain positive recognition of the fact that a picture is, for those who own it and look at it, essentially a diversion. Levity and triviality could hardly go further, in a certain sense; and yet they are redeemed by one's feeling that behind the talent displayed there is a great frankness of temperament. In this point this little Roman school of light painters seems to us vastly superior to that multitudinous host of French and Belgian artists who for so many years have been inundating us with solemn representations of beflounced ladies tying their bonnet ribbons and warming their slipper toes. These things have always been elaborately inane; the reiterated sight of one, for six months, on the parlour wall, is a circumstance to imperil the most tranquil nerves and embitter the most philosophic temper. But for these little Romans, whose names we forget, it seems to us we should always have a certain friendliness; they have, themselves, so much good humour. Some of them paint, too, with extraordinary cleverness. The model, for the most part, is the same stale, half-rakish, half-dowdy damsel, pretending not to beauty, but at most to an exhilarating ugliness; the draperies, too, the brocaded satins and the embroidered crape shawls, and the mantillas, and slippers and fans, look as if they were serving many a turn and being tossed from hand to hand; but the pose is so knowing, the composition so expressive, the lustre of the stuffs and the liquidity of the colour so striking, that you are quite willing to say that there is a small pleasure as well as a great pleasure in the arts, and that this is a very pretty case of the former. Nothing can be more charming, as a mere vehicle, than water-colours as these frivolous Romans handle them. In clearness, brightness, richness, fluidity, they leave nothing to be desired.

It must be confessed, however, that all this is very well chiefly so long as one doesn't talk too much about it. And yet if we said that the pictures at the Academy offered us an essentially worthier theme, we should be afraid of saying more than we can make good. Mr. Gray's picture[1] hung in the place of honour, and, as regards size, was the most considerable performance in the room. Though an ambitious picture, this struck us as a not especially felicitous one; it is a singular congregation of *pièces rapportées*. One has a curious sense of having seen the separate parts before, in some happier association. The eagle and the flag (which are rather awkwardly and heavily contrived) possess, indeed, the merit of originality; but the other things have each an irritating air of being a kind of distorted memory of something else. The young woman's body, her arms, her head, the landscape behind her, the sky, are very old friends; but somehow, on this occasion, they are not looking their best. It describes Mr. Gray's picture not unjustly, we think, to say it is a superficial *pastiche* of Titian. This is especially true of the management of colour. The artist has contrived very cleverly to recall Titian's deep-hued azures, to a casual glance; but at the end of a moment you perceive that

[1] This picture is in the Academy building, 1083 Fifth Avenue, New York.

this sumptuous undertaking rests on a very slender expenditure. Mr. Eastman Johnson, whom we mentioned just now in conjunction with Mr. Gray, is a painter who has constant merits, in which we may seek compensation for his occasional errors. His 'Milton and his Daughters' is a very decided error, and yet it contains some very pretty painting. Like Mr. Gray, Mr. Johnson here seems to us to have attempted to paint an expensive picture cheaply. To speak of the work at all kindly, we must cancel the Milton altogether and talk only about the daughters. By thus defilializing these young ladies, and restoring them to their proper sphere as pretty Americans of the year 1875, one is enabled to perceive that their colouring is charming, and that though the sister with her back turned is rather flat, rather vaguely modelled, they form a very picturesque and richly-lighted group. One of Mr. Johnson's other pictures, a young countrywoman buying a paper of pins from an old peddlar, is a success almost without drawbacks. Mr. Johnson has the merit of being a real painter—of loving, for itself, the slow, caressing process of rendering an object. Of all our artists, he has most coquetry of manipulation. We don't know that he is ever really wasteful or trivial, for he has extreme discretion of touch; but it occasionally seems as if he took undue pleasure in producing effects that suggest a sort of lithographic stippling. The head of the woman, pretty as it is, in the picture just mentioned, is a case in point; her dress, and the wall beyond it, are even more so. But the old hawker, with his battered beaver hat, his toothless jaws and stubbly chin, is charmingly painted. The painting of his small wares and of the stove near him, with the hot white bloom, as it were, upon the iron, has a Dutch humility of subject, but also an almost Dutch certainty of touch. For the same artist's lady in a black velvet dressing-gown, fastening in an earring, we did not greatly care, in spite of the desirable mahogany buffet against which she is leaning. Mr. Johnson will never be an elegant painter—or at least a painter of elegance. He is essentially homely.

Mr. Bridgeman's interior of an American circus in France was painted in that country, with a *brio* intensified possibly by national pride. It is an extremely clever little composition, and the most elaborate figure-piece in the exhibition. The group of the rider of the two horses abreast, with the young lady kicking out a robust leg from her aerial station on his thigh, holds together, moves together, with remarkable felicity. The diffused yellow daylight under the tent, falling on the scattered occupants of the benches beyond the ring, and upon the various accessories, is very cleverly rendered, though much of the painting is rather thin and flat. The picture dates, we observe, from 1870, when it appeared with success, we believe, in the Paris Salon. We hope that it does not sound harsh to express a regret that Mr. Bridgeman should not now be showing us a work subsequently composed, in which we should find all the performance of which this was the promise. Of Mr. Homer's three pictures we have spoken, but there would be a good deal more to say about them; not, we mean, because they are particularly important in themselves, but because they are peculiarly typical. A frank, absolute, sincere expression of any tendency is always interesting, even when the tendency is not elevated or the individual not distinguished. Mr. Homer goes in, as the phrase is, for perfect realism, and cares not a jot for such fantastic hair-splitting as the distinction between beauty and ugliness. He is a genuine painter; that is, to see, and to reproduce what he sees, is his only care; to think, to imagine, to select, to refine, to compose, to drop into any of the intellectual tricks with which other people sometimes try to eke out the dull pictorial vision—all this Mr. Homer triumphantly avoids. He not only has no imagination, but he contrives to elevate this rather blighting negative into a blooming and honourable positive. He is almost barbarously simple, and, to our eye, he is horribly ugly; but there is nevertheless something one likes about him. What is it? For ourselves, it is not his subjects. We frankly confess that we detest his subjects—his barren plank fences, his glaring, bald, blue skies, his big, dreary, vacant lots of meadows, his freckled, straight-haired Yankee urchins, his flat-breasted maidens, suggestive of a dish of rural doughnuts and pie, his calico sun-bonnets, his flannel shirts, his cowhide boots. He has chosen the least pictorial features of the least pictorial range of scenery and civilization; he has resolutely treated them as if they *were* pictorial, as if they were every inch as good as Capri or Tangier; and, to reward his audacity, he has incontestably succeeded. It makes one feel the value of consistency; it is a proof that if you will only be doggedly literal, though you may often be unpleasing, you will at least have a stamp of your own. Mr. Homer has the great merit, moreover, that he naturally sees everything at one with its envelope of light and air. He sees not in lines, but in masses, in gross, broad masses. Things come already modelled to his eye. If his masses were only sometimes a trifle more broken, and his brush a good deal richer—if it had a good many more secrets and mysteries and coquetries, he would be, with his vigorous way of looking and seeing, even if fancy in the matter remained the same dead blank, an almost distinguished painter. In its suggestion of this blankness of fancy the picture of the young farmer flirting with the pie-nurtured maiden in the wheat field is really an intellectual curiosity. The want of grace, of intellectual detail, of reflected light, could hardly go further; but the picture was its author's best contribution, and a very honest, and vivid, and manly piece of work. Our only complaint with it is that it is damnably ugly! We spoke just now of Mr. La Farge, and it occurs to us that the best definition of Mr. Homer to the initiated would be, that he is an elaborate contradiction of Mr. La Farge. In the Palace of Art there are many mansions!

In the Academy, also, there are many portraits. Some of them are fabulously bad, several respectable, and two or three very clever. The one of which we have retained the pleasantest memory is that excellent figure of a young girl in white, by Mrs. Loop, for which every one evidently feels a great friendship. We do not mean to be offensive when we say the picture was, in its cool discretion of manner, remarkably good for a woman. The model, to begin with, was delightful, and the picture was, in its way, thoroughly complete; notably so, for instance, in the excellent rendering, the drawing, the modelling of the young girl's charming smile. To paint a marked smile which does not speedily become to the spectator a rigid, importunate grin, is a proof of extreme ability. There were two very clever things sent from Munich by American artists—Mr. Chase and Mr. David Neal. Mr. Chase's 'Dowager' is an old lady (an admirable model) in a sixteenth-century coif and bodice, whose leathery, wrinkled, bloodless complexion and swollen veins are very picturesquely and yet very soberly painted. Mr. Neal has even more cleverness, but we don't know that he has more verity. His very handsome person in a sixteenth-century ruff struck us as hardly more than a particularly happy example of regular school ability. They are evidently very clever in Munich, and we are sure that they could teach a less gifted student than Mr. Neal to turn out an article not sensibly less brilliant than this lady in the ruff. (He must be certain, indeed, to give his lady the ruff; that is an essential point.) Have they not perhaps similarly taught Mr. Neal, with his brilliant gifts, to do a trifle less well than he might on a deeper line? But these are mysteries.

We choose a wrong moment moreover for harbouring evil thoughts of the Munich school, for we have lately had evidence that a great talent of the most honourable sort may flourish beneath its maternal wing. The good people of Boston have recently been flattering themselves that they have discovered an American Velasquez. In the rooms of the Boston Art Club hang some five remarkable portraits by Mr. Frank Duveneck of Cincinnati. This young man, who is not yet, we believe, in his twenty-fifth year, took his first steps in painting in the Bavarian capital, and it is hardly hyperbolical to say that these steps were, for a mere lad, giant strides. He came back a while since, if we are not mistaken, to his native city, where his genius was not highly appreciated, and where depressing obscurity was his portion, until aesthetic Boston held out a friendly hand. It is of course of supreme importance that Mr. Duveneck should not be talked about intemperately, though we shall be surprised if his head is not too firmly set upon his shoulders to be easily turned.

We speak in reason when we say that the half-dozen portraits in question have an extraordinary interest. They are all portraits of men—and of very ugly men; they have little grace, little finish, little elegance, none of the relatively superfluous qualities. But they have a most remarkable reality and directness, and Velasquez is in fact the name that rises to your lips as you look at them. It is very evident that in so far as there is any question of Velasquez in the matter, the analogy of Mr. Duveneck's talent with that of the great Spaniard is a natural, instinctive one. His models for the pictures in Boston are far from having the Spanish stateliness of aspect or the sixteenth-century bravery of costume. One of them is a plain old agricultural character, we should say, of Quakerish rigidity and of an extremely plebeian type, seated squarely in a straw-bottomed arm-chair and staring out of the picture, at full length, with startling vividness. Another is a young man in a shabby coat and a slouched hat, holding a stump of a cigar, a fellow art student of the author, presumably—less remarkable than the first, yet full of rough simplicity and truth. A third is a head of a German professor, most grotesquely hideous in feature and physiognomy, looking a good deal, as to his complexion and eyeballs, as if he had just been cut down after an unpractical attempt to hang himself. There is little colour in these things save a vigorous opposition of black and white, or of shaded flesh-tints and heavy browns; yet they are strikingly solid and definite. Their great quality, we repeat, is their extreme naturalness, their unmixed, unredeemed reality. They are brutal, hard, indelicate, and as the maximum of the artist's effort they would be almost melancholy; but they contain the material of an excellent foundation—a foundation strong enough to support a very liberal structure. What does Mr. Duveneck mean to build upon it? He is most felicitously young, and time will show. We frankly confess that we shall take it hard if he fails to do something of the first degree of importance.

The Academy contained the usual proportion of landscapes, and these landscapes contained the usual proportion of mild merit. The average merit, as we say, was mild, but it was recognizable as merit. We flourish as yet decidedly more in our handling of rocks and trees and blue horizon-hills than in our dealings with heads and arms and legs. At the Academy were a great many very pretty rocks and trees, a great many charming wavelets and cloudlets. Some of the rocks were most delectable —those, for instance, of Mr. Thomas Moran, in his picture of certain geological eccentricities in Utah. The cliffs there, it appears, are orange and pink, emerald green and cerulean blue; they look at a distance as if, in emulation of the vulgar liberties taken with the exposed strata in the suburbs of New York, they had been densely covered with bill-posters of every colour of the rainbow. Mr. Moran's picture is, in the literal sense of the word, a brilliant production. We confess it gives a rather uncomfortable wrench to our prosy preconceptions of the conduct and complexion of rocks, even in their more fantastic moods; but we remember that all this is in Utah, and that Utah is terribly far away. We cannot help wishing that Mr. Moran would try his hand at something a little nearer home, so that we might have a chance to congratulate him, with a good conscience, not only upon his brilliancy, but upon his fidelity. This is a satisfaction we were able to enjoy with regard to Mr. Jervis McEntee, the author of the landscape which most took our own individual fancy—a pond in a little scrubby, all but leafless wood, on a gray autumn afternoon. There are some children playing on the edge of it; a sort of blurred splinter of cold sunlight is peeping out of the thick low clouds and touching the stagnant, shallow pool. It is excellent in tone; it is a genuine piece of melancholy autumn; we felt as if we were one of the children grubbing unaesthetically in the ugly wood, breaking the lean switches, and kicking the brown leaves. There are other things which would be worth mentioning if we were attempting to speak of the Exhibition in detail. It may seem disrespectful, from a certain point of view, to allude to such performances as Mr. Bierstadt's 'California in Spring' and Mr. Cropsey's 'Sidney Plains' as 'details'; they take up much space on the walls; but they have taken little (and even that we grudge them) in our recollections. Mr. Church had two or three pictures at the Academy—small for him, and for him, too, rather feeble. But, in compensation, he had at the same time a large and elaborate landscape at Goupil's—a certain 'Valley of Santa Isabel', in New Granada. We know of nothing that is a better proof of the essential impotence of criticism, in the last resort, than Mr. Church's pictures. One can't say what one means about them; the common critical formulas are too inflexible. It would be the part of wisdom perhaps to attempt and to desire to say nothing; simply to leave them to their tranquil destiny, which is apparently very honourable and comfortable. If you praise them very highly, you say more than you mean; if you denounce them, if, in vulgar parlance, you sniff at them, you say less. It is the kind of art which seems perpetually skirting the edge of something worse than itself, like a woman with a taste for florid ornaments who should dress herself in a way to make quiet people stare, and yet who should be really a very reputable person. As we looked at Mr. Church's velvety vistas and gem-like vegetation, at Goupil's, we felt honestly sorry that there was any necessity in this weary world for taking upon one's self to be a critic, for deeming it essential to a proper self-respect to be analytical. Why not accept this lovely tropic scene as a very pretty picture, and have done with it? A very pretty picture, surely, it was, and a very skilful, and laborious, and effective one. The valley of Santa Isabel melts away into the softest violet glow—the most cunning aerial perspective. The great, heavy, yellow tropic sun sinks down into the wine-coloured mountains as if exhausted and athirst with his own prodigious heat, and his level rays come wandering forward down the mile-long gorges, and floating over the lustrous mountain lake in the middle distance, and flinging themselves in the flower-strewn grass in the foreground, in the most natural fashion in the world—natural, we mean, when nature is in her theatrical, her demonstrative, her exhibitory moods. Certainly if we were able to handle a brush, we should not use it, in some places (especially in our mysterious, deep-toned boskages, and our rich, multitudinous leafage), exactly as Mr. Church does; but his own brush is an extremely

accomplished one, and we should be poorly set to work to
quarrel with the very numerous persons who admire its brilliant
feats.

It is in order, in speaking of what has been visible at Goupil's
(where, during the winter, there have been several noticeable
things), to make some mention of a couple of pictures which for
a month or two occupied the places of honour. One of these was
a large composition by Mr. Boughton, our chief American representative of the fine arts, we believe, in London. In calling it
a composition we speak perhaps with culpable laxity. It was
entitled, at any rate, 'The Heir-Presumptive', and it is certain
that it had a little boy in the middle, taking a walk in an ancestral
park with his governess. Behind him was a negro servant leading
a white pony, before him was an old labourer doffing his hat.
The little boy, the governess, the servant, the pony, and the
labourer were figures of a fatally meagre execution, and sadly at
loss to acquit themselves of their pictorial duties, in the midst of
this huge expanse of empty canvas. They looked like the little
mannikins which a landscape painter touched into a foreground
at the last moment, before his signature, maliciously magnified
and trying to play at being real figures. What misguided friend
or insidious enemy is it that is forever prompting Mr. Boughton
to meddle with figures? His attempts in this line are painfully
amateurish; his drawing, his colour, his modelling strike us as
almost grotesquely weak. On the other hand, Mr. Boughton is
a landscape painter of a quite exquisite temper, as this same
picture showed; and it was to praise his landscape, and not to
criticize his figures, that we mentioned the work. Here was a
fine old English baronial chase, seen on a morning of early
winter, with the huge leafless oaks standing sturdily grouped,
the pale sky, with its thin yellow lights, showing through the
coarse lacework of the boughs, and the damp English atmosphere
making vague deposits along the brown earth and the rotting
leaves. The canvas was too large for the subject, and (apart from
the infelicity of the figures) the scene was a trifle vacuous and
monotonous; but it had a charming touch. Looking about after-

ward at the usual little French landscapes on Goupil's walls, with their high average of superficial cleverness, we were not arrested in the reflection that there is something inherently superior in the English sentiment of landscape, when it has really mastered its means. It has a story to tell—it has a mystery (sometimes very slender) to reveal. Unfortunately, it generally stammers and stumbles, and the mystery is liable to make a comical figure. It was hardly necessary to perceive that Mr. Boughton's little figures were of the cut-paper school, to relish the consummate vividness of those of Mr. Kämmerer in his 'Beach at Scheveningen'. These are mostly fine ladies, from the Hague and other elegant capitals, who have drawn together their chairs on the firm sand, and, as they sit there facing the glittering, tumbling sea, let the cold northern light filter down through their tense parasols, over their very well-made dresses, their silks, their muslins, their long-gloved hands, their agreeable faces, and luxurious, idle attitudes. Mr. Kämmerer is a young Hollander, we believe, who has lately stepped into Parisian fame. There is something cold, hard, a trifle dry in his manner; but in his way he is a master. We risked an invidious comparison, just now, between the continental and the English schools, in the field of landscape; but now we feel bound to add that they order this matter, of which Mr. Kämmerer's picture is an example, vastly better in France. If one compares it with Mr. Frith's treatment of analogous subjects, one sees that the advantage of delicacy, of taste, of science is on the side of the foreign artist. We are tempted to add another word for the foreign artists—the more so as we broke ground above upon the subject of the actual art possessions of Boston. There is now to be seen at the gallery of the Athenaeum in that city (beside the famous pictures of the Duke of Montpensier) a collection of French and Italian pictures owned by Mr. Quincy Shaw. They are worth going a distance to see. The Italian works are a beautiful Cima da Conegliano, a small but interesting Tintoretto, and a superb Paul Veronese. This last picture is a treasure—a triumph; a triumph, we mean especially, for American empty-handedness in this line. It is a complete and admirable specimen of the master; a broad, authentic, untarnished page from the book of Venetian glory. The French pictures are a series of Troyons and Millets; the former brilliant, but not, to our mind, particularly interesting; the latter dusky, laboured, concentrated, and of extreme interest.

DUVENECK AND COPLEY

1875

WE SPOKE in these columns some weeks since of Mr. Frank Duveneck[1] and the portraits from his hand exhibited at the Boston Art Club. These have been followed by three more, visible during the last month at the rooms of Messrs. Doll & Richards. We expressed some doubts as to whether further acquaintance with what Mr. Duveneck had done would confirm the very high opinion we had formed of his talent, but these doubts have been wholly removed. Two, at least, of the three pictures in question are superior to any of the half-dozen exhibited in the spring. One of them is a head of an old man with a fur-cap, a large, bony, and sanguinary nose, and a mangy-looking scrap of beard—a forlorn, grotesque personage, very strikingly rendered. This picture is skilful and forcible, but it differs less appreciably in kind from ordinary clever work than its companions. These are extremely remarkable. One is a full face of a young man in a broad, black hat—an Italian, we believe, and fellow-student, in Munich, of the artist—painted with admirable richness and solidity. Mr. Duveneck is altogether masterly in his combination of breadth of handling with complete preservation of the essence of his subject. His painting gives us, so to speak, the excitement of adventure and the certitude of repose. The third picture is a half-length of a lady in a brown dress and scarf, and a white cambric hat, holding a fan, with the body in profile and the face

[1] In 1886 Duveneck was married to James's young friend Elizabeth Boott, 'the infinitely civilized and sympathetic, the markedly *produced* Lizzie.' Her father Francis Boott of Boston, Massachusetts ('An Italianate bereft American with a little moulded daughter in the setting of a massive old Tuscan residence'), supplied the 'germ' of Gilbert Osmond in *The Portrait of a Lady*. One of Duveneck's portrait subjects about 1880 was Henry James, Senior.

three-quarters full. This was the first female subject by Mr. Duveneck we had seen, and it is quite the finest of his portraits; this, too, in spite of the fact that only the face is finished. This face strikes us as a very considerable achievement. The consummate expressiveness of the eyes, the magnificent rendering of flush and bloom, warmth and relief, pulpy, blood-tinted, carnal substance in the cheeks and brow, are something of which a more famous master than Mr. Duveneck might be proud. The figure is, moreover, full of movement, spirit, and style; its lightest touches tell of a talent which has excellent reason for self-confidence. Mr. Duveneck is essentially a portraitist; it is hard to imagine a more discriminating realism, a more impressive rendering of the special, individual countenance. That analogy with Velasquez, proportions considered, of which we formerly spoke, strikes us afresh in the works to which we now allude. It is not too much to say that in the portrait of the lady it is, in a very noble sense, deceptive.

We cannot forbear speaking on this same occasion of a very fine portrait by Copley, now also visible at the establishment of Messrs. Doll & Richards. Copley at his best is an admirable painter, and this picture of Mrs. Skinner,[1] painted in Boston almost exactly a hundred years since, was certainly unsurpassable by the artist himself. The lady leans her elbows on a small polished mahogany tea-stand; one hand holds a blue flower, the other, with the fingers extended, supports one of her temples. She is in full dress, with a great deal of admirably painted lace at her bosom and on her sleeves, and her pale blond hair is rolled over an immense cushion. She is not beautiful, and one of the sources of interest of the picture is its intimation that the bloodless, nervous, attenuated type of American woman was not more exceptional among our great-grandmothers than among our wives and sisters. Copley's model in this case—her stately apparel apart—looks as if she might have stepped out of a Boston street-car. The colour of the picture has turned somewhat sallow with time, but its essential characteristics as a first-class

[1] Copley's portrait of Mrs. Skinner is now in the Boston Museum of Fine Arts.

piece of portraiture have not been damaged. For direct, exact reality, Copley almost ranks with the very first, and such a portrait as this satisfies us in so many ways that we are almost puzzled to say what else we demand. When a head is so definite and solid and living as this, we are tempted to believe that it is all it can be. We finally perceive, however, that it can be a little more graceful and a little more suggestive. Even in so happy a performance as the portrait of Mrs. Skinner, Copley remains a trifle hard and rigid; here and there his surfaces are more like carving than painting. As for suggestiveness, he rendered perfectly and exhaustively all that he saw, and he saw nothing that he could not render. He was definite, as we say; but that adventurous vision of the indefinite which has brushed with its wing all the very greatest works of art is never reflected here. Copley was by no means a Holbein, but he holds a very honourable place in the ranks over which Holbein presided as supreme genius. We have called attention to the portrait of Mrs. Skinner because, in these days of complex aims and half-successes, there is something extremely refreshing in the spectacle of a simple aim begetting an absolute triumph.

THE AMERICAN PURCHASE OF

MEISSONIER'S 'FRIEDLAND'

1876

THERE has been much notice taken during the last fortnight of a new picture by Meissonier,[1] which has been on exhibition first at the rooms of an eminent dealer, and then at the Club des Mirlitons. Any new work by M. Meissonier is of course noticeable, but the present one has a special claim to distinction in the fact that it is the largest picture that has ever proceeded from the hand of that prince of miniaturists. Besides, as the future possessors of it, you should know something about it. The picture has been bought by Mr. A. T. Stewart of New York for the prodigious sum, as I see it affirmed, of 380,000 francs. The thing is exceedingly clever, but it strikes me as the dearest piece of goods I have ever had the honour of contemplating. It has, I believe, what they call in France its 'legend'—that little nebulous body of anecdote which hovers, like the tail of a comet, in the rear of every nine days' wonder. The picture was seen in an embryonic condition by Sir Richard Wallace, and purchased in anticipation for 200,000 francs—one-half of which was deposited as a pledge in the hands of the dealer. But time elapsed, and Sir Richard Wallace thought better of his bargain; he took back his offer and his $20,000. Meanwhile the picture was completed, and the price also. It was offered to Mr. Stewart for $60,000. He accepted, but this was not all. The dealer bethought himself that this small parallelogram of canvas would pay a duty of $8,000 at the New York Custom-house, and he accordingly annexed this trifle to the bill of sale. Then it appeared that M. Meissonier

---

[1] 'Friedland, 1807' is now in the Metropolitan Museum, New York.

desired to retain the right to exhibit the picture in the Salon of next year, and that the cost of bringing it back across the seas for this purpose would be a matter of $8,000 more. Why it should cost so much to transport a deal box containing a light canvas from New York to Paris is not immediately apparent. It occupies less space than the most emaciated human being and it eats nothing. But the fare of the picture was superadded to the amount already mentioned, and the American purchaser laid down without flinching—always according to the 'legend'—the round sum of 380,000 francs. The picture represents an immense amount of labour, and of acquired science and skill, and one takes, moreover, an acute satisfaction in seeing America stretch out her long arm and rake in, across the green cloth of the wide Atlantic, the highest prizes of the game of civilization. And yet, in spite of these reflections, M. Meissonier's little picture seemed to me dear, as I have said, at $76,000. It must be added, however, that in dealing with so high a talent as Meissonier's, it is very hard to fix the line of division between the fair value and the factitious value. The ability is so extreme, so consummate, so defiant of analysis, that it carries off with an irresistible assurance any claims it may choose to make. To paint so well as that, you say as you stand and look, must be so difficult, must be impossible—to anyone but Meissonier; and if Meissonier is unique, why should he not command the prices of unique things? If there were only one sewing-machine in the world, for instance, who can say what might be the pecuniary conditions annexed to its changing hands? And then I humbly confess that if a certain number of persons have been found to agree that such and such an enormous sum is a proper valuation of a picture, a book, or a song at a concert, it is very hard not to be rather touched with awe and to see a certain golden *reflet* in the performance. Indeed, if you do not see it, the object in question becomes perhaps still more impressive—a something too elevated and exquisite for your dull comprehension. M. Meissonier's picture represents one of those Napoleonic episodes which he has so often treated, and of which he has so completely mastered the costume and the

historical expression; he entitles it simply '1807'. The work is a
yard and a half long and I suppose about three-quarters of a
yard high. It is probable that the painter considers it his greatest
achievement, for he has evidently spent a world of care and
research upon it. The critics in general, apparently, are not of
this mind; most of them are of the opinion that the success, on
the whole, is not proportionate to the attempt. The artist, I
imagine, has desired not so much to represent a particular battle
as to give a superb pictorial expression of the glory of Napoleon
at its climax. It was about in 1807 that it reached its zenith; then
there were no clouds nor intermissions nor lapses. The battle of
Eylau was fought in 1807, but it took place, if I remember
rightly, in the winter, and the ground, in M. Meissonier's picture,
is covered with the deep verdure of June. At any rate Napoleon
stands on a mound in the middle distance, beyond which, beneath
a brilliant, lightly dappled sky, a mighty battle is going on.
Around him are his marshals and his aides, embroidered on all
their seams, as the phrase is, choking in their stocks and glittering
with their orders. The Emperor strides his white horse, and sits
like a Caesar on a monument, to return the salute of the troops
that are sweeping past him. M. Meissonier paints him at the
moment when he was probably handsomest, the mid-season between the meagreness of his earlier years and the livid corpulence
of his later ones. He looks in this portrait, small as it is, prodi-
giously like a man to believe in. The foreground of the picture,
to the right, is occupied by a troop of cuirassiers, who are
galloping into action; they are the *morituri* who salute the
Caesar Imperator, and they form the real subject of the work.
They are magnificently painted, and full, I will not say of movement—Meissonier, to my sense never represents it—but of force
and completeness of detail. This colonel is exactly passing the
spectators, to whom, as he twists himself in his saddle to lift his
sabre and bellow forth his 'Vive l'Empereur!' he turns his back.
His pose, with its stiffened, elongated leg, its contortion in the
saddle, its harmony with the thundering gallop of the horse, is
admirably rendered. Behind him come plunging and rattling the

others, with their long swords flashing white in the blue air, their heads thrown back and turned to the Emperor, their mouths wide open, their acclamations almost audible, their equipments flapping and jingling, and their horses straining and clattering in a common impetus. They are trampling through the high, poppy-strewn grass, where the crushed flowers seem already like the spatter of blood. To the left there is a slight interval, filled, in the distance, with the gleam of manoeuvring squadrons, beyond which comes riding forward a group of gorgeous hussars. It bothered the spectators a little that they should look as if they might come into collision, diagonally, with the cuirassiers. They are riding slowly, however, and they may sit under their great furred bonnets and watch the charge. All this goes on in a glare of sunshine; there are no clouds, no shadows; nothing but high lights and unrelieved colours. This sustained unity of light, as it were, is, I take it, a great achievement, and must have won much applause from people who have attempted similar feats. The picture has extraordinary merits, but I have seen works of a slighter ability that have pleased me more.

It is hard, however, to admire it restrictively without seeming to admire it less than one really does. It seems to me it is a thing of parts rather than an interesting whole. The parts are admirable, and the more you analyse them the better they seem. The best thing, say, is a certain cuirassier, and in the cuirassier the best thing is his clothes, and in his clothes the best thing is his leather straps, and in his leather straps the best thing is the buckles. This is the kind of work you find yourself performing over the picture; you may go on indefinitely. That great general impression which, first and foremost, it is the duty of an excellent picture to give you, seems to me to be wanting here. M. Meissonier is the great archaeologist of the Napoleonic era; he understands to a buttonhole the uniform of the Grand Army. He is equally familiar with the facial types, and he renders marvellously the bronzed and battered physiognomies that scowl from the deep shadow of shakos and helmets. Each man is perfect, but when M. Meissonier has made him—an elaborate, accomplished historical image—he has done his utmost. He feels under no necessity to do anything with him, to place him in any complex relation with anything else, to make any really imaginative uses of him. This suggests to the observer a want of something which he thinks it a great pity a painter of M. Meissonier's powers should not possess—a want intellectual, moral, spiritual; I hardly know what to call it. He resents the attempt to interest him so closely in costume and type, and he privately clamours for an idea. It is this 'idea' that is somehow conspicuous by its absence in M. Meissonier's pictures; and yet in so eminent a painter you cannot help looking for it. But, to my sense, they are dry and cold. Look at them beside a Gérôme, indeed, and they seem to bloom and teem with high suggestions; but look at them beside a Delacroix or a Millet and they appear only brilliantly superficial. It is a difference like the difference to the eye between plate glass and gushing water.

TWO PICTURES BY DELACROIX

1876

TWO VERY interesting pictures of Eugène Delacroix have for some time been visible at Durand-Ruel's. One is an immense affair, painted in his early youth—a Sardanapalus upon his funeral pile;[1] it takes early youth to attack such subjects as that. The luxurious monarch is reclining upon his cushions on the summit of a sort of brazen monument, and his jewels and treasures and dishevelled wives are heaped in confusion about him. The subject was not easy, and Delacroix has not solved its difficulties; much of the picture is very bad, even for a neophyte. But here and there a passage is almost masterly, and the whole picture indicates the dawning of a great imagination. One of the women, half-naked and tumbling over helpless on her face against the couch of her lord, with her hands bound behind her, and her golden hair shaken out with her lamentations, seems, in her young transparent rosiness, like the work of a more delicate and more spiritual Rubens. The other picture, painted in 1848, an 'Entombment of Christ',[2] is one of the author's masterpieces, and is a work of really inexpressible beauty; Delacroix is there at his best, with his singular profundity of imagination and his extraordinary harmony of colour. It is the only modern religious picture I have seen that seemed to me painted in good faith, and I wish that since such things are being done on such a scale it might be bought in America. It is very dear, but it is to be had, considering what it is, for nothing, compared with Meissonier's '1807'.

[1] Now in the Louvre.
[2] Now in the Boston Museum of Fine Arts.

THE IMPRESSIONISTS

1876

AN EXHIBITION for which I may at least claim that it can give rise (at any rate in my own mind) to no dangerous perversities of taste is that of the little group of the Irreconcilables—otherwise known as the 'Impressionists' in painting. It is being held during the present month at Durand-Ruel's, and I have found it decidedly interesting. But the effect of it was to make me think better than ever of all the good old rules which decree that beauty is beauty and ugliness ugliness, and warn us off from the sophistications of satiety. The young contributors to the exhibition of which I speak are partisans of unadorned reality and absolute foes to arrangement, embellishment, selection, to the artist's allowing himself, as he has hitherto, since art began, found his best account in doing, to be preoccupied with the idea of the beautiful. The beautiful, to them, is what the supernatural is to the Positivists—a metaphysical notion, which can only get one into a muddle and is to be severely let alone. Let it alone, they say, and it will come at its own pleasure; the painter's proper field is simply the actual, and to give a vivid impression of how a thing happens to look, at a particular moment, is the essence of his mission. This attitude has something in common with that of the English Pre-Raphaelites, twenty years ago,[1] but this little band is on all grounds less interesting than the group out of which Millais and Holman Hunt rose into fame. None of its members show signs of possessing first-rate talent, and indeed

---

[1] In the summer of 1856 James saw 'the first fresh fruits of the Pre-Raphaelite effloresence', he tells us in *A Small Boy and Others*. 'The very word Pre-Raphaelite wore for us that intensity of meaning, not less than of mystery, that thrills us in its perfection but for one season, the prime hour of first initiations.'

the 'Impressionist' doctrines strike me as incompatible, in an artist's mind, with the existence of first-rate talent. To embrace them you must be provided with a plentiful absence of imagination. But the divergence in method between the English Pre-Raphaelites and this little group is especially striking, and very characteristic of the moral differences of the French and English races. When the English realists 'went in', as the phrase is, for hard truth and stern fact, an irresistible instinct of righteousness caused them to try and purchase forgiveness for their infidelity to the old more or less moral proprieties and conventionalities, by an exquisite, patient, virtuous manipulation—by being above all things laborious. But the Impressionists, who, I think, are more consistent, abjure virtue altogether, and declare that a subject which has been crudely chosen shall be loosely treated. They send detail to the dogs and concentrate themselves on general expression. Some of their generalizations of expression are in a high degree curious. The Englishmen, in a word, were pedants, and the Frenchmen are cynics.

LES MAÎTRES D'AUTREFOIS

1876

IT WILL not surprise the readers of M. Fromentin's earlier compositions to learn that this is a very interesting book. Those persons who remember his two strangely pictorial little volumes on the East—*Un Été dans le Sahara, Une Année dans le Sahel* —will have retained a vivid impression of his descriptive powers and his skill in evoking figures and localities; while the admirers of the charming novel of *Dominique*—a singularly exquisite and perfect work, which has had no successor—must have kept an equally grateful record of his art of analysing delicate moral and intellectual phenomena. These three modest volumes have hitherto constituted what is called in France the author's literary baggage. The work whose title we have transcribed, and which is somewhat more massive than its predecessors, has just been added to the list, and upon this evidence (*Les Maîtres d'Autrefois* has attracted great attention) M. Fromentin the other day presented himself as a candidate for the French Academy. He was not elected, and one may, while admiring his writings, think perhaps that his application was a trifle premature. The quality of his productions is exquisite, but the quantity is as yet slender. It must be added, however, that M. Fromentin has had occupations other than literary. He is a distinguished painter, and a great many of his refined, if somewhat pallid, renderings of Eastern scenes have been seen in America. We prefer his books to his pictures, and we have greatly enjoyed the volume before us. We recommend it to those lovers of art who have visited the great Dutch and Flemish pictures in the cities in which they were painted; and we recommend it even more to persons who have the journey through Holland

and Belgium still before them. It would be even more useful, perhaps, as an incitement than as a reminder.

M. Fromentin begins with Rubens, to whom he devotes the longest section in his volume, talks briefly of Van Dyck, passes on to Jacob Ruysdael and the principal Dutch genre-painters, expatiates largely upon Rembrandt, and touches finally (returning to Belgium) upon Van Eyck and Memling. We repeat that his whole volume is extremely interesting, but it strikes us as curious rather than valuable. We have always had a decided mistrust of literary criticism of works of plastic art; and those tendencies which have suggested this feeling are exhibited by M. Fromentin in their most extreme form. He would deny, we suppose, that his criticism is literary and assert that it is purely pictorial—the work of a painter judging painters. This, however, is only half true. M. Fromentin is too ingenious and elaborate a writer not to have taken a great deal of pleasure in the literary form that he gives to his thoughts; and when once the literary form takes the bit into its teeth, as it does very often with M. Fromentin, the effect, at least, of over-subtlety and web-spinning is certain to be produced. This over-subtlety is M. Fromentin's fault: he attempts to say too many things about his painters, to discriminate beyond the point at which discriminations are useful. A work of art has generally been a simpler matter, for the painter, than a certain sort of critic assumes, and M. Fromentin, who has painted pictures, ought to know that they are meant before all things to be enjoyed. The excess into which he falls is not of the same sort as that which is so common with Mr. Ruskin—the attribution of various incongruous and arbitrary intentions to the artist; it is rather a too eager analysis of the material work itself, a too urgent description of it, a too exhaustive enumeration of its constituent particles. Nothing can well be more fatal to that *tranquil* quality which is the very essence of one's enjoyment of a work of art. M. Fromentin, like most French writers on aesthetic or indeed on any other matters, abounds in his own sense. He can say so much so neatly and so vividly, in his admirable French style, that he loses all respect for the unsayable—the better half, we think, of all that belongs to a work of art. But his perception is extraordinarily just and delicate, and his power of entering into a picture is, in a literary critic, very rare. He enters too much, in our opinion, into the technical side, and he expects of his readers to care much more than should be expected even of a very ardent art-lover for the mysteries of the process by which the picture was made. There is a certain sort of talk which should be confined to manuals and note-books and studio records; there is something impertinent in pretending to work it into literary form—especially into the very elegant and rather self-conscious literary form of which M. Fromentin is master. It is narrow and unimaginative not to understand that a very deep and intelligent enjoyment of pictures is consistent with a lively indifference to this 'inside view' of them. It has too much in common with the reverse of a tapestry, and it suggests that a man may be extremely fond of good concerts and yet have no relish for the tuning of fiddles. M. Fromentin is guilty of an abuse of it which gives his book occasionally a somewhat sickly and unmasculine tone. He is, besides, sometimes too inconclusive; he multiplies his descriptive and analytic touches, but we are at loss to know exactly what he has desired to prove.

This is especially the case in the pages upon Rubens, which contain a great many happy characterizations of the painter, but lack a 'general drift', an argument. M. Fromentin indulges in more emotion on the subject of Rubens than we have ever found ourselves able to do, and his whole dissertation is a good example of the vanity of much of the criticism in the super-subtle style. We lay it down perplexed and bewildered, with a wearied sense of having strained our attention in a profitless cause. There is a limit to what it is worth while to attempt to say about the greatest artists. Michael Angelo and Raphael bid defiance to more than a moderate amount of 'keen analysis'. Either Rubens was a first-rate genius, and in this case he may be trusted to disengage him-self freely from his admirers' impressions; or else he was not, and in this case it is not worth while to split hairs about him.

M. Fromentin, speaking roughly, takes Rubens too seriously by several shades. There are fine painters and coarse painters, and Rubens belonged to the latter category; he reigned in it with magnificent supremacy. One may as well come to this conclusion first as last, for all the ingenuity in the world will not avert it. Rubens was, in painting, an incomparable *improvvisatore*; almost always a great colourist, often extremely happy in composition, he never leaves us without a sense that the particular turn the picture has taken, the cast of a certain face, the attitude of a certain figure, the flow of a drapery or the choice of a gesture, has been an accident of the moment. Hence we have in Rubens a constant sense of something superficial, irreflective, something cheap, as we say nowadays. His intentions had often great energy, but they had very little profundity, and his imagination, we suspect, less delicacy than M. Fromentin attributes to it. He belongs, certainly, to the small group of the world's greatest painters, but he is, in a certain way, the vulgarest of the group. No other of its members has produced anything like the same amount of work of which the quality discredits and compromise the remaining and superior portion. M. Fromentin has some excellent remarks about his portraits, of which he recognizes the coarseness and the limited value. 'Suppose Holbein', he says, 'with Rubens's *clientèle*, and you immediately see before you a new human gallery, very interesting for the moralist, equally admirable for the history of life and the history of art, and which Rubens, one must admit, would not have enriched by a single type.' M. Fromentin has, however, a charming paragraph about the magnificent 'St. George' of the Church of St. James of Antwerp—the church containing the tomb of the painter; a paragraph we are glad to quote as an example of the admirable way in which the author often says things:

'One day, towards the end of his life, in the midst of his glory, in the midst, perhaps, of his repose, under an august title, under the invocation of the Virgin, and of the only one of all the saints to whom it seemed to him lawful to give his own image, it pleased him to paint in a small frame (about two yards square) what there had been venerable and seductive in the beings whom he had loved. He owed this last tribute to those of whom he was born, to those women (his two wives) who had shared and embellished his beautiful and laborious career, charmed it, ennobled it, perfumed it with grace, tenderness, and fidelity. He gave it to them as richly and in as masterly a way as was to be expected from his affectionate hand and his genius in the fullness of its power. He put into it his science, his piety, and a rarer degree of care. He made of the work what you know—a marvel, infinitely touching as the work of a son, a father, and a husband, and for ever memorable as a work of art.'

M. Fromentin has some admirable pages upon the origin of Dutch art, and the conditions upon which it came into being: 'Genius shall consist in prejudging nothing, in not knowing that you know, in letting yourself be taken by surprise by your model, in asking of it alone how it shall be represented. As for embellishing, never; ennobling, never; chastening, never: these are so many lies as so much useless trouble. Is there not in every artist worthy of the name a certain something which takes upon it this care naturally and without effort?' His chapters upon Paul Potter, Cuyp, Ruysdael, Terburg, and Metsu are in our opinion the most felicitous in the volume; they are full of just discrimination and interesting suggestion. He ranks Ruysdael immediately after Rembrandt, a classification of this enchanting painter with which we have no quarrel; but we are not sure that with regard to him, too, he may not be accused of looking for midday (as the French say) *à quatorze heures*. But he characterizes him charmingly. He says very justly that there are a great many things which we should like to know about his life and person which it is impossible to ascertain; his history is obscure, and the questions are unanswerable. But would the idea come to us, he adds, of asking such questions about any of the other Dutch painters? 'Brilliant and charming, they painted, and it seems as if this were enough. Ruysdael painted, but he lived, and this is why it is desirable to know how he lived. I know but three or four men who are to this degree personally interesting—Rembrandt, Ruysdael, Paul Potter, perhaps Cuyp. This is more than enough to class them.' Upon Rembrandt M. Fromentin expatiates largely and very ingeniously; but we should say of these chapters as of his remarks upon Rubens, that the author goes through a great critical motion without arriving at any definite goal. He strikes a great many matches, and often rather bedims the subject. The great picture at Amsterdam, best known by its French name of the 'Ronde de Nuit', is a very strange work if you will, but nothing is gained by making it out stranger than it is and exhausting the vocabulary of hopeless aesthetic conjecture on its behalf. The note of M. Fromentin's view of Rembrandt is struck by his saying that he 'revealed one of the unknown corners of the human soul', and by his adding, at the close of his remarks, that he was 'a pure spiritualist—an ideologist'. Some readers, doubtless, will be more struck with the felicity of this definition than we have been. It is not the unknown, we should say, that Rembrandt represents, but the known, the familiar, the common, the homely. His subjects, his scenes, his figures are almost all taken from common life, and where they are not they are brought into it. He was an alchemist: he presents them in that extraordinary envelope of dense light and shade which is the familiar sign of his manner; but in this it is the execution that is rare to our sense—incomparably rare, certainly—rather than the conception. But to whatever degree in detail M. Fromentin's readers may dissent from him, they will do justice to the brilliancy of his work. Its acuteness and delicacy of perception are altogether remarkable and its manner most exquisite. It has a peculiar charm.

THE NATIONAL GALLERY

1877

SINCE I was last in London the new rooms of the National Gallery have been thrown open to the public; this took place in the month of August last. The noble collection at Trafalgar Square is at last arranged and distributed in a manner worthy of itself and of the nation. The new halls are some half-dozen in number; all of them are spacious and some are of great extent. Their general aspect and style of decoration recall the new galleries of the Louvre, though they are perhaps a trifle less lofty and less splendid than the Louvre. They are, however, airy, well-ordered apartments, and the pictures appear to as great an advantage as the London daylight allows. They are less crowded than at the Louvre, and few of them are hung inconveniently as regards the level of the eye. Even the Salon Carré is not more impressive than the spacious chambers allotted to the half a dozen Italian works, among which Michael Angelo's 'Entombment' stands supreme. Of course there have been a complete rearrangement and reclassification of the pictures; and all the works of the English school, which (comprised chiefly within the collection bequeathed to the nation by Mr. Vernon) had for so long found shelter at the South Kensington Museum, have now been accommodated at Trafalgar Square in the old rooms. We will not say that they gain by this close neighbourhood to their Italian and Flemish brethren; but, judged by themselves, they make a various and creditable show. I refreshed my memory, in particular, of a certain 'Portrait of Two Gentlemen', by Sir Joshua Reynolds; before this beautiful work the depressed Anglo-Saxon, wandering from the presence of the Moronis, hard by, may hold up his head. The Turners have been rehung, many of them in the long room in which Paul Veronese's superb 'Alexander' used to form the most brilliant feature; and I observe that the extraordinary 'Storm, Steam, and Speed' (if that is just the title), which was formerly much *en évidence*, is now suspended quite above the line.

THE OLD MASTERS AT
BURLINGTON HOUSE
1877

AMERICAN travellers who, during the last few years, have passed through London during the midwinter months, will remember having lost a sense of the gloom which at that period characterizes the British metropolis, during the hour or two that they may have spent in the rooms of the Royal Academy. This institution eight years ago established the practice of collecting during the dull season such privately-owned specimens of the great schools of painting as their possessors were willing for a item to part with. The result has been, year by year, an extraordinary testimony to the art-wealth of Great Britain, as well as to the liberality of those persons in whose hands it resides, to say nothing of the opportunity (just mentioned) for the fog-smitten wanderer to pass out of the January darkness of Piccadilly into the radiant presence of Titian and Rubens. As the successive exhibitions have unfolded themselves, however, it has been remarked that there is an end to everything, even to the picture-list of English castles and Mayfair mansions, and that before very long all the Titians and Rubenses, all the Van Dycks and Gainsboroughs, will have taken their turn. The fund upon which the Royal Academy can draw is not inexhaustible. However this may be, it is certainly not yet exhausted; the exhibition of the present year very comfortably proves it. And yet I believe it had been foretold that on this occasion the display would prove so meagre as to amount to a confession of defeat. It is doubtless not so brilliant as it has been in some former years—I remember the collection of 1870, for instance, as altogether superb—but if it really consists of the dregs of the country's wealth, it must be said that they are such dregs as no other country could furnish. The exhibition of last year was remarkable for its full representation of English portrait-painters of the last century, there being no less than thirty Reynoldses and nineteen Gainsboroughs. Another painter, little known to the world at large, the strong, deep, mellow Romney, affirmed himself in a number of works with a vividness which was almost a revelation. Gainsborough is present on this occasion in nineteen portraits, but Sir Joshua is reduced to twenty-one, and they are not all of the first excellence. Neither, indeed, are the Gainsboroughs; and between a fine Gainsborough and an indifferent one the distance is almost immeasurable. The Romneys are few in number, but they are striking and interesting, and British portraiture receives further support from an unexpected quarter. Sir Henry Raeburn, who was some thirty years the junior of the great trio I have mentioned, and who did his best work in the early part of the present century, is represented by a number of works which lead one almost to revise one's old assumption that Scotchman and artist (as regards the plastic arts) are a necessary contradiction in terms. (It is true that, besides the Raeburns, there are a couple of delightful and familiar little Wilkies—the 'Rabbit on the Wall' and the 'Gentle Shepherd', which remind us that their author was as genuine an artist as Van Ostade or Terburg.) In the way of foreign portraiture there are two or three admirable Van Dycks and several highly respectable specimens of the Venetian school. There are some small but charming early Tuscan pictures, and there are a couple of highly characteristic Rubenses. There is a capital show of great Dutchmen—three or four Tenierses and Van Ostades, two Hobbemas, and two specimens of the thick-shadowed Nicholas Maas, all of the first water. Landscape is not very richly represented, although there are two Turners, a very fine Constable, and three or four large Cuyps. There is also a specimen—precious for rarity if nothing else—a figure-piece by Turner.

The most delightful pictures, to my mind, in the exhibition

are the two or three best Gainsboroughs. The portrait of Johann
Fischer, the composer, is very well known; it hangs habitually
at Hampton Court, and was lent by the Queen. He is leaning,
cross-legged, against a harpsichord, on which his elbow rests,
with a pen in his hand, and looking up with an expression so
genial and gentle, and, at the same time, so acute that we feel
it to have a direct kinship with that ecstasy of St. Cecilia which
Raphael has portrayed for us. Gainsborough's model is listening,
mentally, to some very charming air, and the portrait is admirably complete and human, and full of that easy reality which is
the mark of the painter at his best. The portrait of a young Lord
Methuen, lent by the present wearer of that title, is perhaps not
so strong a performance, but it is a most delightful figure: a
youth of twenty, with a handsome, delicate, regular face, presented in full, leaning on a pedestal and clad in one of those much-
wrinkled, light-blue satin doublets, surmounted with a vandyke
collar, which Gainsborough was fond of touching off so handsomely. A little of the blue of the doublet has perhaps wandered
off into the tone of the face, but the portrait is a model of wholesome grace and unaffected elegance. Both of these pictures, however, are thrown into the shade by a large 'family group' representing a lady and gentleman, whose names apparently have not
been ascertained, going for a walk in the country with their little
girl: the magnificent picture and the happy, sympathetic people!
The figures but partly fill the large canvas, the left-hand side of
which is occupied by a brown-toned landscape of much more
solidity than the streaky umbrage which Gainsborough usually
offers us for backgrounds. The lady, in crumpled blue silk,
passes her hand into her husband's arm, while he, as he steps
forward holding his cocked hat in his outstretched hand, and
turning his face slightly and tenderly to his wife, points out the
beauties of the prospect in the neatest last-century prose. The
airy, diminutive little girl, held in her mother's left hand, nestles
against the blue petticoat, and, looking out of the shadowy
drapery with admirably childish eyes, seems alone to be conscious of the spectators. The husband is a very handsome fellow,

with keen, expressive eyes and a nose a trifle Judaic; and the *speaking* look in his face—the look as if words were audibly coming from it—is rendered with extreme felicity. Charming in every respect, too, is his modest, virtuous, ladylike English wife, with her auburn hair and her ill-fitting dress. The whole picture has an amplitude, a grasp of life itself, and a·rich, dark harmony of colouring, which must place it among the artist's few supreme masterpieces. The numerous other Gainsboroughs are far from having this value. They are evidently, for the most part, mere 'pot-boilers', upon which the minimum of care has been bestowed. They are, in general, full-lengths—which means that a pair of very wooden legs has been added to a pair of extremely mechanical arms. The colouring is cold and waterish, and the accessories in the highest degree sketchy and scratchy. It is the work of a brilliantly successful man who can afford to be a trifle impudent. But it must be added that with Gainsborough, even when the whole picture seems at first very bad, the head and face rarely transgress a certain limit of badness. The painter's natural refinement takes refuge in the countenance, which is always evidently a good deal of a likeness and, through fine rapid touches, something of a piece of painting. The charm of Gainsborough is indefinable; there is always something amateurish about him, and one feels like calling him the first (beyond all comparison) of the amateurs. It is not the charm of vigour, but the charm of facility, and of a correctness and softness of style so perfect that they never had occasion to dream of mannerism.

The only Sir Joshua which I have space to mention is a capital portrait of Doctor Burney, the historian of music, Mme. d'Arblay's father. There is also a large portrait of two small children, sprigs of the nobility, which would be charming if the colour had not turned to a disagreeable black. There are three sketches by Romney of his frequent model Lady Hamilton, very bold and expressive of the lady's enchanting beauty, and there is a large portrait by the same hand of a certain Margravine of Anspach, which is noble and gravely elegant, and which also, like its companions, has a reddish glow of colouring suggestive of our own Allston. Allston, however, was a talent of higher flights than Romney. The Raeburns are singularly solid and estimable works—the works of a genuine and accomplished painter. Some of the heads of old men—quiet-faced, canny Caledonians—are full of individual character, and painted with masterly breadth and mellowness; some of the women, too, are extremely pleasing, with their sober grace and their mild picturesqueness. There is an admirable head of the painter himself, with his chin in his hand and the eyes of a man of genius. When Sir Henry Raeburn has to render a hand, an arm, a leg, he usually draws it far better than Gainsborough, or even than Sir Joshua; but his manly and respectable work lacks a certain charm which one always find in theirs. The touch of fancy is absent; it is all plain, nutritive prose. There was lately gathered together in Edinburgh a complete collection of Raeburn's works, and the exhibition excited, I believe, much patriotic pride. This was highly proper; but to have passed an hour there, I should say, would have been, for a southern visitor, a good deal like attending a session of the national Kirk. It is Presbyterian art!

I have left myself insufficient space to speak of the other noticeable works. In the way of portraits there is a masterpiece by Franz Hals—a Dutch lady in a black dress and a huge ruff. Anything more living as portraiture, or more brilliantly clean as execution, it would be hard to imagine. Then there is one of the fine Van Dycks I spoke of—a certain Duke of Richmond of Charles I's time. He is dressed in black satin, with wrinkled stockings of pale, faded blue, and he rests his right hand upon the head of a great deerhound which is seated on his haunches beside him, and which leans his long nose against his thigh and looks up with a canine softness that is admirably indicated. The gentleman's yellow hair falls upon his satin mantle, and his face, which is not handsome, is touchingly grave. Such a give-and-take of gentlemanliness between painter and model is surely nowhere else to be seen. Several of the Italian pictures would be worth specifying. The large Rubens, lent by Lord Darnley, a 'Queen Tomyris with the head of Cyrus',[1] is, like so many Rubenses, extremely entertaining on a first glance; but it proves on a longer inspection to be rather inexpensively 'got up'. The picture contains a certain turbaned Turk, however, with a long beard falling over his gown of plum-coloured satin, who straddles importantly and sticks out his paunch while he looks at the bleeding head in the pail, which only Rubens could have painted, though doubtless the model could still be found among the portly pashas at Constantinople who are planted with some such majesty as that across the westward path of Russia.

[1] Now in the Boston Museum of Fine Arts.

THE PICTURE SEASON IN LONDON

1877

WITH the advance of the spring and the development of the season, in London, the streets (in the West End) begin to present to the eye of an observant stranger a great many new characteristics. The dusky metropolis takes on, here and there, in spots, a perceptible brightness, and as the days elapse these spots increase and multiply. At last they produce a general impression of brilliancy. Thanks to this combined effect, the murky Babylon by the Thames becomes cheerful and splendid. At the climax of the season, of a fine, fresh day in June, the West End exhibits a radiance which, to my sense, casts into the shade even the charming brightness of Paris. The brightness of Paris is, as I say, charming; it is a very pretty spectacle; it flashes and twinkles, and laughs, and murmurs. Stand on the edge of the Place de la Concorde, at the bottom of the Champs-Élysées, on any fine-weathered Sunday in the late spring—on a day when there are races beyond the Bois de Boulogne—and you will feel the full force of all the traditions about Paris being the gayest, easiest, eagerest, most pleasure-taking of capitals. The light has a silvery shimmer, the ladies' dresses in the carriages a charming harmony, the soldiers' red trousers a martial animation, the white caps of the *bonnes* a gleaming freshness. The carriages sweep in a dense line up the long vista of the Champs-Élysées, amid the cool, fresh verdure, and the lines of well-dressed people sitting on neat little yellow chairs; the great mass of the Arc de Triomphe rises with majestic grace, transmuted by distance into a sort of violet shadow; the fountains sparkle and drizzle in the vast sunny *place*; the Seine sweeps by in an amber flood, through a channel that gleams like marble beneath the league-long frontage of the splendid Louvre, and beyond that, crowning the picturesque purple mass before which the river divides, the towers of Notre-Dame stand up and balance in the opposite distance with the softened majesty of the Arch.

All this is irresistibly pretty. You feel that it was made to please. It has a kind of operatic harmony, and the impresario has thoroughly understood his business. But in that fine intermission of the London gloom of which I speak there is something more impressive, more interesting. It was not made to please, and it doesn't think of the spectators. It pleases by accident, by contrast, and by the immensity of its scale. It is an enormous, opulent society expanding to the enjoyment of the privileges and responsibilities of wealth and power, with nothing of that amiable coquetry of attitude toward the public at large which seems somehow to animate the performers in the Parisian spectacle. Except that part of it which takes place in the Park, the London spectacle goes forward in the midst of ugly accessories —smoke-blackened houses, an undeveloped architecture, dingy and hungry-looking population—but for ten weeks it overbears these things by its mass and brightness, and makes you believe that you are in the city of pleasure, and not in the city of pain. Then the flunkied chariots, with flower stacks in front, stand locked together in the genteel neighbourhoods; then the admirable types of English beauty look forth with quiet eyes from the shadow of lace-fringed parasols; then the rosy women sit flushed and panting on glossy thorough-breds along the misty, red-earthed vistas of the Park; then the juvenile members of a hereditary aristocracy diffuse themselves over the slopes of Piccadilly, and excite the admiration of the passing stranger by figures which tell of rowing matches, and garments which hint at Poole.

Then, in the mansions of Mayfair and Belgravia, the window-sills are bright with wondrous tulip beds, and the thresholds and porticoes flamboyant with still more wondrous footmen; then the streets are bedizened with motley placards and the names of all the great singers, and players, and actors, and painters, confront you at every turn, with thrilling familiarity; then the amateur coaches, driven by the gentleman of leisure and heralded by the mellow horn of the scarlet-coated guard, come rattling up to the classic door of Hatchett's; then the plumes and diamonds of bare-shouldered duchesses nod at you from the gilded coaches which, in drawing-room days, are waiting to deposit their noble burden in the presence of its gracious sovereign; then, too, the Life Guards and the Blues, the 'finest men' in the world, come flashing and clashing on their sable chargers from attendance on the same august personage. Then, at the hour of the vast pink sunset which filters upward so picturesquely through the hovering London exhalations, every rattling hansom contains a hurrying diner-out in a beautifully tied choker, and then, later, when the pale starlight twinkles down feebly into the dim, innumerable streets, the lines of lamp-lit broughams at the doors of houses given up to a 'crush', stretch away into neighbouring parishes. These are a few of the features of that external manifestation of the London 'season' which I just now spoke of as impressive. No single one of them, doubtless, will seem to deserve so exalted an epithet, but such certainly is, upon a simple Western mind, the effect of their aggregation. Such a vast amount of human life, so complex a society, so powerful a body of custom and tradition stand behind them, that the spectacle becomes the most solidly brilliant, the most richly suggestive, of all great social shows.

It was not, however, of its general suggestiveness that I meant to speak in making this allusion to it. It was one of its more trivial incidents—a mere detail in that daily multiplication of visible detail which, from Easter onward, goes forward in the London streets. The pitiful old men who perambulate in portable stocks increase a hundredfold. I mean by this those ragged starvelings who are induced, by pecuniary considerations, to merge that small remnant of individuality which survives the levelling action of soot without and whisky within in the conspicuous neutrality of advertising mediumship. We only know them as we know the tortoise, by their shell. This shell is a kind of two-sided pyramid, from which their chins emerge, and from which, from the knee downward, their legs depend. Or it might be likened to a sort of over-starched shirt, with the skirts left flying, upon the rigid bosom and back whereof the attractions of concerts and galleries are inscribed in letters of crimson and azure. The wearers stand on the street corners or stroll along the kerbstone for days, weeks, and months together; though occasionally, I suppose (to carry out our metaphor), they may be observed to have affected a change of linen. In the London streets their number is always great, but after Easter it becomes greater than ever. This season ushers in a quickened activity in those two forms of entertainment on whose behalf they chiefly appeal—the concerts and the picture shows.

Judged by the testimony of the wooden-shirted fraternity, the English are both the most musical and the most pictorial of races. There are half a dozen concerts every day; there is a special 'exhibition' in every print shop. Every song, every singer, every picture, is the subject of a special placard, and you thus walk about in a wilderness of aesthetic mementoes. If you are a perfect stranger, you will at first be led to suppose that you are in a city whose native inspiration is a kind of *résumé* of the arts of modern Germany, medieval Florence, and ancient Athens. If you are an older inhabitant, you will not be led into this illusion, but I think I may say that your reflections will be, on this ground, only a few degress less interesting. You are not among the greatest artistic producers of the world, but you are among the greatest consumers. The supply is for the most part foreign, but the demand is extremely domestic. The evidences of the demand are, in England, to a certain extent always before one's eyes; but in London, among the various vernal phenomena, they are not the least striking. They are a part of that redundancy of luxury of which the 'season' is an expression. The English are as largely addicted to intellectual luxury as to material; and these things may, I suppose, come under the former head, or in other words under that of 'culture'.

I am conscious at this point of the temptation to wander off into a long parenthesis and note down a few of my impressions of this same intellectual luxury—enumerate a few of those more particularly social tributes to culture which strike an observant foreigner. But remembering that it is only with the sidelight projected from picture shows that I am concerned, I content myself with the briefest allusion. An American could not be long in England before he discovers that its inhabitants are a much more 'accomplished' people than ourselves—that in those graceful arts which mitigate the severity of almost obligatory leisure they are infinitely more proficient. I should say that, in the educated classes, eight English persons out of ten have some small speciality of the artistic, scientific, or literary sort. Of course I include both sexes, but I do not include the purely muscular and athletic, or, more correctly, the purely sporting members of society; these should not properly be numbered in the educated classes. The others either sketch, or 'play', or sing, or botanize, or geologize, or write novels; they are amateur antiquaries, entomologists, astronomers, geographers, photographers, engravers, or wood-carvers. If they are nothing else, they are addicted to private theatricals. But these, perhaps, should be accounted a form of athletics. The ladies in particular cultivate their little private plot of aesthetic or scientific learning; thereunto impelled in a large measure, I imagine, by that peculiarly English institution of country life which is so beautiful, so stately, so respectable, and so dull. '*Que faire en un gîte à moins que l'on n'a songé?*' What can you do in a country-house unless you sketch, or make music, or scribble? The answer to this question sometimes takes the shape of an offhand affirmation that country-houses are always filled with visitors; but the stranger is free to suspect that this is true only as regards the minority of rural residences and the scantier portion of the year. Even if his glimpses of these enchanting spots have been infinitely briefer than his desire, he will probably have gathered our impression that, for many months together, the hours are as spacious as the great smooth-rolled lawns, and the days as long as the neatly gravelled avenues.

English culture, then, in so far as it is a luxury, is a child of leisure; whereas leisure, in America, has not yet reached that interesting period at which the parental function begins to operate. We have, it is true, a great many young ladies who 'play', but we have, as compared with the English, a very small number who sketch, either in oil or water colours, who write three-volume novels, or produce historical monographs. For my own part, I regret it; for I subscribe to the axiom that culture lends a charm to life. But I have a friend, a compatriot, with whom I often discuss these matters, who takes a very different view, and who pretends that (speaking particularly for instance of the sketching) it is better not to sketch at all than to sketch badly. He here makes, as you see, two questionable assumptions: one is that we Americans do not sketch at all, the other is that the English sketch badly. In fact I should say that we do sketch a little, and that the English often sketch very well. They certainly sketch a great deal; you will hardly find an English family, I think, of which one member at least is not a client of Messrs. Windsor and Newton, the people who manufacture those delightful little miniature gingerbread-pans of cobalt and crimson lake.

My friend has a theory that English sketching is not only no proof of aesthetic talent in the people, but that it is positive proof of the absence of this gift. 'It is a proof of their leisure, of their culture, of their luxury, of their wisdom, of their prudence, of their propriety, of their morality, of anything on that line that you will', he always says. 'But it is not a proof of their having the painter's disposition. If they had the painter's disposition, they couldn't stand that amount of amateurishness. Observe that they always frame their sketches and hang them on the walls. It is therefore not simply the process that they value, as teaching them (as it is the pertinent fashion now to say) how to look, how to use their eyes—it is the result as well. In nine cases out of ten the result is grotesquely amateurish—the drawings are, seriously speaking, pitiful. But the English can stand that; *we* couldn't. We feel we couldn't; therefore we don't risk it. The English have the grossness which is proof against offence; we have the delicacy which shrinks from it. In other words, the English have not, as a people, the artistic sense, and we have it in a certain degree.'

To this I always make a point of replying that if, as a society, we don't sketch, it is not because we won't, but because we can't; and if we don't hang indifferent water colours on our parlour walls, it is because we have not got them to hang. If we had them, I say, we should be only too happy. It is mere want of culture, I say, and not our native delicacy. Delicacy is shown, not in barren abstinence, but in beautiful performance. This I say, and a great deal more; but I confess I don't convince my friend, which, however, hardly matters, for he is sometimes very bitter against the English, and always judges them from the foreign point of view. Among the other things I say is that, besides, all English sketching is not bad, by a good deal; that I have seen a great deal that is very charming, and that I believe in the existence of a great deal more. I believe that there are charming things done, so quietly and privately, in those beautiful rural homes of which I was speaking just now—at those wide Elizabethan windows that look out on far horizons of their own. To this my friend answers that when I get to talking theoretically about what 'must' be produced in English country-houses I become very fantastic; and indeed I think it possible that I go too far. Still, I by no means give up my theory that there are water-colour sketches suspended in many of them more beautiful than any that I have seen.

The reader, however, must have perceived that what I started to say was that the taste for art in England is at bottom a fashion, a need of luxury, a tribute even, as my friend says, to propriety; not an outgush of productive power. So the reflective stranger concludes, after having gone the rounds of everything in the way of an exhibition that the season offers him; and so, if he had time to make the reader perform the same interesting tour, he would expect the latter to conclude with him. But if art is a fashion in England, at least it is a great fashion. How these people have always needed, in a certain sort of way, to be entertained; what handsome things they have collected about them; in the absence of production, on what a scale the consumption has always gone on! A great multiplicity of exhibitions is, I take it, a growth of our own day—a result of that democratization of all tastes and fashions which marks our glorious period. But the English have always bought pictures in quantities, and they certainly have often had the artistic intelligence to buy good ones. In England it has not been the sovereigns who have purchased, or the generals who have 'lifted', and London accordingly boasts of no national collection equal to the gallery at Dresden or the Louvre. But English gentlemen have bought—with English bank notes —profusely, unremittingly, splendidly. They have stored their treasures in their more or less dusky drawing-rooms, so that the people at large have not, on the whole, been much the wiser; but the treasures are at any rate in the country, and are constantly becoming more accessible. Of their number and value the exhibitions held for several years past, during the winter, in the rooms of the Royal Academy, and formed by the loan of choice specimens of the old masters, have been a liberal intimation. These exhibitions give a great impression of the standing art-wealth of Great Britain, and of the fact that, whether or no the English people have painted, the rest of the world has painted for them. They have needed pictures; it is ungracious to look too narrowly at the grounds of the need. Formerly it was supplied almost exclusively by the lordly operation of purchase; now it is gratified by the simpler process of paying a shilling to an extremely civil person in a front shop and passing into certain maroon-draped *penetralia*, where the London daylight is most artfully economized, and where a still more civil person supplies you with a neat literary explanation of the pictures, majestically printed on cardboard, and almost as clever as an article in a magazine.

They do all this wonderfully well in London. I always appreciate it; but then, perhaps, I am too appreciative. I have just come out of a place in Bond Street, which struck me as a particularly characteristic example of its class. The exhibitions in Bond Street, indeed, are legion, and are surpassed (if surpassed) in number only by those in Pall Mall. In this case I saw by the outside announcements that a great religious work by Sir Noel

Paton, R.S.A., LL.D., was on view within, and I furthermore perused a statement, glued to the middle of the plate-glass window, that the picture had, on Thursday, May 10, been conveyed to Marlborough for inspection by H.R.H. the Prince of Wales. Here was a combination of attractions not to be resisted. A religious picture, painted by a baronet, a Royal Scottish Academician (I believe that is the meaning of the first batch of initials), and a Doctor of Laws, and further consecrated by exposure to the awful gaze of royalty—a glimpse of such a work was certainly cheap at a shilling. '*C'est pour rien*', said that friend whom I just now quoted, who happened to be with me, and who interlards his conversation most unconsciously with disjointed scraps of French. We paid our respects—that is, our shilling—to the blonde young lady posted *ad hoc* in the front shop, and then we were inducted by two blond gentlemen—very 'fine men', as they say in England—to the compartment in the rear. This was a charming little place, draped in maroon-coloured stuff, which was elaborately fluted and festooned, and lighted by concealed gas-burners, which projected a mellow glow upon a single picture disposed at the end of the apartment.

The title of the picture was 'Christ the Great Shepherd'—a title whose latent significance, together with the beauties of the work, was set forth on a large card, which was placed in our hands by the attendants. We were instructed by this document that, the Christ being clad, like most Christs, in garments of red and blue, the former colour represented love and the latter wisdom, and that both of these qualities are necessary to the character of a perfect man. Sir Noel Paton's Christ is walking through a rocky country, with a radiance round his head, and a little lamb in his arms, toward whom he gently bends his face. The little lamb is very good; it occurs to me that, the painter being a Scottish Academician, the picture was perhaps painted in the Highlands, where there are great opportunities for making ovine studies. As regards the subject, my companion took occasion to remark that he accepted all representations of Jesus on easy terms; his admiration of the type depicted was so great, his sentiment about it so vivacious, that his critical sense was suspended. If the painter was at all clever, the battle meanwhile was won. I called his attention shortly after this to the interest of looking at a picture by a Doctor of Laws; I think I even remarked upon the beauty of the frame. At all events, I talked about everything being so comfortably arranged. By this time his good humour of a few minutes before appeared to have evaporated. 'Yes', he said, in his incorrigible French; '*il n'y a que la peinture qui manque.*'

This has been a very good year, from the sightseer's point of view, inasmuch as it has witnessed the inception (I believe that is the proper word in such cases) of an artistic enterprise of an unusually brilliant sort. I suppose it is correct to speak of the Grosvenor Gallery as primarily an artistic enterprise; for it has had its origin, on the part of its distinguished proprietor (Sir Coutts Lindsay), rather in the love of pictures than in the love of money. Sir Coutts Lindsay is himself a very clever painter, and I see no warrant for the ill-natured intimation which I heard put forth somewhere, that he built the Grosvenor Gallery in order to have a place to exhibit his own productions. These works would make a very honourable figure at the Royal Academy. In so far as his beautiful rooms in Bond Street are a commercial speculation, this side of their character has been gilded over, and dissimulated in the most graceful manner. They are the product of a theory that there is a demand for a place of exhibition exempted both from the exclusiveness and the promiscuity of Burlington House, in which painters may communicate with the public more directly than under the academic dispensation, and in which the more 'peculiar' ones in especial may have a chance to get popular. Sir Coutts Lindsay is his own counsel, his own jury, and his ambition, I believe, is to make of the Grosvenor Gallery a sort of *Fortnightly Review*, or more correctly, *Nineteenth Century*, among exhibitions. He plays the same part as the thoroughly 'catholic' editor of the latter periodical, who invites the lion and the lamb to lie down together, allows an equal space in his pages to Cardinal Manning and Mr. Huxley.

There are people who expect the Grosvenor Gallery to be simply, for a year or two, a success of curiosity, and then to go the way of all those other brilliant failures in the attempts to entertain this mighty metropolis, whose more or less mouldering relics are scattered over its thankless bosom—the Crystal Palace, the Alexandra Palace, the Westminster Aquarium, the Albert Hall.[1] Then there are people who hold that it corresponds to an essential yearning of the public heart; that it will become a permanent institution, pursue a glorious career, and reimburse the owner for the £100,000 it has cost him. I am unable to hold the scales on so momentous a question, and can only say that for the present the place is very pretty and elegant, and the pictures, in general, are very clever. A good many of them are from foreign hands, and it is interesting to see the work of continental artists in juxtaposition to that of Englishmen. A whole long wall in the first room is covered with the contributions of MM. Heilbuth and James Tissot, who are probably (with a single exception) the most brilliant members of the large colony of foreign painters established in London, and basking in the golden light, not of the metropolitan sky, but of British patronage.

Tissot is a Belgian and Heilbuth is a sort of Gallicized German, whose speciality is Graeco-Roman 'restorations'. Both are extremely clever, but M. Tissot is perhaps more brilliantly so. He is a painter of modern manners, and he generally chooses a subject which it takes a kind of *tour de force* to render. One of his pictures represents a corner of the deck of one of the Queen's ships at Portsmouth, with two ladies and a young officer leaning over the side and looking down at a boat containing a party of their friends, which is putting off.[2] They are women of high

[1] The Grosvenor Gallery, 135 New Bond Street, provided exhibitions of art until 1890. For an account of its foundation and vicissitudes, see *Notes From a Painter's Life* by C. E. Hallé (1909).

[2] 'The Deck of the H.M.S. Calcutta' is now in the Tate Gallery. In 1878 James described Daisy Miller's frock in terms which recall his description of Tissot's 'pretty woman.'

'She was dressed in white muslin, with a hundred frills and flounces, and knots of pale coloured ribbon.'

fashion, and dressed in garments, which have come straight from
Brussels; the one in front, in particular, who twists her perfect
figure with the most charming gracefulness as she rests her
elbows on the bulwark, and, with her head a little thrown back,
smiles down lazily and luxuriously at her friends. She wears a
dress of frilled and fluted white muslin, set off with a great
number of lemon-coloured bows, and its air of fitting her well,
and, as the ladies say, 'hanging' well, is on the painter's part a
triumph of perception and taste. M. Tissot's taste is highly
remarkable; what I care less for is his sentiment, which seems
sterile and disagreeable. Like so many other pictures representing
the manners of the day, his productions suggest a curious and, I
confess it seems to me, an insoluble problem. What is it that
makes such realism as M. Tissot's appear vulgar and *banal*, when
an equal degree of realism, practised three hundred years ago,
has an inexhaustible charm and entertainment? M. Tissot's pretty
woman, with her stylish back and yellow ribbons, will, I am convinced, become less and less charming and interesting as the
years, or even the months, go on. Certain I am, at any rate, that
I should not be able to live in the same room with her for a week
without finding her intolerably wearisome and unrefreshing.
This is not of necessity because she is dressed in the costume of
a particular moment; the delicious Dutch painters, Terburg and
Metsu, Mieris and Gerard Douw, dressed their ladies in the
current fashions of their time, and we find their satin and silver,
their velvet and swansdown, their quilted hoods, and their
square-toed shoes, delightful still. The only thing I can say about
it is that the realism of the Dutch painters seems soft, and that of
such men as M. Tissot seems hard. His humour is trivial, his
sentiment stale. Is there then to be no more *delightful* realism?
I sometimes fear it.

M. Heilbuth is very real, and he is a good deal softer than
his companion, but his Roman skies are strangely grey and cold,
and his pictures have to an inordinate degree that deplorable look
of being based upon photographs, which is the bane of so much
of the clever painting of our day. The painters have used photo-

graphs so much in their work that the result is tainted by that hideous inexpressiveness of the mechanical document. You see that the picture has been painted by a short cut. But I have not the heart to bear too hardly on M. Heilbuth; he recalls so many of those delightful things that compose our Roman memories— the benignant *monsignori* with their purple petticoats and stockings, and their servants in ancient liveries made to fit the household in general; the little crop-headed seminarists, marshalled into a crooked file like a long, innocuous serpent, and petticoated, too, beyond their years; the stately nurses of well-born babies, with their embroidered head-cloths, their crimson bodices, the silver daggers in their coarse back hair, and the gold beads on their ample brown bosoms.

Putting aside the remarkable productions of Mr. Burne-Jones, of which I will presently speak, the most interesting work at the Grosvenor is that of Mr. G. F. Watts, the first portrait painter in England. Mr. Watts is serious and manly, gravely and profoundly harmonious in colour, and full of style in drawing. Though he has made his reputation by his portraits, which constitute his usual work, I believe he has a great longing to deal with 'subjects'. He has indulged it in one of the pictures at the Grosvenor, and the result certainly justifies him. 'Love and Death' is an allegory, an uncomfortable thing in painting; but Mr. Watt's allegory is eminently pictorial. On a large canvas a white draped figure, with its back to the spectator, and with a sinister sweep of garment and gesture, prepares to pass across a threshold where, beside a rosebush that has shed its flowers, a boy figure of love staggers forth, and, with head and body reverted in entreaty, tries in vain to bar its entrance. The picture has a certain graceful impressiveness, and the painter has rendered with peculiar success the air of majestic fatality in the pale image which shows no features.

Next this work hangs the portrait of an admirable model, Mrs. Percy Wyndham. 'It is what they call a "sumptuous" picture', said my companion. 'That is, the lady looks as if she had thirty thousand a year.' It is true that she does; and yet the picture has a style which is distinctly removed from the 'stylishness' of M. Tissot's yellow-ribboned heroine. The very handsome person whom the painter has depicted is dressed in a fashion which will never be wearisome; a simple yet splendid robe, in the taste of no particular period—of all periods. There is something admirably large and generous in the whole design of the work, of which the colouring is proportionately rich and sober. For the art of combining the imagination and ideal element in portraiture with an extreme solidity, and separating great elegance from small elegance, Mr. Watts is highly remarkable.

I will not speak of Mr. Whistler's 'Nocturnes in Black and Gold' and in 'Blue and Silver', of his 'Arrangements', 'Harmonies', and 'Impressions', because I frankly confess they do not amuse me. The mildest judgement I have heard pronounced upon them is that they are like 'ghosts of Velasquezes'; with the harshest I will not darken my pages. It may be a narrow point of view, but to be interesting it seems to me that a picture should have some relation to life as well as to painting. Mr. Whistler's experiments have no relation whatever to life; they have only a relation to painting. Nor will I speak of Mr. Millais's three heads of youthful specimens of aristocratic loveliness, because I am certain that his beautiful models (daughters of the Duke of Westminster) must have measured out to him whatever ire may flow from celestial minds. That Mr. Millais's brush has at its worst a certain indefeasible manliness there is no need of affirming; this the artist has been proving to us any time these ten years. Neither will I stop longer before Mr. Holman Hunt's 'After-Glow in Egypt' than to pay my respects to its beauty of workmanship, and to wonder whence it is, amid all this exquisitely patient labour, that comes the spectator's sense of a singular want of inspiration. Do what he will, Mr. Holman Hunt seems prosaic. At the end of the room in which this picture hangs the crowd is perceptibly thicker than elsewhere, and, glancing over people's heads, you are not slow to perceive an excellent reason for their putting them, as the phrase is, together.

Here hang, more than covering a complete wall, the productions of Mr. Edward Burne-Jones, who is quite the lion of the exhibition. Mr. Burne-Jones's lionship is owing partly to his 'queerness' and partly to a certain air of mystery which had long surrounded him. He had not exhibited in public for many years, and people had an impression that in private prosperity his genius was growing 'queerer' than ever. This impression will probably have found itself justified. To say everything that Mr. Burne-Jones's pictures suggest is to undertake much more than I have either space or ability for; I must content myself with calling them by far the most interesting things in the Grosvenor Gallery. They are seven in number, each of them is large and elaborate, and they represent altogether an immense amount of labour, science, and skill. In my own opinion they place their author quite at the head of the English painters of our day, and very high among all the painters of this degenerate time. I hasten to add that this is the opinion of a spectator not at all in sympathy with the school of art, if school there is, to which Mr. Burne-Jones belongs, not at all inclined to look at things after that morbidly ingenious fashion which seems to me the sign of this school, and able therefore to enjoy its productions only with a dozen abatements. But after these abatements are made there remains in Mr. Burne-Jones a vast deal to enjoy. It is the art of culture, of reflection, of intellectual luxury, of aesthetic refinement, of people who look at the world and at life not directly, as it were, and in all its accidental reality, but in the reflection and ornamental portrait of it furnished by art itself in other manifestations; furnished by literature, by poetry, by history, by erudition. One of Mr. Burne-Jones's contributions to the Grosvenor is a very charming picture entitled 'Venus's Mirror', in which a dozen young girls, in an early Italian landscape, are bending over a lucid pool, set in a flowery lawn, to see what I supposed to be the miraculously embellished image of their faces. Into some such mirror as this the painters and poets of Mr. Burne-Jones's turn of mind seem to me to be looking; they are crowding round a crystal pool with a flowery margin in a literary landscape, quite like the angular nymphs of the picture I speak of.

I can easily imagine what these artists find there being intolerable to some people, and in so far as it offers itself as subject-matter for painting, can conceive of their having no patience with it. 'It is not painting', I hear them say, 'and it has nothing to do with painting. It is literature, erudition, edification; it is a superior education, a reminiscence of Oxford, a luxury of culture. Painting is a direct rendering of something seen in the world we live in and look at, we love and admire, and in that sense there is certainly no painting here.' A part of this is very true. What such a critic brutally calls the reminiscences of Oxford occupies a very large place in Mr. Burne-Jones's painting, and helps it to give us that feeling that the painter is thinking, not looking, which the critic in question finds so irritating. But it is equally certain that such a remarkable work as the 'Days of Creation',[1] such a brilliant piece of simple *rendering* as the 'Beguiling of Merlin',[2] could not have been produced without a vast deal of 'looking' on the painter's part. It is just the difference between Mr. Burne-Jones and a weakly master, that while the brilliantly suggestive side of his work holds a perpetual revel of its own, the strictly plastic side never really lapses. It never rises beyond a certain point; his figures, for instance, to my eye, always seem flat and destitute of sides and backs. If it rose beyond this point, the painter would, with his great suggestiveness, be one of the very greatest of artists. His amateurishness of drawing, his lack of being pledged to a single personal type, diminish considerably the weight of his impressiveness; but they have a chance for much that is exquisitely beautiful in execution, and, in particular, for the display of an admirable art of colour.

Mr. Burne-Jones's most important contribution, the 'Days of Creation', is a series of six small pictures in a single frame. The fullness of their mystical meaning I do not profess to have fathomed, but I have greatly enjoyed their beauty. They consist of different combinations of seven female figures, each of whom

[1] Now in the Fogg Museum, Cambridge, Mass.
[2] Now in the Lady Lever Gallery, Port Sunlight, England.

(save one) bears in her two hands a wonderful image of the globe we inhabit, and represents one of the stages of the process of creation: the light and darkness, the sun and moon, the heavens, the earth, the birds of the air, the human race. Each is accompanied by the mystic nymphs who have figured before, and who are crowded behind her into the narrow canvas, after a fashion which displays the artist's extreme ingenuity and grace of composition. The great burnished ball, its sides embossed with planets and birds, is in each case a beautiful piece of painting, and the folded wings of the angels, overlapping and nestling against each other as they press together, are rendered with even greater skill. Out of this feathery wall rise the angels' faces— faces upon which the artist's critics will find it easy to concentrate their dissatisfaction. We have seen them more or less before in that square-jawed, large-mouthed female visage which the English Pre-Raphaelite school five-and-twenty years ago imported from early Florence to serve its peculiar purposes. It has undergone various modifications since then, and in Mr. Burne-Jones's productions we see its supreme presentment. Here, it must be admitted, it looks very weary of its adventures—looks as if it needed rest and refreshment. But it still serves admirably well what I have called the peculiar purpose of its sponsors; it still expresses that vague, morbid pathos, that appealing desire for an indefinite object, which seems among these artists an essential part of the conception of human loveliness.

In the 'Days of Creation' this morbid pathos, this tearful longing, are expressed with wonderful grace. You may, of course, quarrel with Mr. Burne-Jones for desiring to express it, and especially for expressing it so much. He expresses in fact little else, and all his young women conform to this languishing type with a strictness which savours of monotony. I call them young women, but even this is talking a grosser prose than is proper in speaking of creatures so mysteriously poetic. Perhaps they are young men; they look indeed like beautiful, rather sickly boys. Or rather, they are sublimely sexless, and ready to assume whatever charm of manhood or maidenhood the imagination desires. The manhood, indeed, the protesting critic denies; that these pictures are the reverse of *manly* is his principal complaint. The people, he declares, look debauched and debilitated; they suggest a flaccid softness and weakness. Soft they are, to my sense, and weak and weary; but they have at the same time an enchanting purity, and the perfection with which the painter has mastered the type that seems to say so much to his imagination is something rare in a day of vulgar and superficial study. In the palace of art there are many chambers, and that of which Mr. Burne-Jones holds the key is a wondrous museum. His imagination, his fertility of invention, his exquisiteness of work, his remarkable gifts as a colourist, cruelly discredited as they are by the savage red wall at the Grosvenor—all these things constitute a brilliant distinction.

The Royal Academy is, I believe, this year pronounced a rather poor academy; but such, I also believe, is the regular verdict. Every annual exhibition, as its day comes round, is thought to be rather worse than usual. I am not in a position to compare the Academy with itself, having seen hitherto but a single specimen of it. The most I can do is to compare it with the Paris Salon. This, indeed, I found myself doing spontaneously, as I walked through the brilliant chambers of Burlington House. I call them brilliant advisedly, for the first impression that one receives is that of extraordinary brightness of colour. The walls of the Salon, by contrast, seem neutral and dusky. What shall I say that the next impression is? It is too composite and peculiar to be easily expressed, but I may say that, as I roamed about and eyed the pictures on the 'line', it defined itself, on my own part, by a good deal of inoffensive smiling. My smiles were by no means contemptuous; they denoted entertainment and appreciation; yet the sense of something anomalous and inconsequent had a good deal to do with them.

I had had my private prevision of what the Academy would be. I had indeed not spent four or five consecutive months in England without venturing to elaborate a small theory of what, given the circumstances, it *must* be; and now I laughed to myself

to find that I was so ridiculously right! The only way in which
it differed from my anticipatory image was in being so much
more so. That the people he lives among are not artistic, is, for
the contemplative stranger, one of the foremost lessons of
English life; and the exhibition of the Academy sets the official
seal upon this admonition. What a strange picture-world it
seems; what an extraordinary medley of inharmonious forces!
The pictures, with very few exceptions, are 'subjects'; they
belong to what the French call the anecdotical class. You immediately perceive, moreover, that they are subjects addressed to a
taste of a particularly unimaginative and unaesthetic order—to
the taste of the British merchant and paterfamilias and his excellently regulated family. What this taste appears to demand of a
picture is that it shall have a taking title, like a three-volume
novel or an article in a magazine; that it shall embody in its
lower flights some comfortable incident of the daily life of our
period, suggestive more especially of its gentilities and proprieties and familiar moralities, and in its loftier scope some
picturesque episode of history or fiction which may be substantiated by a long explanatory extract in the catalogue.

The Royal Academy of the present moment unquestionably
represents a great deal of cleverness and ability; but in the way
in which everything is painted down to the level of a vulgar
trivial Philistinism there is something signally depressing. And
this painting down, as I call it, seems to go on without a struggle,
without a protest on the part of the domesticated Muse, with a
strange, smug complacency on the part of the artists. They try of
course to gather a little prettiness as they go, and some of them
succeed in a measure which may be appreciated; but for the most
part I confess they seem to revel in their bondage and to accept
as the standard of perfection one's fitness for being reproduced
in the *Graphic*. Here and there is a partial exception; one complete and brilliant exception, indeed, the Academy of the present
year contains. Mr. Frederick Leighton has always 'gone in', as
the phrase is, for beauty and style, and this year he has defined
his ideal even more sharply than usual by sinking it in sculpture.

His 'Young Man Struggling with a Python'[1] is quite the eminent work of the exhibition. It is not only a wonderfully clever piece of sculpture for a painter, but it is a noble and beautiful work. It has that quality of appealing to our interest on behalf of form and aspect, of the plastic idea pure and simple, which is characteristic of the only art worthy of the name—the only art that does not promptly weary us by the pettiness of its sentimental precautions and the shallowness of its intellectual vision. Whenever I have been to the Academy I have found a certain relief in looking for a while at this representation of the naked human body, the whole story of which begins and ends with the beautiful play of its muscles and limbs. It is worth noting, by the way, that this is to the best of my recollection the only study of the beautiful nude on the walls of the Academy. In the Salon last year, I remember, every fifth picture was a study of the nude; but I must add that that nude was not always beautiful.

It must be allowed that quite the most full-blown specimens of that anti-pictorial Philistinism of which I just now spoke are from the hands of the older Academicians. (I am speaking only of pictures on the 'line'; above it and below it one may find things a little better and a good deal worse.) Some of these gentlemen are truly amazing representatives of the British art of thirty and forty years ago, and there is something cruel in their privilege of Academicians, admitting them into the garish light of conspicuity. There is a portrait by Sir Francis Grant, President of the Academy, of a young lady on horseback, on a manorial greensward, which surely ought to be muffled in some kind of honourable curtain. The productions of Mr. Horsley, Mr. Cope, Mr. Ward, Mr. Redgrave, Mr. O'Neil, are an almost touching exhibition of helplessness, vulgarity, violent imbecility of colour. Of the younger painters it may very often be said that they have the merits of their defects. M. Taine, in his *Notes on England*, pointed out these merits with his usual vigour. 'It is impossible to be more expressive, to expend more effort to address the mind through the senses, to illustrate an idea or a truth, to collect into

[1] Now in the Tate Gallery.

a surface of twelve square inches a closer group of psychological observations. What patient and penetrating critics! What connoisseurs of men!' This is very true; if there is something irritating in the importunately narrative quality of the usual English picture, the presumption is generally that the story is very well told. It is told with a kind of decent good faith and *naïveté* which are wanting in other schools, when other schools attempt this line. I am far from thinking that this compensatory fact is the highest attribute of English art. It has no relation to the work of Gainsborough and Reynolds, Constable, Flaxman, and Turner. But in some of the things in the present Academy it is very happily illustrated.

I found it illustrated, indeed, in the spectators quite as much as in the pictures. Standing near the latter with other observers, I was struck with the fact that when these were in groups or couples, they either, by way of comment, said nothing at all or said something simply about the subject of the picture—projected themselves into the story. I remember a remark made as I stood looking at a very prettily painted scene by Mr. Marcus Stone, representing a young lady in a pink satin dress, solemnly burning up a letter, while an old woman sits weeping in the background. Two ladies stood near me, entranced; for a long time they were silent. At last—'*Her mother was a widow!*' one of them gently breathed. Then they looked a little while longer and departed. The most appreciable thing to them was the old woman's wearing a widow's cap; and the speaker's putting her verb in the past tense struck me as a proof of their accepting the picture above all things as history. To this sort of appreciation the most successful picture of the year, Mr. Long's 'Egyptian Feast', appeals in a forcible and brilliant manner. A company of the subjects of the Pharaohs are collected at a banquet, in the midst of which enter certain slaves, who perform the orthodox ceremony of dragging round the hall, over the polished tessellated floor, as a *memento mori*, the lugubrious simulacrum of a mummy. It is literally the skeleton of the feast, and the purpose of the picture is the portrayal of the various attitudes and facial expressions produced in the assistants by this reminder of mortality. These are represented in each case according to the type of the figure, always with much ingenuity and felicity. From the painter's own point of view the picture is extremely successful; but the painting is of a light order.

Of what order is the painting, by Mr. Millais, of an immense ulster overcoat, flanked by a realistic leather valise and roll of umbrellas, and confronted by a provisional young lady with clasped hands and a long chin, the whole being christened 'Yes'? A lithograph on a music sheet, mercilessly magnified—such is the most accurate description of this astonishing performance. Mr. Millais has a very much better piece of work on exhibition at one of the private galleries, an 'Effie Deans', in which M. Taine's 'expressiveness' is forcibly exemplified. But I prefer his large landscape at the Academy, 'The Sound of Many Waters', possibly because, after all this emulation of the *tableau vivant*, it has the merit of having no expressiveness at all. The best picture in the Academy is one of a series of four by M. Alma Tadema, that Anglicized Hollander and extremely skilful painter whose contributions 'to Burlington House' have for some years past attracted so much attention. These things are called the 'Seasons'; they are all admirably clever, but the scene representing 'Summer' is in its way a marvel. M. Alma Tadema's people are always ancient Romans, and in this case he has depicted a Roman bath in a private house. The bath is of yellow brass, sunk into a floor of yellow brass, and in the water, up to her shoulders, sits an ugly woman with a large nose, crowned with roses, scattering rose-leaves over the water, and fanning herself with a large, limp, yellow ostrich-plume. On a narrow bench, against a mosaic wall, sits another ugly woman, asleep, in a yellow robe. The whole thing is ugly, and there is a disagreeable want of purity of drawing, sweetness of outline. But the rendering of the yellow stuffs and the yellow brass is masterly, and in the artist's manipulation there is a sort of ability which seems the last word of consummate modern painting.

THE NORWICH SCHOOL

1878

IN SPEAKING, a year ago, of the loan exhibition which now regularly takes place in the rooms of the Royal Academy during the months preceding the great show of the pictures of the year, I had occasion to say that the very rich stock of art-treasures from which these assemblages are drawn shows as yet no sign of being exhausted. In the light of the exhibition of the present year this remark needs, perhaps, to be slightly modified. The stock is doubtless not nearly exhausted, but the milk-pan, if I may be allowed in such a connection so vulgar an expression, has been pretty well skimmed. The first-rate things scattered among private collections over the length and breadth of this most richly-furnished country have, for the most part, taken their glorious turn upon the winter-lighted walls of Burlington House. There are, doubtless, some great prizes remaining, but they are not very numerous. The Titians, Rubenses, Rembrandts, Van Dycks, the precious specimens of the Dutch painters, the flower of the Reynoldses and Gainsboroughs, have already obeyed the invitation. This year there are two or three superb Rembrandts; but it is apparent that for the future (unless they begin at the top of the list again) the exhibitions must be pitched in a minor key. To-day, in the absence of great Italians, we have a room devoted to the 'Norwich School'. I do not mention this fact invidiously, for the Norwich room is very interesting. I allude to it simply to indicate that London picture-lovers must begin and clip a little the wings of expectation. It has been the custom with these exhibitions to have, on each successive year, a speciality—the earmark of the particular exhibition. At first this distinguishing stamp was given by the greater masters; there was the Titian year, the Rubens year, the year when the early Tuscan painters came out with peculiar force. Then there was the Reynolds year, and the Gainsborough year; and there was even, a twelvemonth since, what it would be tolerably correct to call the Raeburn year. At the present moment, I suppose, one may talk of the Norwich year. The works of the painters who achieved the unique distinction of reflecting their eminence upon an English provincial town three-quarters of a century ago are ranged together in the first room; and although there are names in the exhibition much more familiarly known to fame than those of John Crome, Cotman, Stannard, Vincent, Stark, there is no part of it more interesting than that occupied by this modest but exquisite group. The founder of the so-called Norwich School was John Crome—'Old Crome'—a man of genius who, among manifold difficulties, spent the greater part of his life cultivating landscape art in the neighbourhood of a little English episcopal city, at what would be termed to-day—at least from the artistic and even the landscape point of view—a very Philistine period of its history. He gathered about him a number of not unworthy pupils, appreciative observers of humble scenery, who, under his wholesome influence and with the minimum of patronage, succeeded in founding the sole local subdivision in the history of English painting. John Crome is a very charming painter, and each of his companions has an interest of his own; but to a stranger, I think, almost the chief merit of the group will be historic or social—found in the simple fact that it held its own and flourished in a situation in which there can have been the least possible human inspiration towards taking the pictorial view of things. It is hard to imagine an assemblage of painters, united by a common ideal, holding well together in an English cathedral town even at this emancipated and Ruskinized day; but to reflect that something of that kind happened during those dusky years of the Napoleonic wars, when England was shut up to her purely British and unaesthetic self, is to find one's self confronted with a genuine marvel. There are no less than twenty-seven of Old Crome's landscapes in the exhibition (I do not know how he came to gain his sobriquet; he lived but to the moderate age of fifty-two), and most of them are extremely delightful. With two exceptions (rather infelicitous memorials of a journey to Paris), they are illustrations of the homely Norfolk scenery—the moist meadows and brown-coated moors, the canal-like rivers, the thatched and gabled cottages, the shallow harbours of the region in which he was born. He had evidently had some observation of the Dutch masters of land-scape, and he had zealously appropriated their teachings. There is a certain 'View on the Wensum', a small expanse of stagnant-looking river, shut in by brick-walled houses with pointed roofs, which would require very little more perfection of detail to make it pass for a Van der Heyden. Crome is seen at his best, however, in the rendering of open spaces—of heath and furze and scrubby trees, and morning and evening skies. Near the picture just named hangs an admirable 'Distant View of Nor-wich', taken in the late afternoon, with the mass of the city lying large and vague in the early dusk, and the spire of the cathedral —a loved landmark—rising far into a sky of remarkable mellow-ness and airiness. There are also two other little pictures—a certain view of 'St. Martin's Gate' and another on 'The Back River'—of old steep-roofed, ruddy-walled houses, reflected in thick, quiet water that are full of a Dutch minuteness and reality. The perfect Dutch skill and taste are wanting; but there is a great charm of colouring, and most of the pictures, like those of the Dutch masters, have suffered very gratefully the action of time. They have a sort of rich brown bloom—a sober glow. I have not space to speak in detail of Crome's followers; but I must spare an allusion to James Stark, who in a small way, with his thin woods, his crooked roads, his timbered cottages, his gray skies, and his unambitious love of foliage, reminds one even vividly of Hobbema. Stark is very charming, though doubtless a little finical and common. Cotman is also charming, with the advan-tage of being stronger and more breezy; a fine Cotman, indeed —for instance, a certain 'Windmill', in this same room, with a great watery, wind-stirred sky—is a very noble piece of work.

In the way of landscape the exhibition contains three or four other excellent things. One of the two Turners—a 'Trout Stream', lent by Lord Essex—may be so spoken of, in virtue of its superb rendering of a gigantic gray cloud lifted up into the air and returning upon itself, like a waterspout. Of the un-equalled art with which, in a subject like this, Turner contrasted with his pregnant vapour-masses the lighted spaces of the sky, this picture is a sufficient illustration. In connection with Cot-man's 'Windmill', I should mention a picture by Rembrandt bearing the same title; or rather, I may say, it will be more con-siderate of the English painter to mention it apart. The Rem-brandt, which is one of the artist's strongest landscapes and is the property of the fortunate Lord Lansdowne, represents a mill standing almost in profile upon a low cliff that overlooks a river. The picture is very dark, and in the way in which the stunted tower of the mill stands up against the sky, and its clumsy arms spread themselves in the faded, ruddy evening light, while the lower part of the subject is bathed in the usual brown Rem-brandtesque mystery, there is an ample suggestion of the painter's characteristic magic. A picture that need not fear juxtaposition even with Rembrandt is an admirable specimen of a Dutch painter who is rarely encountered—John de Capella: a gray, moist harbour-scene; the edge of a pier near which a boat is unloading, and an expanse of quiet water, with other boats vaguely seen beyond it. This small picture is a masterpiece; the look of the monotonous sky, stuffed, as it were, with small rain-clouds; of the warm, damp air, with softened, muffled sounds passing through it, is a marvel of quiet skill. There are two or three good specimens of the better-known Dutch landscape-painters—a couple of interesting Jacob Ruysdaels and of desir-able Hobbemas. In relation to Rembrandt, I must speak of certain portraits from his great hand, which are presumably to be accounted the gems of the exhibition. One is a superb por-trait of himself as a young man—painted in 1635; the other a head of a Jewish rabbi, which is present at Burlington House in two editions. One of these latter works has been contributed by

the Duke of Devonshire, the other by Lord Powerscourt, and
the second being an inferior replica—or a picture, at the best,
much injured by time, or possibly by cleaning—the presence of
its competitor may, in vulgar parlance, be pronounced 'rough
on' the Duke of Devonshire's fellow-peer. The portrait is in
Rembrandt's greatest manner, and represents an old man with
a much-twisted turban, an upper lip shaven like that of an
American legislator, a large, ugly face, magnificently wrinkled
and withered, and a big jewelled clasp glowing upon the bosom
of his furred and dusky robe. The picture is full of that profundity of life which we find in Rembrandt's greatest works.
There are naturally many other portraits; but with the exception
of a beautiful head of a gentleman, auburn-haired and refined, by
Rubens, there is nothing of absolutely the first importance. The
Titians are, I should say, apocryphal, and the Van Dycks, though
decidedly striking, not of supreme excellence. The same may be
said of the Gainsboroughs and Sir Joshuas, which are, as usual,
abundant. The exhibition, with regard to Gainsborough, is
chiefly but a reminder of the difference existing between good
and indifferent specimens of this too prolific painter. Still, one
takes a pleasure even in a collection of fairish Gainsboroughs, by
reason of the large proportion of charming faces among his
models. He painted some very weak pictures, but he never fairly
sacrificed a face. There are two interesting Romneys—portraits
of his perpetual model, Lady Hamilton, which, though the
painting is of an almost primitive baldness, are highly suggestive
of the lady's extraordinary, innocent-looking loveliness. She had
evidently a genius for 'sitting'. There are many more interesting
things which I have no space to commemorate, and I must content myself with a mere allusion to the brilliant winter-exhibition
of the Grosvenor Gallery. This is composed of drawings and
water-colours by masters not living, and in the department of
drawings is especially strong. The Queen has lent a great many
from the treasures of Windsor, most of which are of high value.
But supreme among them and easily surpassing everything else
—even two or three noble designs of Michael Angelo and

several beautiful sketches of Raphael—are a series of deeply-interesting heads by Leonardo da Vinci. These things, as drawings, strike me, in their union of the grand and the exquisite, of intellectual intention with brilliant handiwork, as beyond price.

RUSKIN'S COLLECTION OF
DRAWINGS BY TURNER
1878

THERE HAS for a long time been no more interesting exhibition in London than the little collection of drawings by Turner, the property of Mr. Ruskin, which is now to be seen in Bond Street.[1] I call it a 'little' collection because, although the result of many years of ardent activity on Mr. Ruskin's part, it has been much curtailed by his liberality in parting with some of its most valuable features, many of which he has given away to the two Universities. In its decimated condition, however, it contains many treasures. The interest of the exhibition is increased, moreover, by the fact that Mr. Ruskin is just now lying very ill, and that telegrams and bulletins relating to his condition are suspended in the room, and also by the fact that the catalogue consisted of a collection of notes made by the owner of the drawings. This catalogue is extremely characteristic, containing, as it does, amid much exquisite criticism and much that is a genuine help to enjoyment, many of those incongruous utterances of which the illustrious art-teacher has of late been so prolific. I may add that a portion of it appears to have been dictated at the moment when Mr. Ruskin felt the approach of his illness, and that these pages bear the marks of this condition to a degree which makes it seem almost a cruelty—an irony—to have published them. A drawback, on the other hand, is that the drawings are hung quite without method and without any reference to their chronological order. The room, which is small,

[1] In the Fine Art Society's Galleries, 148 New Bond Street. These drawings were again exhibited in the same Galleries in 1900.

is also densely crowded with (apparently most appreciative) visitors. But in spite of drawbacks it is possible to obtain an abiding impression of the genius of this mightiest of all painters of landscape. I have not space to enumerate these drawings, which are chiefly in water-colours. They are divided in the catalogue into groups which correspond to decades in the painter's life, and to which Mr. Ruskin has affixed characteristic headings: '2d Group—The Rock-Foundations; Switzerland, 1800-1810. 3d Group—Dreamland; Italy, 1810-1820. 4th Group—Reality; England at Rest. 5th Group—Reality; England Disquieted. 6th Group—Meditation; England Passing Away. 8th Group— Morning; By the Riversides'. The English series in this list is decidedly the richest and finest, though the most valuable drawing in the collection is undoubtedly the splendid little 'Rouen' from the 'Rivers of France'. Turner rarely surpassed what he achieved within the few inches' space of this small sheet, rarely rendered more wonderfully the immensity and the impressiveness of nature than in the diminutive brush-work of this crimson western sky or the onward flow of this almost microscopic Seine. In the English drawings the subjects are usually of extreme loveliness, and worthy of Turner's transfiguring vision. That imaginative quality with which he invests his work is often such as to make the reader of the catalogue admit those ultra-metaphysical intentions which Mr. Ruskin attributes to him. From what Mr. Ruskin says about the beauty and delicacy of the work, as simple work, he at any rate rarely ventures to differ. And this is the lesson of these admirable drawings—the feeling they impart, that idealism like Turner's has for its main condition of beauty the fact that it rests upon a solidity of execution which almost defies ultimate analysis. In these water-colours of his healthiest time everything is equally light, clear, and unerring. There is never (save occasionally in the figures) a touch of violence. At the moment at which I write Mr. Ruskin continues seriously ill; but the crisis of his malady—which his almost violent activity during the last few years appears to have rendered inevitable—has, I believe, been passed. There are few persons who will not be interested in hearing of the recovery of a writer whose eccentricities of judgement have been numerous, but for whom, at least, it can be claimed that he is the author of some of the most splendid pages in our language, and that he has spent his life, his large capacity for emotion, and his fortune in a passionate—a too passionate—endeavour to avert, in many different lines, what he believed to be the wrong and to establish his rigid conception of the right.

THE GROSVENOR GALLERY

1878

THE second summer exhibition of the Grosvenor Gallery, which opened a week ago, is pronounced quite as good as the first, if not rather better. This fact is worth noting, for there had been plenty of people ready to declare that this novel enterprise was all very well for once, but that it could not keep itself up. It is really not at all apparent why the Grosvenor Gallery should find the struggle for existence so arduous, and the supposition rests upon a vague idea, diffused to an amusing degree, that it had undertaken to be excessively 'peculiar'. What form its peculiarities are liable to assume most people would find it hard to say; but they have, at least, a strong impression that this exhibition will somehow not be as other exhibitions are. They go there with the expectation of finding something very strange and abnormal; and it is certain that as a general thing they must be grievously disappointed. The last time I entered I heard a lady confessing to this sentiment in rather an amusing manner; she was passing out, with a gentleman, as I came in. 'I am rather disappointed, you know; I expected the arrangement of the pictures would be more unusual.' I wondered in what fashion this good lady had supposed the productions of Mr. Burne-Jones and Mr. Watts would be arranged—hung upside down, or with their faces to the wall? There is, it would seem, but one manner of arranging pictures at an exhibition, and to this time-honoured system the Grosvenor has rigidly adhered. As for the pictures themselves, some of them are very good, and reflect substantial credit upon British art. From this point of view the exhibition, as a whole, is much more glorious than the show at the Royal Academy, which has but just opened, and of which I will speak on another occasion. If on the one hand it is much smaller, on the other it is not disfigured by the presence of any member of that contingent of the old-fashioned Academicians who, at Burlington House, offer so painful and humiliating a reminder of the depths of vulgarity to which English art had sunk thirty or forty years ago. The painters represented at the Grosvenor this year are almost the same names that figured in last summer's catalogue; the artist most conspicuously absent is, perhaps, Mr. Holman Hunt. This year, as last, Mr. Burne-Jones is easily the first, and his several works are far away the most interesting and remarkable things in the exhibition. To the visitors in quest of 'peculiarity' they are, as usual, a particularly opportune spectacle.

Mr. Burne-Jones's contribution consists of two large pictures —'Laus Veneris' and 'Le Chant d'Amour'—and eight smaller ones, several of which were painted some years ago. I have space to speak only of the large things, which are certainly, as yet, the painter's strongest works. 'Laus Veneris' represents a wonderful royal lady in a flame-coloured robe, seated among her maidens, who are singing to her the praise of love, and accompanying themselves on quaint musical instruments. A long, low open window behind the maidens reveals a company of gentlemen in white armour, on white horses, who, as they pass, peer curiously and wistfully into the splendid room. The lady is leaning back wearily, with one arm thrown up and passing over her head, whose dense tresses are all unfolded, while she has lifted off her terrible great crown and placed it before her in her gorgeous lap. She has the face and aspect of a person who has had what the French call an 'intimate' acquaintance with life; her companions, on the other hand, though pale, sickly, and wan, in the manner of all Mr. Burne-Jones's young people, have a more innocent and vacant expression, and seem to have derived their langour chiefly from contact and sympathy. 'Le Chant d'Amour' is a group of three figures, seated, in rather an unexpected manner, upon the top of a garden wall. The middle one is a young woman in a white satin dress, kneeling upon a blue cushion before a small organ, over whose keys her white fingers move. On the right, behind the organ, a young angel, of uncertain sex, plies the instrument with wind from a pair of bellows; on the left sits a melancholy youth in armour, with a dark brown face, leaning on his hand, with his legs folded beside him, listening to the melody produced by his two companions. These two pictures are open to the same sort of criticism that was freely bestowed upon the artist last year. It will be a matter of course to say that the subjects are unreal, the type of figure monotonous and unpleasant, the treatment artificial, the intention obscure. There is much to be said about Mr. Burne-Jones every way; but the first thing to be said, it seems to me, is that no English painter of our day has a tithe of his 'distinction'. After that there is more to say than I have space for. If his figures are too much of the same family, no English painter of our day has mastered a single type so completely and made it an image of so many different things. In colour, the two pictures of which I have spoken are a great achievement; they have extraordinary beauty. They are extremely different, and only a master could offer us such contrasts. The 'Laus Veneris' is pitched in a high key—a key given by the wondrous flame-coloured robe of the heroine fretted with little circular figures in relief. The colours are all brilliant, the shadows thin, the whole impression that of bright surfaces in a strong light. 'Le Chant d'Amour' on the contrary, looks at first like some mellow Giorgione or some richly-glowing Titian. The tone is full of depth and brownness, the shadows are warm, the splendour subdued. As a brilliant success in the way of colour it is hard to know which picture to place first; each of them, at any rate, bears in this respect the great stamp—the stamp of the master for whom the play of colour is a freedom, an invention, a source of thought and delight. In the way of design the strongest point in these two works is the attitudes of the two principal figures—the grand weariness and, at the same time, absorption of posture of the medieval Venus, and the beautiful, rapt dejection of the mysterious young warrior. It must be admitted that the young warrior, with his swimming eyes, has a certain perplexing femineity of expression; but Mr. Burne-Jones does not pretend to paint very manly figures, and we should hardly know where to look for a more delicate rendering of a lovesick swain. The fault I should be inclined to charge upon Mr. Burne-Jones's figures is that they are too flat, that they exist too exclusively in surface. Extremely studied and finished in outline, they often strike one as vague in modelling—wanting in relief and in the power to detach themselves. They are, however, so wonderfully elegant that I should not insist upon that. The compositions of which they form part have the great and rare merit that they are *pictures*. They are conceptions, representations; they have a great *ensemble*.

There are some other excellent things at the Grosvenor, though I should greatly hesitate to name among them the numerous contributions of Mr. G. F. Watts. Mr. Watts has been for thirty years one of the first—perhaps, indeed, the very first—of English portrait-painters; but in the evening of his days he has taken to allegory, and it must be declared that in this pursuit his zeal has decidedly outrun his discretion. His big, mystical 'Love and Death', last year, had indeed a great deal of nobleness, and might, all things considered, be pronounced a success. But this season Mr. Watts is really too big and too mystical: he appears to me, in vulgar parlance, quite off the scent. There is a good deal of fine colour and of what may be called the intention of imagination in his two large canvases, 'Time and Death' and 'Mischief', but there is still more of a certain dense confusion and of an indefinable something which reminds the spectator that nothing is so precious as good taste, or, in its absence, so much missed.

Two American painters are substantially represented. I may seem to stretch a point, indeed, in speaking of Mr. James Whistler as an American painter, for it is not fair to attach to Mr. Whistler any label that serves for anyone else. He is quite sole of his kind. He covers a large space of wall with an array of his usual 'harmonies' and 'variations', 'arrangements' and 'nocturnes'. 'I don't know', was the answer of a friend to whom I had uttered some restrictive criticism of these performances; 'I think they are very pleasant things to have about.' This seemed to me an excellent formula. Mr. Whistler's productions are pleasant things to have about, so long as one regards them as simple objects—as incidents of furniture or decoration. The spectator's quarrel with them begins when he feels it to be expected of him to regard them as pictures. And, even as 'objects', it is hard to feel strongly about them; for Mr. Whistler paints in a manner to make it difficult to attach a high value to individual pieces. His manner is very much that of the French 'Impressionists', and, like them, he suggests the rejoinder that a picture is not an impression but an expression—just as a poem or a piece of music is. Mr. George H. Boughton proceeds in a very different manner, and his results are always charming. More exactly than any one else he preserves the balance between landscape and figures; with him it is always difficult to say whether the group or the background constitutes the subject. This is pretty sure to be one of two things—a study of the costume of the early years of the present century, or a study of the English rustic ('navvy' or ploughboy) and his brawny sweetheart. At the Academy, this year, Mr. Boughton shows us the big bonnets and pelisses, the scanty skirts and long mittens, of the year 1810; he understands these things in perfection and paints them charmingly. At the Grosvenor he exhibits, beside an excellent landscape with a single figure, a rustic pastoral with a large element of landscape—a couple of huge-armed swains in corduroys, at the edge of a stone-quarry, contending with the hammer (they are trying to crack a big block) for the favour of a thick-necked and thick-wristed maiden who sits watching them like the queen of beauty at a tournament. In all Mr. Boughton's work, and especially in his partiality for a certain bright soberness of colour, there is something very refined and discreet.

Mr. Millais is present at the Grosvenor in two contributions—one of the sort that is spoken of at present as representing him at his best; the other looking very much like the work of a vulgar and infelicitous imitator. The better of these two pictures is a portrait, entitled 'Twins'—two young girls of eighteen or twenty stiffly posed and drawn, but very freely painted, and looking out of the canvas as Mr. Millais can so often teach his figures to look. It is kinder not to speak of the other example of this strangely unequal painter—a painter whose imperfectly great powers always suggest to me the legend of the spiteful fairy at the christening feast. The name of Mr. Millais's spiteful fairy is vulgarity; but, fortunately (it must be added), the good fairies are *au complet*. The trio of clever foreigners—MM. Tissot, Alma Tadema, and Heilbuth—are in force; and I must find space to mention two young Englishmen (or, as I believe, Scotchmen) who have this year 'revealed' themselves—Mr. Gregory, with a really superb portrait of a gentleman, and Mr. Cecil Lawson, with two very large and ambitious, but very original and interesting, landscapes.

THE ROYAL ACADEMY

1878

I BELIEVE that every year the Academy is pronounced 'rather worse than usual'; but I suspect that there is little doubt that the exhibition of 1878 is decidedly weak. It is not an exhibition from which it would be agreeable to the indigenous mind to think that a Frenchman, a German, even an Italian, should derive his ultimate impression of contemporary English art. There is a great deal of vulgarity, of triviality and crudity, and of that singular 'goodiness', as one may say for want of a better word, with a certain dose of which the average English painter appears to have discovered it to be needful to flavour his picture in order to make it palatable to the average English purchaser. Even if the pictures were better at the Academy, there would, to a visitor from another country, be something more interesting than their technical merit: I mean the evidence they should offer as to the English mind and character—the English way of thinking and feeling about all things, art included. M. Taine has often been quoted as to the *moralizing* character of English art; not that he is the only person who has ever noticed it, but because he appears, in his very suggestive *Notes sur l'Angleterre*—a book which was, I believe, the result of a very short visit on the author's own part, but which a long stay on the part of a foreign reader only seems to render more pregnant—to have expressed it better than anyone else. At all events, I never go into an exhibition of English pictures without being strongly reminded of M. Taine; I put on his spectacles; I seem to see so well what he meant. With M. Taine's spectacles you immediately see that the exhibition is only in a secondary sense *plastic;* that the plastic quality is not what English spectators look for in a picture, or what the artist has taken the precaution of putting into it. The artist must tell a story or preach a sermon; his picture must not be an image, but, in some fashion or other, a lesson; not a reproduction of form and colour, but of life and experience.

The only strongly 'plastic' pictures I can think of in the present Academy are the charming 'Nausicaa' and 'Winding the Skein' of Mr. Frederick Leighton, both representations of antique figures, of which the interest is in attitude and outline. It is impossible to be more graceful and elegant, and more keenly artistic, than Mr. Leighton; he strikes me as one of the few English painters who have had an artistic training that would be considered thorough by a high French standard. His taste and discretion are infallible, and he has a love of purity and clearness of outline which it does one good to encounter. But in Mr. Leighton's plasticism there is something vague and conciliatory; it is as if he thought that to be more plastic than that would not be quite gentlemanly. He may, however, I think, be said to be the one painter of eminence who bridges over the gulf existing between French and English art. He has an exquisite sense of form, and he has, in addition, the merit of being what I have called gentlemanly to a degree that is rare among the devotees of form on the other side of the Channel. His 'Winding the Skein' (two Greek girls, on a terrace, against the sky) is quite the most strictly beautiful—indeed, I think the only very beautiful—work in the Academy.

In any exhibition in which Mr. Millais appears, Mr. Millais is always the strongest genius present; though his pictures on particular occasions may be by no means the best. But it is interesting to see how he, rich and strong in the painter's temperament as he is, shirks, as it were, and coquets with, the plastic obligation, and plays into the hands of the public desire for something more amusing or more edifying. Mr. Millais always knows thoroughly well what he is about, and when he paints very badly he is certainly aware of it, and of just how it serves his turn; indeed, I may say that to paint so badly as Mr. Millais occasionally does a great deal of knowledge must be brought to bear. Of course, in his portraits there is less begging of the question—less of a tendency to solve the problem on side-issues—than in his 'subjects'; but even in his portraits it is amusing to see the tendency crop up, as in the case of the sketch of the beautiful Mrs. Langtrey—the lady whose photographs, in every possible attitude and costume, are in all the shop-windows, and who appears to be, with the London public, in the remarkable position of a person whose beauty has become legendary—become a household word, even in her lifetime. Mrs. Langtrey's admirable beauty is quite of the antique, classical, formal, and, to return to the word I began with using, plastic order: but Mr. Millais paints her as if he meant to make her pass for the heroine of a serial in a magazine, and, to carry out the impression, calls his picture 'A Jersey Lily'—the lady being a native of that fortunate island. A much better, indeed, a very fine, portrait of Mrs. Langtrey is contributed by Mr. Poynter, who has rendered admirably the serene, un-modern character of her beauty, and has given her a costume which helps her to look like some splendid human flower of the Renaissance, or of some other period at which there were no serial novels.

Mr. Millais's best thing, by far, is an admirable portrait of Lord Shaftesbury, of whom there is another excellent portrait by a young painter of solid promise, Mr. John Collier. 'Painted for the Bible Society', says the catalogue; and there could not be an image more perfectly in harmony with such a label. If the great thing for a painter is to lay his hand upon a characteristic model, Mr. Millais has been most fortunate in his sitter, and he has shown himself quite worthy of his luck. It is an admirable piece of really psychological painting. Lord Shaftesbury's face is an excellent example of the British countenance as, in nine cases out of ten, this immitigable mask presents itself to foreign observation—that 'biblical' countenance which has the privilege of irritating the lively perception of the Latin, the Slav, and other Bohemian races; very dry on one side, but on the other inspiring unlimited confidence. Mr. Millais has rendered with remarkable skill both the dryness and the cleanness. He has also a landscape

—'St. Martin's Summer', a wild Scotch brook in a tangle of
autumnal foliage—containing some admirable painting, but with
a curiously motionless and photographic quality. Then he has
the 'Princes in the Tower', who are of course very much
noticed—two charmingly pretty boys, in black velvet, with an
impromptu turret staircase behind them. This is a sort of thing
which Mr. Millais sometimes does admirably; of how well he is
capable of doing it 'The Bride of Lammermoor', now on exhibition by itself, is this year (just as the 'Effie Deans' was last year)
a very brilliant example. In these things the artist attempts to be
subtly dramatic, to represent the finest shades of expression of
the human face. The attempt is perfectly legitimate, and, as I
have mentioned M. Taine, I may recall the tribute that he pays
to the wonderfully delicate skill of which English painters are
capable in these experiments, which he considers their strongest
point. 'The Princes in the Tower' is a fair specimen of this skill,
but the scene from Scott's novel is a really extraordinary one; I
wish I had more space to speak of it. It represents Lucy Ashton,
in a forest glade, leaning on the arm of her lover after he has
saved her from the aggression of the wild bull. Her face—an
exquisite piece of painting—is a marvellous study of girlish
agitation, and that of the sombre young Master of Ravenswood
is not less remarkable. Mr. Millais is, by the way, almost always
greatly to be congratulated on his models; he evidently has his
'pick' of handsome people. It would be hard to find a lovelier
specimen of English girlish beauty than his Lucy Ashton, or a
more magnificent young man than her companion. But, as it
seems to me, he makes figures of them, and nothing more; he
does not make pictures, in the sense that Mr. Burne-Jones does.
The figures are lighted anyhow, or not at all; they are not seen
in relation to the rest of the canvas, which looks as if it were
rubbed in, after the fact, in the most perfunctory manner.

In one of the rooms at the Academy there is a dense crowd of
people, pressing closely together, under the rigid surveillance of
a policeman, who beseeches them to 'move on' in tones which
resound the livelong day. Is it, then, so difficult to detach one's

self from the work of Mr. Frith, after one has caught a happy glimpse of it? I can hardly answer this question on the evidence of the 'Road to Ruin' (the title of his present contribution), for, thanks to the crowd and the policeman, I saw very little of it. I perceived, however, that it consists of five small pictures, which form a kind of contemporary edition of Hogarth's 'Rake's Progress'—the downward career beginning with a card-party at college of a young man about town. At the end, with a livid face and bloodshot eyes, he is locking the door, preparatory to an operation indicated by a suicidal-looking pistol on the centre-table. I could see also that Mr. Frith had apparently lost nothing of the peculiar ability which formerly made a policeman the indispensable adjunct of his 'Derby Day' and his 'Railway Station'. But it would take M. Taine to speak properly, and, as it were, scientifically, of Mr. Frith. I have not pretended to speak of many of his fellow-contributors, and I can think of no other work that it is a serious wrong not to mention. M. Alma Tadema has a great piece of flesh-modelling, and one of his consummately-skilful 'restorations' of Roman costumes and antique interiors. Mr. Boughton, Mr. Orchardson, and Mr. Marcus Stone are very charming; Mr. Long, representing a large workshop of Egyptian girls, in the Ptolemaic time, making up little effigies of Isis and Osiris, is very brilliant; Mr. Pettie paints portraits of gentlemen in ancient doublets and tartans very bravely. Of some of the elder Academicians—Sir Francis Grant, the president, Messrs. Horsley, Cope, Hart, O'Neil, etc.—it is but common humanity not to speak. Their contributions, raggedly and cruelly squaring themselves upon the 'line', must be seen to be believed in. American art (and American nature, I may add), are represented in a large view of Colorado scenery by Mr. Albert Bierstadt. The picture is unfavourably hung.

ON WHISTLER AND RUSKIN

1878

THE London public is never left for many days without a *cause célèbre* of some kind. The latest novelty in this line has been the suit for damages brought against Mr. Ruskin by Mr. James Whistler, the American painter, and decided last week. Mr. Whistler is very well known in the London world, and his conspicuity, combined with the renown of the defendant and the nature of the case, made the affair the talk of the moment. All the newspapers have had leading articles upon it, and people have differed for a few hours more positively than it had come to be supposed that they could differ about anything save the character of the statesmanship of Lord Beaconsfield. The injury suffered by Mr. Whistler resides in a paragraph published more than a year ago in that strange monthly manifesto called *Fors Clavigera*, which Mr. Ruskin had for a long time addressed to a partly edified, partly irritated, and greatly amused public. Mr. Ruskin spoke at some length of the pictures at the Grosvenor Gallery, and, falling foul of Mr. Whistler, he alluded to him in these terms:

For Mr. Whistler's own sake, no less than for the protection of the purchaser, Sir Coutts Lindsay ought not to have admitted works into the gallery in which the ill-educated conceit of the artist so nearly approached the aspect of wilful imposture. I have seen and heard much of cockney impudence before now, but never expected to hear a coxcomb ask 200 guineas for flinging a pot of paint in the public's face.

Mr. Whistler alleged that these words were libellous, and that, coming from a critic of Mr. Ruskin's eminence, they had done him, professionally, serious injury; and he asked for £1,000 damages. The case had a two days' hearing, and it was a singular and most regrettable exhibition. If it had taken place in some Western American town, it would have been called provincial and barbarous; it would have been cited as an incident of a low civilization. Beneath the stately towers of Westminster it hardly wore a higher aspect. A British jury of ordinary taxpayers was appealed to to decide whether Mr. Whistler's pictures belonged to a high order of art, and what degree of 'finish' was required to render a picture satisfactory. The painter's singular canvases were handed about in court, and the counsel for the defence, holding one of them up, called upon the jury to pronounce whether it was an 'accurate representation' of Battersea Bridge. Witnesses were summoned on either side to testify to the value of Mr. Whistler's productions, and Mr. Ruskin had the honour of having his estimate of them substantiated by Mr. Frith. The weightiest testimony, the most intelligently, and apparently the most reluctantly, delivered, was that of Mr. Burne-Jones, who appeared to appreciate the ridiculous character of the process to which he had been summoned (by the defence) to contribute, and who spoke of Mr. Whistler's performances as only in a partial sense of the word pictures—as being beautiful in colour, and indicating an extraordinary power of representing the atmosphere, but as being also hardly more than beginnings, and fatally deficient in finish. For the rest, the crudity and levity of the whole affair were decidedly painful, and few things, I think, have lately done more to vulgarize the public sense of the character of artistic production. The jury gave Mr. Whistler nominal damages. The opinion of the newspapers seems to be that he has got at least all he deserved—that anything more would have been a blow at the liberty of criticism. I confess to thinking it hard to decide what Mr. Whistler ought properly to have done, while —putting aside the degree of one's appreciation of his works— I quite understand his resentment. Mr. Ruskin's language quite transgresses the decencies of criticism, and he has been laying about him for some years past with such promiscuous violence that it gratifies one's sense of justice to see him brought up as a disorderly character. On the other hand, he is a chartered libertine—he has possessed himself by prescription of the function of a general scold. His literary bad manners are recognized, and many of his contemporaries have suffered from them without complaining. It would very possibly, therefore, have been much wiser on Mr. Whistler's part to feign indifference. Unfortunately, Mr. Whistler's productions are so very eccentric and imperfect (I speak here of his paintings only; his etchings are quite another affair, and altogether admirable) that his critic's denunciation could by no means fall to the ground of itself. I wonder that before a British jury they had any chance whatever; they must have been a terrible puzzle. The verdict, of course, satisfies neither party: Mr. Ruskin is formally condemned, but the plaintiff is not compensated. Mr. Ruskin too, doubtless, is not gratified at finding that the fullest weight of his disapproval is thought to be represented by the sum of one farthing.

ON ART-CRITICISM AND

WHISTLER

1879

I MAY mention as a sequel to the brief account of the suit Whistler v. Ruskin, which I sent you a short time since, that the plaintiff has lately published a little pamphlet[1] in which he delivers himself on the subject of art-criticism. This little pamphlet, issued by Chatto & Windus, is an affair of seventeen very prettily-printed small pages; it is now in its sixth edition, it sells for a shilling, and is to be seen in most of the shop-windows. It is very characteristic of the painter, and highly entertaining; but I am not sure that it will have rendered appreciable service to the cause which he has at heart. The cause that Mr. Whistler has at heart is the absolute suppression and extinction of the art-critic and his function. According to Mr. Whistler the art-critic is an impertinence, a nuisance, a monstrosity—and usually, into the bargain, an arrant fool. Mr. Whistler writes in an off-hand, colloquial style, much besprinkled with French—a style which might be called familiar if one often encountered anything like it. He writes by no means as well as he paints; but his little diatribe against the critics is suggestive, apart from the force of anything that he specifically urges. The painter's irritated feeling is interesting, for it suggests the state of mind of many of his brothers of the brush in the presence of the bungling and incompetent disquisitions of certain members of the fraternity who sit in judgement upon their works. 'Let work be received in silence,' says Mr. Whistler, 'as it was in the days to which the penman still points as an era when art was at its apogee.' He is very

[1] *Whistler v Ruskin, Art and Art Critics*, by J. A. McNeill Whistler, The White House, Chelsea, Dec. 24, 1878.

scornful of the 'penman', and it is on the general ground of his being a penman that he deprecates the existence of his late adversary, Mr. Ruskin. He does not attempt to make out a case in detail against the great commentator of pictures; it is enough for Mr. Whistler that he is a '*littérateur*', and that a *littérateur* should concern himself with his own business. The author also falls foul of Mr. Tom Taylor, who does the reports of the exhibitions in *The Times*, and who had the misfortune, fifteen years ago, to express himself rather unintelligently about Velasquez. 'The Observatory at Greenwich under the direction of an apothecary!', says Mr. Whistler, 'the College of Physicians with Tennyson as president! and we know that madness is about. But a school of art with an accomplished *littérateur* at its head disturbs no one, and is actually what the world receives as rational, while Ruskin writes for pupils and Colvin holds forth at Cambridge. Still, quite alone stands Ruskin, whose writing is art, and whose art is unworthy his writing. To him and his example do we owe the outrage of proffered assistance from the unscientific—the meddling of the immodest—the intrusion of the garrulous. Art, that for ages has hewn its own history in marble, and written its own comments on canvas, shall it suddenly stand still, and stammer, and wait for wisdom from the passer-by? —for guidance from the hand that holds neither brush nor chisel? Out upon the shallow conceit! What greater sarcasm can Mr. Ruskin pass upon himself than that he preaches to young men what he cannot perform! Why, unsatisfied with his conscious power, should he choose to become the type of incompetence by talking for forty years of what he has never done!'[1] And Mr. Whistler winds up by pronouncing Mr. Ruskin, of whose writings he has perused, I suspect, an infinitesimally small number of pages, 'the Peter Parley of Painting'. This is very far, as I say, from exhausting the question; but it is easy to understand the state of mind of a London artist (to go no further) who skims through the critiques in the local journals. There is no

---

[1] This quotation, as reprinted here, conforms with the text of Whistler's pamphlet; in the *Nation* it differed in several particulars, chiefly of punctuation.

scurrility in saying that these are for the most part almost incredibly weak and unskilled; to turn from one of them to a critical feuilleton in one of the Parisian journals is like passing from a primitive to a very high civilization. Even, however, if the reviews of pictures were very much better, the protest of the producer as against the critic would still have a considerable validity. Few people will deny that the development of criticism in our day has become inordinate, disproportionate, and that much of what is written under that exalted name is very idle and superficial. Mr. Whistler's complaint belongs to the general question, and I am afraid it will never obtain a serious hearing, on special and exceptional grounds. The whole artistic fraternity is in the same boat—the painters, the architects, the poets, the novelists, the dramatists, the actors, the musicians, the singers. They have a standing, and in many ways a very just, quarrel with criticism; but perhaps many of them would admit that, on the whole, so long as they appeal to a public laden with many cares and a great variety of interests, it gratifies as much as it displeases them. Art is one of the necessities of life; but even the critics themselves would probably not assert that criticism is anything more than an agreeable luxury—something like printed talk. If it be said that they claim too much in calling it 'agreeable' to the criticized, it may be added on their behalf that they probably mean agreeable in the long run.

THE ROYAL ACADEMY AND
THE GROSVENOR GALLERY
1879

I FIND by counting the advertisements on the first page of *The Times* that more than a dozen exhibitions of pictures contend at the present moment for the patronage of the London public, but in the small space of this letter I can only speak—and that very briefly—of the two principal houses. The Academy and the Grosvenor have been open since the beginning of the month. The absence of what the French call *grande peinture*—painting in which style plays a part—is as striking as ever at the former institution, where anecdotical art and little pictures addressed directly to the pocket of purchasers who demand a great deal of familiar point hold undisputed sway. I can recall only two or three things at the Academy that have any pretension whatever to nobleness. One of these is a large canvas by the new President, Sir Frederick Leighton, an 'Elijah in the Wilderness', representing the brawny prophet asleep on a rock and visited by the angel who brings him a jug of water and a loaf. This picture was one of the ornaments of the English department at the Paris Exhibition of last year; but in spite of this fact, of its ambitious intention, and of an execution as brilliant in many ways as Sir Frederick Leighton has accustomed us to look for, it cannot be called a success or commended as an example of the author's best skill. With Mr. Poynter's 'Nausicaa and her Maidens', however, it does solitary duty at the Academy as an appeal to interest on simple grounds of beauty of design. Mr. Poynter's picture, which was much talked about in advance, has proved, I believe, a general disappointment. It was known that some of the most

178

beautiful women of the London world—in which so many
beautiful women are to be found—had stood to the artist for
the figures (by which I mean the faces) of Nausicaa's companions,
so that on the day of the private view people flocked to the
picture with the interesting hope of recognizing beneath the
desultory drapery of the Homeric period the aristocratic heroines
of the photograph shops. These ladies, however, are not thought
to have been favourably represented, and indeed the picture
strikes me as having a good deal of almost inexplicable awk-
wardness and ugliness. It is a very different affair from the same
artist's charming representation of the 'Race of Atalanta', which
was exhibited a few years since—a work with which it challenges
comparison by its shape and style. The painting seems dry and
dull, the colour harsh and displeasing, the composition by no
means happy. Of course, when young ladies are playing at ball
they are obliged to stand at a considerable distance from each
other, and this fact has introduced into Mr. Poynter's picture a
series of empty spaces, blank intervals, to which he has not
always succeeded in imparting interest. In the case of the most
considerable of these *lacunae* he has resorted to the expedient of
representing a little naked boy, bounding across the field of
vision with as wide a stride as possible. But in point of fact this
little naked boy is the principal object in the picture; he jumps,
as the French say, at the eyes, and there is something almost
ludicrous in his exaggerated gambol. The redeeming point in
Mr. Poynter's canvas is a certain elevation of intention, a search
for nobleness and suggestiveness of line and form, a care for style.

Two pictures for which it would perhaps be claimed that they
rank themselves under the head of *peinture de style* are the
'Esther' and the 'Vashti' of Mr. Long, who at several successive
exhibitions has attracted attention by clever archaeological representations of oriental subjects. The two works I have just
mentioned ought to have been hung in juxtaposition; but, for
reasons not obvious to the casual visitor, they are separated by
the space of several rooms. They are imaginary dramatic portraits of the two Biblical ladies whose names they bear; but in

spite of a certain sort of skilful elaboration of touch they strike me as capital—indeed, as quite inimitable—examples of the trivial tendency of contemporary English art. Mr. Long has, I believe, a great reputation; he makes a great figure in the London picture-market, and this fact, in the presence of his light, thin, small, undeveloped manner of painting, with its lack of breadth and boldness, of light and shade, is a measure of the standard and the taste that prevail here. Neither in France nor in Germany would Mr. Long pass as an important or even as a particularly competent painter.

There is usually at the Academy a so-called 'picture of the year'—a picture that has a thicker crowd in front of it than any other. If I say that this distinction has not this year fallen very obviously upon any particular work it will, perhaps, seem but another way of saying that the crowd at Burlington House has been everywhere so dense that it is hard to say that the spectator is more tightly squeezed in one place than in another. But I suppose it would be a fairer statement to recognize the rather evenly balanced claims to conspicuity of two very clever productions of Mr. Fildes and Mr. Pettie, who may be said to divide between them the distinction of which I just spoke. Mr. Fildes's 'Return of the Penitent' has the honours of a crowd, and it very well deserves them, being a very strong and brilliant example of that relish of a human interest which is the most marked characteristic of the British school. It represents a group of country people in a village street—an old farmer leading his big cart-horse back from the plough, three or four old and young women, a couple of children—who have stopped to stare at a young girl who has prostrated herself at the door of a rustic dwelling, and who, as it stands sternly closed against her, lies there huddled together with her head buried in a passion of grief and shame. We are left to perceive that she has lost her maiden innocence, and that, having been deserted by her lover, she has made her way back to her father's house only to find herself treated as an outcast, or left at least to do public penance on the doorstep. The penance is very public indeed, and the incidents it brings with it are indicated by Mr. Fildes with that moral ingenuity, as I may call it for want of a better name, which English painters have so largely at their command in the treatment of such subjects, and which, as a general thing, fills their public with a kind of comfortable sympathy. Mr. Fildes's picture, which is large and abounds in detail, contains some very charming painting—it is indeed charmingly painted throughout, and the different figures with their various gossiping, pitying, criticizing attitudes, are excellently studied and full of significant touches. The thing possesses in a word, in a high degree, the story-telling quality which marks the maximum of so much of the English art of the day. But, at the risk of seeming very dry and cynical, I must say that I find it hard to express my sense of the latent bad taste of such a performance—of a certain quality in it which would make it a misery to possess the picture and have it hanging constantly before one's eyes. The vulgarity of feeling which has prompted the painter to twist into a pictorial effect a subject altogether moral and dramatic, and seeming bruised and injured by the violence done it—this vulgarity is not flagrant or visible on the face of the work; but after one has looked at the picture for three minutes it becomes quite confounding, and one turns away from so much misapplied cleverness with something of the annoyance produced by the sight of a serious social blunder.

Mr. Pettie in his 'Death Warrant' has less of a story to tell, and his picture is more of a picture. A young king (who may be Edward VI of England) is seated at the council-table with his old ministers, one of whom offers him a parchment and pen; which he, looking away and with the tears rising to his blue eyes, neglects to take. Mr. Pettie is a colourist, and a warm and powerful one. He inclines rather to the abuse of reds and yellowish browns, but he has done nothing so fine as this important work, in which the heads of the old men, bald, bearded and sagacious, are treated in a thoroughly painter-like way. Mr. Millais, who is usually first spoken of in connexion with any exhibition of the Royal Academy, may almost be said on this occasion to be conspicuous by his absence. He has no composition this year, and of his several portraits only one is of striking interest. It is true that this one—a remarkable rendering of the at once strange and familiar physiognomy of Mr. Gladstone[1]—is a brilliant success. The resemblance is extreme, although the expression of the face is singular and a little pushed in the direction of parody. I have heard the thing cleverly described as 'Mr. Gladstone repenting that he had not become after all a Bishop'. He stands with his features rather rigid and his eyes uplifted and filled with a sort of visionary glow; but it must be remembered that light animation is at no time the characteristic of his countenance, and that his eyes are always extraordinary. Mr. Millais has apparently wished to offer an image of his mystical, theological, episcopal side; but at any rate he has produced a very manly, masterly, simple piece of portraiture. There is no detail save in the head; the body is scarcely treated at all. But the thing has the great quality—it lives, it looks, it expresses something. It is true that what it expresses will perhaps gratify Mr. Gladstone's enemies as much as his friends.

At the Grosvenor (which, with its beautiful rooms, its thinner attendance, and its interspaced, low-hung pictures, is a very agreeable change from the material conditions of the Academy) Mr. Burne-Jones is, as usual, the chief 'actuality'. He makes a less striking appearance this year than the two preceding ones; but his contributions are important and highly characteristic. I have no space to describe either the 'Annunciation' or the four smaller pictures, in which the painter has told, with the accompaniment of a running motto ('The heart desires, The hand refrains, The Godhead fires, The Soul attains'), the story of Pygmalion and Galatea. These things are open to all of the same criticism which has been lavishly bestowed at any time upon their author, and which, in spite of his reputation for having established what is called in London a 'craze', strikes me as being much in excess of any adulation that he has received. At the same time they have, to my mind, as much as ever the great merit—the merit of having a great charm.

[1] Now in the National Portrait Gallery, London.

THE LETTERS OF

EUGENE DELACROIX

1880

IT IS PROBABLE that few people would contest the proposition that, of the modern schools of painting, the French is the most complete; but, on the other hand, there would probably be many dissentients to the idea, that, of this brilliant school, Eugène Delacroix is the most eminent member. He has passed into the rank of one of the 'glories' of France, and yet he belongs to the class of artists who gratify the few rather than the many. We may believe that no small part of the patriotic amateurs who boast of him as a national genius take him upon trust. Like Turner, he enjoyed during his life but a moderate share of his meed of honours; he profited less by his reputation than those have done who, since his death, have gathered the emoluments, both intellectual and financial, of having appreciated him. Comparisons are odious, and it would profit little to say that Delacroix did better work than this one or that among his contemporaries. They were a band of resolute workers, and it should be borne in mind of them—as it should always be of the representative members of any school of art—that they helped each other, owed much to each other. Nothing tends more to make an observer doubt whether human nature be worth his hopes than the absence, among men engaged in a common undertaking, of a certain mutual respect. Art is really but a point of view, and genius but a way of looking at things. The wiser the artist, and the finer the genius, the more easy will it be to conceive of other points of view, other ways of looking at things, than one's own. At any rate, a person whose sole relation to

183

pictures is a disposition to enjoy them can rest upon his personal impressions; and in the case of the writer of these lines such an impression has been conscious of no chilling responsibilities. I have felt no obligation to determine for my own comfort Delacroix's place in the hierarchy of painters, or to ascertain the figure he would present if he should be made to constitute the apex of a pyramid of prostrate rivals. I have not lately had the opportunity to refresh my memory of his works; but as I recall, one by one, those which I knew at an earlier time, a vivid sense of the rare quality of his genius comes back to me. He belongs to the family of the great masters of the past—he had the same large, liberal way of understanding his business. He was far from being their equal in skill and science—he was not another Titian, nor another Tintoretto; he was not even a modern Rubens. But he was of the same artistic strain as these great painters; for him, to do a thing at all meant to do it grandly. He had an imagination which urged and inflamed him, and never allowed him to rest in the common and the conventional. He was a great colourist and a great composer: in this latter respect he always reminded me of Tintoretto. He saw his subject as a whole; not as the portrait of a group of selected and isolated objects, but as an incident in the continuity of things and the passage of human life. Like Tintoretto, he must be judged as a whole; like Tintoretto, too, he must be judged with the imagination. What it is the imagination finds in him I do not pretend always to settle; but the burden of his message to it is almost constantly grave. He intimates that life is a perplexing rather than an amusing business; and it is very possible that in so doing he is unfaithful to his duty as a painter—the *raison d'être* of these gentry being, constructively, the beautifying of existence, the conservation of enjoyment. But there is plenty of beauty in Delacroix—woe, indeed, to the painter in whom there is not! His vision of earthly harmonies leaves nothing to be desired; only his feeling about it, as he goes, is that of a man who not only sees, but reflects as well as sees. It is this reflective element in Delacroix which has always been one of the sources of his interest, and I am not ashamed to say that I like him in part for his moral tone. I know very well that I appear to be uttering a grievous solecism, and that in the opinion of many people a painter has no business with a moral tone or a sentimental intention. Such people are very right in one sense, and there is no doubt that every artist's first and bounden duty is to be an artist. But an artist, after all, has some of the common attributes and privileges of humanity, and it were a pity to multiply the negative points of his function. A painter is none the worse for being of a reflective temperament, or for having a good deal of feeling about the things he represents. In such questions as this, it is easy to say more than one intends, or than one is sure of. So it is enough to express the belief that a large part of the legitimate value of the pictorial power of such painters as Tintoretto and Delacroix lies in their having felt a good deal about the things they represented. In the arts, feeling is always meaning, and so I think we do not go too far if we permit ourselves to allude to the moral and psychological side of Delacroix. It is very true that people who are jealous of the rights of 'execution' have a tolerably easy reply to this. 'Oh, very well,' they may say, 'we concede that a painter may mean something, so long as no one can tell what he means. If that is your idea, you are welcome to it, and much good may it do you!'

I am afraid that this is my idea to a greater degree than this meagre expression of it can hope to rescue from ridicule. I remember that when I had occasion to see the productions of Delacroix more frequently than I now do, it seemed unnecessary to go further than to say that he made his reflections: it seemed beside the mark to try and give a name to this metaphysical emanation of his work. I had a vague sense that it proceeded from a serious mind—perhaps even from a melancholy nature. By contrast this gave an air of the trivial and superficial—almost of the vulgar—to the work of some of his extremely accomplished companions. I think there is no question that, on the whole, the artist we value most is the artist who tells us most about human life. This large reference to human life appeared to be the merit of Delacroix, so that he became, to my perhaps rather too fanciful vision, the most interesting of contemporary painters. Delacroix was not fond of Ingres, and there is a passage in one of his letters in which, in indicating (it must be admitted rather contemptuously) the limitations of this refined but shallow genius, he points out the reasons of his own effectiveness. 'You have made a perfect article upon Ingres', he writes to a critic; 'you have touched the real chord. No one up to this time had indicated that radical vice, that absence of heart, of soul, of reason, of everything that touches *mortalia corda*, that capital defect which leads only to the satisfaction of an empty curiosity, and to the production of Chinese works, which his are, *minus* the *naïveté*—a quality still more absent than all the rest.'

It is the presence of heart, and soul, and reason, of something that touches *mortalia corda*, which constitutes half the charm of Delacroix. For the rest, he is a magnificent executant—a singularly powerful and various colourist. If it were not for the fear of seeming pedantic, I should risk the assertion that he belonged to the class of synthetic rather than of analytic painters; but I instantly withhold it when I remember what beautiful parts, what splendid details, are to be found in many of his pictures. If he poetically describes himself in the passage I have just quoted, he may be said to complete the description in the following short extract, which occurs in a letter addressed to another critic:

I am afraid to say that what you have written in your article is extremely just, because it redounds to my benefit. What you say of colour and colourists has never been much said. Criticism is like many other things—it dawdles about over what has been already said, and never gets out of the rut. That famous 'Beautiful', which some people see in the winding line, and others in the straight line—they have all made up their minds to see it in nothing but lines. I am at my window, and I see the most beautiful landscape; the idea of a line never comes into my head. The lark sings, the river glitters, the foliage murmurs, but where are the lines which produce these charming sensations? They can see proportion and harmony only between two lines; the rest, for them, is chaos, and the compass only is judge.

Yes, Rubens draws—yes, Correggio draws; but neither of these men have any quarrel with the ideal. Without the ideal there is neither painting, nor drawing, nor colours; and what is worse than being without it is to have that second-hand ideal which those people go to school to acquire, and which would make us hate our very models.

Delacroix had, with the highest degree of spontaneity, the ideal. I do not pretend, however, to describe or definitely to estimate him as an artist. It was because the man was distinguished, as well as the painter, that there was a promise of lively interest in these letters. They are, indeed, interesting; but they are perhaps at the same time a little disappointing. Almost any clever Frenchman is a good letter-writer: of the many functions to which his admirable tongue easily adapts itself, there is none in which it appears to greater advantage than in the play of epistolary conversation. The letters of Delacroix have the generic quality; as regards vivacity and natural grace they would be very good letters for an Englishman. But one expects a good deal from a French letter-writer who is at once an illustrious artist and a man of general ideas. Delacroix was a colourist, but his letters are less pictorial than might have been expected. They have little humour, little jocosity, little of that charming brightness which made the feature of those of Henri Regnault, published a few years ago.[1] He was a man of imagination—of the richest; but he had not high spirits. He guided the chariot of his invention with a powerful hand, but he was not addicted to cracking his whip.

His life bears the stamp of that Parisian monotony which in the career of distinguished Frenchmen is always so striking to English readers. Paris, and Paris alone, is the world of their celebrities; they find it sufficient, and they know nothing else. Most Englishmen, in the process of acquiring a reputation, make the acquaintance of a considerable part of the globe; they travel, and compare, and lay foreign lands under contribution. The same, for stronger reason, is the case with Americans of corresponding rank; both of our English kinsmen and of ourselves it may be said that we often become conspicuously national only

[1] Reviewed by James in the *Nation*, 2 January 1873, 13-15.

by leaving home. Of course, in this matter a great deal depends upon the character of this home; and if it is a question of being tethered forever in the same pasture and making one's world of a single town, there is no doubt that Paris serves the purpose wonderfully well, especially for an artist. Delacroix, strange to say, never went to Italy, and never saw the great gallery at Madrid, and yet he could say to himself that he knew a good deal about Titian and Velasquez. There remains, however, something almost displeasing to an Anglo-Saxon mind in the fact that he should have lived to the age of sixty-five, and attained to the enjoyment of emoluments and honours, without having thought it necessary to cross the Alps and enlighten his eyes with the supreme examples of the art he so robustly practised. He made, indeed, two or three journeys. At the age of twenty-seven (in 1825) he went over to London and spent a portion of a summer. Later, in 1832, he accompanied a French commissioner upon a diplomatic errand to Morocco, where he gathered in a few weeks those impressions of Eastern life which during the rest of his career were so frequently reflected in his work. He continued all his life to paint the East, and one might easily have supposed he had lived there, or that he had often returned to Africa. But he never renewed his impressions. He had laid in his stock of notes and visions once for all, and it served him to the end. It must be added, that, amid all the elaborate Orientalism with which we are deluged nowadays in painting, few pictures strike us as containing more of the essence of the matter than the best Eastern subjects of Delacroix. Several other painters may have done more justice to draperies and pottery, to palm-trees and minarets; but no one else has touched us so with the feeling of the Mahometan world—as any one will admit who vividly recalls those admirable things now placed in the Museum of the Louvre—the 'Femmes d'Alger', and the picture representing, in a sort of well-like, whitewashed room, with wood-work painted in green, a congregation of wedding-guests, muffled in frowsy festive array. This latter production is a marvel of local colour. Such a painter as Gérôme gives us most skilfully the surface of

Eastern life; Delacroix gives us its substance. Later still in life he made a little journey into Holland and Belgium, and in his later years he bought a small property in the country—the estate of Champrosay, near Paris, where, after this, he spent much of his time. He suffered all his days from a painful affection of the throat, and it was to a malady connected with this ailment that he succumbed, in Paris, in the year 1863. He was sixty-five years old; he had never married.

The editor of his letters is M. Philippe Burty, the well-known critic, who has performed his task with excellent judgement. M. Burty was one of several persons appointed by Delacroix, in his will, to sift and classify his enormous accumulation of studies, sketches, and drawings, and prepare them for a public sale. Of this sale, which was held at auction six months after the artist's death, M. Burty says: 'It was an intoxication and a rehabilitation. The world saw and loved Delacroix. The sale, estimated before-hand at 100,000 francs, produced more than 360,000.' And he adds that speculation had nothing to do with it; the competition was wholly between passionate amateurs. He reproduces Delacroix's will, which is touching in the number and minuteness of its personal bequests, but which I mention only in order to quote a special paragraph, which I leave, for the sake of its suggestiveness of expression, in its native French:

Mon tombeau sera au cimetière du Père-La-Chaise, sur la hauteur, dans un endroit un peu écarté. Il n'y sera placé ni emblème, ni buste, ni statue; mon tombeau sera copié très exactement sur l'antique, ou Vignoles ou Palladio, avec des saillies très prononcées, contrairement à tout ce qui se fait aujourd'hui en architecture.[1]

'Art and friendship', says M. Burty, 'had been the motive and the constant mainstay of his life;' and in fact Delacroix strikes the reader of these letters as having had a genius for this latter sentiment not inferior to his more technical gift. His father was

---

[1] *Lettres d'Eugène Delacroix* (1815 à 1863) recueillies et publiées par M. Philippe Burty. Paris, 1878, p. vii.

The quotation, as it appeared in the *International Review*, differed in certain particulars from the text in the Delacroix Letters and has been emended to agree with it.

a man of some distinction, who had been, under the first Republic
and the Empire, both a prefect and a minister; but the son
inherited nothing but a lawsuit which was decided adversely,
leaving him, for all patrimony, 'a pair of silver spoons and forks
and a gilt water-jug'. His father died in 1805, when he was seven
years of age; his mother survived a few years. The boy's vocation
marked itself out from the first, and he began betimes the study
of his art. He had many difficulties, but though he wanted money
he appears not to have wanted friends. Better still, he appreciated
those he had. 'Yes, I am sure', he writes, at twenty, to a cherished
comrade, 'great friendship is like great genius; the memory of a
strong friendship is like that of the great works of genius. What
a life it would be—that of two poets who should love each other
as we love each other! It would be too great for humanity.'
'Farewell, dear friend', he adds in the same letter; 'I leave you
for dinner. It is doubtless very wrong of me; but as we can't live
without dining, and we can't love each other without living, I
shall dine.' There are passages in the letters of his younger years
to his friends which read like speeches addressed to objects of
the passion known more exclusively as the 'tender' one: 'I forget
the principal thing. Answer me instantly, post for post. Send me
another letter, and pass the night in making it long, long! Go to
the stationers, and tell them to press you out some paper—to
press it fine, so that you can put more upon it. There is little time.
Don't neglect this, I beseech you.' That reminds us of one of the
love-speeches in Beaumont and Fletcher. He rings all the changes
upon the sentiment of friendship: 'What do you think I take to
when I wish to pass delicious moments? *Je me recueille*; I forget
everything that surrounds me; I think of all those who are still
dear to me on earth. I am happy, really happy, only when I am
with a friend.' Two years later he begins a letter to the same
friend in the following passionate fashion: 'Holy friendship,
divine friendship, excellent heart! No, I am not worthy of you.
You wrap me about with your friendship; I am your vanquished
one, your captive. Good friend, it is you who know how to love.
I have never loved a man like you; but I am sure that your heart

will be inexhaustible. How rare you are, for your equal is not to be found; how meagre my soul is, weighed against yours!' And again, writing shortly afterwards from the country to this same Pierret, whom he expected soon to find in Paris: 'I embrace you already in idea. Oh, how my heart will beat when I come into the house! I will stop on every floor! Try that day not to have your face in soapsuds—it is so good to kiss each other instantly, at the minute: do you hear?' Many years after (he was forty-four years of age), the same note is struck: 'Preserve yourself, dear friend; let us above all preserve our friendship! Heavens, what a fragile thing it is to keep! How small a thing can blurr the mirror in which two heads are reflected together! How little is needed to disturb or bedim one of these images! Up to this time I have seen you clear and sharp. Make this last, and may you always see me in the same way!'

It would appear, however, that the consolations of friendship did not exclude others of a still intenser sort. There is a letter written in his nineteenth year which is almost amusingly characteristic of what is supposed to be the normal attitude of Young France at this susceptible age. 'I'm in a *drôle de position*. I don't know how it comes about, but I am always on the stairs, and all day long I go down into the court, only to come up again and then to go down. The voice of a certain door that you know sounds every moment in my ear. . . . I stick out my nose and I hear the rustle of a *sylphide*. . . . Honestly, too, it's worth the trouble. . . . The triumph of the head is its outline. Oh, the singular little woman! I don't know what to think.' It must be added that this little romance appears not to have gone very far —no farther than his passing the object of his admiration upon the public staircase and paying her the tribute of a *coup de chapeau*. Indeed, the most serious allusion to the tender passion which these letters contain is a passage in which the writer complains of the unoccupied condition of his heart. The fact that he utters his complaint with a candour which is much more natural in such matters to Frenchmen than to ourselves need not prevent us from finding something touching in it: 'I am unhappy.

I have no *amour*. This delicious torment is wanting to my happiness. I have nothing but vain dreams, which agitate me and do not satisfy me in any way. I was so happy to suffer in loving. There was a kind of stimulus even in my jealousy, and my actual indifference is not the life of a corpse. I am obliged, in order to live in the only manner in which I can live—that is, by my feelings and my heart—to seek these pleasures in painting; to try and wrest them from it. But nature cannot understand all this, and when I fall back upon my empty heart with all the weight of my artificially baffled and diverted *ennui*, I feel that a flame must have fuel, and that I should paint in a very different fashion if I were kept in spirits by the soft warmth of love.' These lines were written in 1821, while Delacroix was still a very young man; but they are interesting as the mark of an artistic nature of the old-fashioned type, which rested upon the conviction, that, for successful production, the whole man must expand in harmony with a sort of flower-like freedom, and which included a perpetual love-affair in its personal scheme, just as it included the growth of knowledge and fame. Whether Delacroix obtained in the long run the sum of affection which he desired, I have no means of knowing; but, as I have spoken of the warmth of his friendships in early life, I may add that this source of sentimental satisfaction was not absolutely undisturbed. 'People imagine', he writes in 1860, 'that friendship is a peaceful divinity, whose gentle chains succeed to those of love when we have settled down to a time of life which gives us, or is supposed to give us, the taste for calm attachments. Nothing is more false. Friendship, dull-coloured and pale as she is, has her storms, and unhappily reconciliations are more difficult.'

Delacroix's short visit to England in his youth left its mark upon his mind and his work; it helped to initiate him still further into the possibilities of that 'romanticism' which in France was about to become a great movement. We may doubt whether, without the impressions that he gathered on English soil, he would have conceived that admiration for Shakespeare, or even for another foreign genius, Goethe, which he subsequently expressed with so much pictorial power. It must, indeed, have been a great pleasure to an imaginative young Frenchman of 'romantic' tendencies to see Shakespeare interpreted by Edmund Kean and Charles Mayne Young. He must have returned to the land of classic art on the stage and on canvas with a rich store of impressions and intuitions. Delacroix took a great fancy to Kean, and went to see him whenever he could. He took a great fancy, too, to English painting, of much of which he always retained a high enjoyment; his own eminently independent spirit found something congenial in the absence of that school-discipline which has always been at once the strength and the weakness of French art. His impressions of English life, however, were not exclusively favourable; and indeed, if the 'intelligent foreigner' finds the London of to-day, in its superficial aspects, a depressing and uncomfortable city, we may imagine what such an observer must have made of the unregenerate metropolis of 1825:

There is decidedly something sad and stiff in all this, which doesn't square with our own France. The cleanliness of some houses and streets is balanced by the dirtiness of others. The women are all ill-arrayed, with dirty stockings and ill-made shoes. What strikes me most is a kind of general paltriness which leads one to think that one is in a country of smaller and more contracted people than our own. I believe that people here are, if possible, bigger gossips and fools than ours—a thing I couldn't have believed without coming here. I don't look at all this as an economist or a mathematician. In this respect they have all sorts of fine qualities, which I leave them. . . . I break a lance for France against every possible Englishman. There is in the blood of this people something savage and ferocious, which comes out horribly in the rabble, which is hideous. After that, it's a famous government. Liberty here is not an idle word. The pride of their nobles and the distinction of ranks is pushed to a point which shocks me infinitely; but some good things result from it.

He saw Sir Thomas Lawrence, whom he always appreciated highly. 'He is the flower of civility and a real painter of great lords. . . . No one has ever made eyes—those of women especially

—as he has done, or those half-open mouths, of a perfect charm.' There is a charming letter about the English painters, written many years later, in 1858, to a friend who was about to go to London, and who had asked Delacroix for information. He speaks of the past and recalls the admiration of his early years:

I have no desire to see London again; I should find none of my old associations, and, more than that, I should not find in myself the same power to enjoy what is done there now. The school itself is changed; perhaps I should have to break a lance for Reynolds and for that ravishing Gainsborough whom you are so right to admire. Not that I am the adversary of what is done now in English painting. I have been struck with the prodigious conscience which the English are able to introduce even into the things of imagination. . . . My impressions of that early time would perhaps be modified to-day. Perhaps I should find in Lawrence an exaggeration of those means of effect which savour too much of the school of Reynolds; but his prodigious delicacy of drawing, the life that he gives to his women, who look as if they were speaking to you, give him, as a portrait-painter, a kind of superiority over Van Dyck himself, whose admirable figures simply 'sit' in tranquillity. The brightness of the eyes, the parted lips, are rendered admirably by Lawrence.

Delacroix speaks also very tenderly of Wilkie and of Constable, and in 1861 he writes an interesting letter to a critic who had asked him for some details about Bonington. This delightful painter, whose reputation has been touched by the distinction imparted, in the case of genius, by early death, may almost be said to have introduced the English art of water-colour into France. The extreme brilliancy with which he used it had, at any rate, given it a vogue to which, after his death at the age of six-and-twenty, none of his successors or imitators so effectively contributed. Delacroix had known him well, having met him originally in England in 1825. 'I knew him well, and I liked him extremely. His British *sang-froid*, which was imperturbable, interfered with none of the qualities which make life agreeable. We all loved him.'

Delacroix's own apprenticeship to fame was, as I have said,

no easier than that of most young artists; and in a letter written in 1828, he expresses a state of feeling very familiar to waiting and struggling genius. In the long, steep staircase of success there is many a step like that on which, in this letter, we see Delacroix pause, wearily, in discouragement, and seat himself.

You seem to think I go out a great deal. Far from it. The few evening parties I go to, by habit, to lose myself and to try not to bore myself, do nothing, on the whole, but fatigue me physically. In most cases I am buttonholed by some d——d fool who talks to me of painting, in a muddle-headed manner, thinking that I shall carry away a lofty idea of his conversation and his capacity. It leads to no relations with women. I am too pale and too thin. The great occupation of my existence—the one which holds in suspense and in check the high and powerful faculties with which, according to some good people, Nature has endowed me—is to succeed in paying my rent every three months and in keeping myself alive in a paltry manner. I am tempted to apply to myself the parable of Jesus Christ, who says that his kingdom is not of this world. I have a rare genius, which doesn't go so far as to make me live in peace like a clerk in a shop. Intellect is the last of the elements which lead to the making of a fortune—and that without paradox, without exaggeration. Imagination, when unhappily this fatal gift accompanies the rest, completes the ruin, finishes the work of blighting, of breaking up in every way, the wretched soul. . . . I must expect no employment or encouragement whatever. Those who are most favourable to me agree to consider me as an interesting madman, whom it would be dangerous to encourage in his eccentricities and oddities.

Delacroix's work was, indeed, sufficiently unacceptable to the official taste of the day; as a painter he flew in the face of all the regular proprieties. To the day of his death he was an object of formal reprobation to the old-fashioned critics who endeavoured to keep alive, like superannuated vestals, the fading flame on the altar of conventionalism; and he was elected to the Institute (Department of the Fine Arts) only after that process of reiterated application to which a stranger wonders to see a Frenchman accommodate the most finely-seasoned vanity in the world. Obscure and insignificant candidates for Academic honours were repeatedly preferred to Delacroix, and he was allotted a place among the official representatives of French art only after he had enjoyed ample opportunity to reflect upon the purely relative character of his merit. As the years went on, however, his reputation established itself, and his profession enabled him to live. Later, it brought him a good deal of honour and profit. He received various orders from the State; he decorated some of the ceilings of the new Louvre, and some of the chapels of the restored churches. His productions commanded high prices, and in the opinion of many judges he was the first painter of the day.

I have no space to trace the different stages of his career—nor, indeed, do these letters, with their interruptions and desultory allusions, afford material for doing so. Delacroix had, at any rate, the satisfaction of living his life in a country and a society in which an artistic career is, on the whole, held in more honour than anywhere else—in which the artistic character is more definitely recognized and more frankly adopted. In France the artist finds himself, *ex officio*, a member of a large and various society of fellow-workers; whatever may be his individual value, his basis or platform is a large and solid one, resting upon social position and public opinion. He has to make his work a success, but he has not, as happens in England, where the vivacity of the artistic instinct appears to have been checked in a mysterious manner by the influence of Protestantism, to justify and defend his point of view. His point of view is taken for granted, and it may be said that his starting-place is the point at which, after much superfluity of effort, the artist in other countries arrives.

I have spoken of Delacroix's journey to Morocco in 1832; he spent a few weeks in Spain on his way home. He was attached to a mission which had been despatched by Louis-Philippe to the Moorish emperor, and in this capacity he enjoyed the sight of a great abundance of local colours. His letters denote an extreme relish of what he beheld, but they are not especially descriptive or demonstrative; it is only here and there that his phrase is pictorial. 'It has been one of the most delightful sensations possible', he writes, after touching on the coast of Spain on his way out, 'to find myself, on leaving France, without having set foot ashore elsewhere, transported into this land of picturesqueness; to see their houses, the cloaks worn by the veriest paupers, by the little children of the beggars, *où tout Goya palpitait autour de moi.*'

Afterwards, at Tangier, he writes: 'I have moments of delicious laziness in a garden at the gates of the town, amid a profusion of orange-trees in flower and covered with fruit. In the midst of this vigorous Nature I am conscious of sensations like those I had in my childhood; perhaps it is the confused remembrance of the sun of the South, which I saw in my early youth, coming back to me. The most that I can do here will be very little in comparison with what there is to be done; sometimes I drop my arms in despair, with the certainty that I shall bring back but a shadow.' He was wrong—he brought back the substance; no pictures of Eastern life, as I have said, are more expressive and suggestive than his. The latter half of his life— the thirty years that followed the episode I have just mentioned —was a long period of tranquil, uninterrupted production. As M. Burty says, it was taken up wholly with work and friendship. Work, with Delacroix, was a passion—he says somewhere that, for him, the absence of it is equivalent to a sickness. There is an interesting passage bearing upon this point in a letter written in 1855—a passage worth quoting entire. He is writing to a female friend:

You ask me where happiness is to be found in this world. After numerous experiments I am convinced that it is to be found in contentment with one's self. The passions cannot give this contentment, for we always desire the impossible—what we obtain fails to satisfy us. I suppose that people who have a solid virtue must possess a large share of that contentment which I make a condition of happiness. For my own part, not being virtuous enough to please myself on that side, I make up for it in the real satisfaction which is given by work. This gives one a genuine well-being, and increases one's indifference to the pleasures which are only pleasures in name, and with which *les gens du monde* are obliged to content themselves. Such, my dear friend, is my little philosophy, and, especially when I am in good health, it has a very certain effect. It must not, however, prevent the little diversions that one may pick up from time to time. A little *affaire de coeur*, when the occasion offers; the view of a fine country, travelling in general— these things leave charming traces in the mind; we recall the emotions that belonged to them after they have passed away, and we can have no others like them. It is a little provision of happiness for the future, whatever the future may be.

There is evidence in other letters that Delacroix's 'little philosophy' was not always absolutely successful, though one of them, indeed, offers an example of the practical application of it. 'As to you, my poor friend,' he writes in 1862 to M. Soulier, one of the oldest of his intimates, 'you are in the same case as myself. The seasons may change, but the oftener they follow each other the more they increase the cause of those thousand afflictions which besiege us and await us still. Our season—ours —is that of old age, which makes us feel every hour of the day the wrong it does us. . . . Often, when I am sad and suffering, I make use of the same means as you do, to relieve myself. I think of the happy moments in which we have known each other and enjoyed so fully each other's society. Many an empty place has been made, but after all we are here still. We must say to ourselves, then, that, with all our pains, we are in the number of the fortunate ones.'

Among the best of Delacroix's friends was Madame George Sand, who published, several years after his death, an interesting little reminiscential sketch of him. There is a charming glimpse of Madame Sand's life at Nohant in a letter of the year 1842. Delacroix writes from under this lady's roof:

I lead a conventual life—a life more and more like itself. No event interrupts its course. We have been expecting Balzac, who has not come, and I am not sorry. He is a chatterbox who would have broken in upon that harmony of doing nothing in which I slumber most agreeably. A little painting, billiards, walking, is more than enough to fill up one's days. There is not even the distraction of neighbours and friends in the country about; everyone hereabouts stays quietly at home and looks after his oxen and his lands. . . . I have talks *à perte de vue* with Chopin, whom I like very much, and who is a man of rare distinction. He is the truest artist I have ever met. . . . The great event of my stay has been a ball given to the peasants on the lawn before the *château*, with the bagpipers of highest repute in the region. The people hereabouts are a remarkable type of gentleness and *bonhomie*; ugliness is rare, though beauty is not absolutely striking; but there is not the feverish look which you see in the country people in the neighbourhood of Paris. The women all resemble those gentle figures which you see only in the pictures of the Old Masters. They are all Saint Annes.

The reader of this passage will venture to differ from the writer, and to regret that on this occasion Balzac should not have presented himself at Nohant. There would be a certain intellectual satisfaction in thinking of four such distinguished specimens of imaginative genius as Madame Sand, Honoré de Balzac, Chopin, and Delacroix spending the summer days together and talking *à perte de vue*. It was among the 'feverish populations' of Paris that Delacroix had been obliged to establish his own rural dwelling. Writing from the house of a friend in Champagne, with whom he was staying in 1862, he makes an invidious comparison between the scenery which surrounds him there and the suburban charms of Champrosay. 'Here I am really in the country. Champrosay is a village in a comic opera. You see no one there but fine folks, or peasants who look as if they had dressed themselves for the stage. Nature herself seems tricked out: I am irritated by all those paltry little gardens and little houses arranged by Parisians. . . . Here in the midst of Champagne I see men, women, cows; all this gives me a gentle emotion and sensations unknown to little townsfolk and to artists who inhabit towns.'

I have said Delacroix passed the later years of his life in the position of an acknowledged master; but it would appear that the assertion needs to be slightly qualified. 'The Salon of 1859', says M. Burty, 'was for Delacroix a veritable Waterloo. The critics on whom he could count the most, *romantiques* of the first or the second stage, abandoned him to the attacks of the triumphant classicists, or else gave him either fool's advice or piteous consolations. Delacroix, deeply wounded, never exhibited again.' It is sad to learn that toward the end of a long, laborious, and distinguished career Delacroix found himself still obliged to 'count upon' the critics; but M. Burty's whole statement (including his mention of Delacroix's 'wounded' condition) is characteristic of the way such things take place in France. In that country criticism is not only a profession, it is a power. Whereas, in other countries, critics are, if I am not mistaken, a little ashamed of their trade, in France they rather pride themselves on it, take their stand upon it, and exercise it very frankly and aggressively. They are often able to give their judgements the importance of literary and artistic events. It is only fair to add, that, in general, they do their work much more skilfully than among ourselves. At all events they carry standards and trumpets and great guns; they belong to camps and schools; they have dogmas, codes, strongholds, to defend. In 1859 they awoke, after a temporary slumber, to a sense of having something—I do not quite know what—to defend against poor Delacroix, an honoured veteran and a national glory. It would be hard to imagine an English artist who should have attained to the rank of a master taking the strictures of the art-reviewers, as we of English speech are mainly acquainted with them, very much to heart; but once granted that in France their word carries weight, it was very natural in Delacroix to feel wronged.

During the last years of his life, with failing health, he fell under the dominion, to an extent which appears unfortunate, of a person whom he had installed in his dwelling as housekeeper. She was devoted to him to the point of jealousy, but she was despotic and meddlesome; she allowed none of his friends save such as she herself approved to have access to him; and at the end, as M. Burty says, *elle fit le vide* around him. He left her in his will a large legacy. To the end of his life, we are told by a cousin of Delacroix, 'he kept his taste for simple habits, and he liked to return to the manners of his youth. He was fond of dinners at the city gate or in the country, with a bottle of common wine; but he was fond of good things too, in a little circle of three or four friends, with the talk turning on painting, philosophy, or good stories.' He was an interesting genius, and this record of his career, imperfect as it is, has a peculiar charm. He had a combination of qualities which are not often seen together; he united in his nature what may be called a masculine and a feminine element. He had a great imagination; he conceived things richly and comprehensively, and yet he was tender, grave, contemplative. He was reserved and delicate, and yet he had in a high degree what the French call *la fougue*—a grand sweep and energy of execution. I have not pretended to enumerate or to describe his productions, of which the interest, increasing greatly on prolonged acquaintance, does not easily lend itself to analysis. As for those more accidental manifestations of the man, we may say in regard to them that the best thing a book can do for its readers is to give them the impression of a certain nobleness. That is what we find here—the presence of a high artistic ideal, untouched by the vulgar or the trivial.

LONDON PICTURES

1882

I CANNOT pretend this year to answer one of the regular questions of the London social season, and say how I think the exhibitions of 1882 compare with those of the previous twelve-month; for the simple reason that I find the exhibitions of 1881 have left no definite impression on my mind. I recall with extreme difficulty last year's Grosvenor Gallery; I attempt, quite without success, to evoke a vision of the Academy. Here and there, it is true, a dim, peculiar canvas on the walls of the latter institution glimmers into momentary distinctness. I remember coming back to London from the Continent quite late in the season, and going to the Royal Academy on one of those stale, close, dusty days that precede the closing of its doors. I was accompanied by a foreign friend, and we wandered through the fatigued looking rooms with a certain langour of attention. Here and there we stopped rather short, as before the portrait of Lord Beaconsfield by Mr. Millais, before the portrait of Matthew Arnold by Mr. Watts.[1] These painters are, in the line of portrait, the most distinguished in England, and the model, in each of the cases I have mentioned, was what a Frenchman would call another English illustration. But what was principally illustrated in both works was the ancient axiom that even Homer sometimes nods. Very bad, strangely, grotesquely bad, were the portrait of Matthew Arnold by Mr. Watts, and the portrait of Lord Beaconsfield by Mr. Millais. My foreign friend, a painter by profession, chose to take the humorous view of the Academy altogether, and to treat even the most brilliant pictures suspended there as productions with which the art of painting was but feebly and

[1] Both these pictures are in the National Portrait Gallery, London.

remotely connected; and indeed it was not easy to pretend that the state of painting was honourable in a country in which two of its foremost representatives were capable of exhibiting such fearful emanations of the brush as those two misbegotten portraits. I was not greatly concerned to defend it, for I may frankly observe that English painting interests me chiefly, not as painting, but as English. It throws little light, on the whole, on the art of Titian and of Rembrandt; but it throws a light which is to me always fresh, always abundant, always fortunate, on the turn of the English mind. It is far from being the most successful manifestation of that mind; but it adds a good deal to our knowledge of it. This assertion, doubtless, makes it the more culpable to have so completely forgotten the contents of last year's exhibitions; I ought to have remembered them for their illuminating virtues; and I am afraid I must say, in mitigation of my fault, that on that occasion the English mind was less happily manifested even than usual. Moreover, it matters very little, for last year's exhibitions have scarcely more actuality than last year's moons. I alluded to them only because one is expected to be able to say, any month of May, with an air of experience, that this is rather a good, or rather a bad, Academy.

I think it is rather a good one; by which I mean that it is somewhat less bad than usual. There are fewer pictures within immediate eyeshot that are no pictures at all than I remember on some former occasions; and the whole exhibition has an air of succeeding tolerably well in what it attempts. It is true that it doesn't attempt anything very tremendous, except in the sense in which it is always tremendous to attempt to paint. But there is painting and painting; there is light work, and there is heavy work. The Academy is essentially light; it does its best not to 'go in', as the phrase is, more for the severely plastic than a Royal Academy of Arts is absolutely bound to do. The pictures for the most part are illustrations, like the little drawings in the magazines or in books. There are no striking experiments in execution, and, save on the part of the distinguished president, no attacking of the nude. Personal colour, personal form, has hardly a votary; but there are multitudinous coats and trousers, and innumerable bonnets and shawls. There are also any number of chairs and tables, of windows and doors, curtains, carpets, side-boards and chimney-pieces; and the usual proportion of green fields and cloudy skies, thatched cottages, and old brick walls, browsing donkeys and waddling geese. These are the stock properties of British art; and with their assistance the British artist is rarely at a loss to point a moral. He is not less anecdotal to-day than usual; but his anecdotes are often very neatly related. The British artist is apt to be an arrant Philistine, but he is by no means without his good points. He is wanting in science; he is wanting even in art; but he has a great deal of observation and a great deal of feeling. As M. Taine, the French critic, long ago took occasion to remark, he is very fond of studying and repres-enting motives and states of mind; he has a turn for psychology; he is often successful in rendering the facial expression of emotions, though indeed since M. Bastien-Lepage exhibited at the Salon that remarkable figure of Joan of Arc, which hangs to-day in the Metropolitan Museum of New York, and showed us with what skill a modern Frenchman could infuse into a set of features the condition and attitude of a soul, it must be admitted that these ingenious feats are not reserved for the English.

I have embarked too soon, however, upon generalizations about the state of affairs at the Academy; for it was my intention to speak first of the Grosvenor Gallery, which is on the whole the more interesting show. It is, at any rate, the pleasanter place to go to. There are fewer pictures, and the same may be said of the visitors—perhaps from this very fact of your shilling's worth being more slender. People with only a shilling to spend on pictures—and there are many people in London in this sad situation—prefer to spend it at the Academy. It occurs to me that the vagueness of my recollection of the Grosvenor last year is owing to the fact that Mr. Burne-Jones had nothing on exhib-ition. Or was it the year before that this melancholy blank occurred? Vagueness prevails, whichever way I turn it; so I fore-see that a twelvemonth hence I shall be very glad to have these notes to refer to. A Grosvenor without Mr. Burne-Jones is a *Hamlet* with Hamlet left out. Mr. Whistler, it is true, is always there, but Mr. Whistler is rather less a sign of the establishment. This year Mr. Burne-Jones is in force, as I count in the catalogue of the exhibition no less than nine of his productions. Most of these, however, are small pieces, and I must speak only of the two principals. The common verdict, I suppose, is that they are as queer as ever—which I am quite willing to agree to, if it be added that they are as charming. They are full of beautiful work, beautiful feeling, an expression of many things. There are many people who declare that they contain only two things—a bad stomach and a perverted mind. Mr. Burne-Jones's figures have a way of looking rather sick; but if illness is capable of being amiable—and most of us have had some happy intimation that it is—Mr. Burne-Jones accentuates this side of the case. This, indeed, I suppose, is the very ground of that accusation about the perversity of his mind; he is accused of delighting in disease, and revelling in woe. The truth is, however, that this kind of talk is very much beside the mark, and I should be inclined to doubt whether the painter's art is very dear to anyone who cannot find much to enjoy in Mr. Burne-Jones. With the exception of Mr. Millais, who is not so much a painter as a master of the brush, he seems to me the only Englishman painting to-day who carries into the business a passion of his own. A whole range of feeling about life is expressed in Mr. Burne-Jones's productions, and I scarcely know of which of his competitors the same can be said. His expression is complicated, troubled; but at least there is an interesting mind in it. And then, in general, it is exceedingly successful and beautiful. He is a deep and powerful colourist; he lives in a world of colour. Amid the hard, loud chatter and clash of so many of his colleagues, the painting of Mr. Burne-Jones is almost alone in having the gravity and deliberation of truly valuable speech. It needs, however, to be looked at good-humouredly and liberally; he offers an entertainment which is for us to take or to leave. It pretends to please us, if we care to be pleased—to touch us in the persuasive, suggestive, allusive,

half-satisfying but more mystifying way in which distinguished
artists of the imaginative class have always appealed to us. He is
not a votary of the actual, and nothing is easier than to pull such
an artist to pieces, from the point of view of the actual. But the
process is idle; the actual does not gain and the artist does not
suffer. It is beside the mark, as I said just now, to say that his
young women are always sick, for they are neither sick nor well.
They live in a different world from ours—a fortunate world, in
which young ladies may be slim and pale and 'seedy' without
discredit and (I trust) without discomfort. It is not a question of
sickness and health; it is a question of grace, delicacy, tenderness,
of the chord of association and memory. Mr. Burne-Jones has
for that chord an exquisite touch. It is easy to accuse him of
turning reality topsy-turvy; but I think he does it less injury
than many of those painters whose relations with it are more
primitive. At any rate, for the author of these lines there is
something in his talent which makes almost anything pass. There
is no very visible reason, for instance, why, in the largest picture
the artist exhibits this year, the lovely Phyllis, forsaken by her
lover, and turned by the kind gods into an almond-tree, should
look as if she had secreted a button, or even a quid of tobacco,
beneath her upper lip; there is no reason why Demophoön, the
guilty lover, passing that way in penitence, and finding himself
suddenly embraced by the arborescent Phyllis, should have hair
of a singular greenish tinge. If there was to be any green hair in
the picture, it surely should belong to the hardly yet revivified
nymph. In spite of all this, Phyllis's lip and Demophoön's hair
are extremely pictorial, and I am willing to believe that they are
indispensable parts of a beautiful scheme. The picture in question
has a strange and touching beauty; though it is of course open
to the grave accusation of representing a monstrosity. The artist
has asked himself why, if a poet may be a painter, a painter may
not be a poet. Phyllis, shut up in the trunk of the tree, has
retained her slim and delicate human shape; she has not merged it
in the blossoming boughs, whose wealth of white flowers is
splendidly rendered by the painter. This charming curtain of

almond blossom hangs over the reunited pair, and mingles with
the tender embrace of the nymph, who flings herself from out her
riven sheath, and hangs upon the neck of the startled Demophoön. The subject was difficult, and there could be no question
of making it 'natural'; Mr. Burne-Jones has had to content himself with making it lovely. It is a large, elaborate study of the
undraped figure, the painter's treatment of which surely gives
sufficient evidence of his knowing how to draw—an accomplishment that has sometimes been denied him. The drawing of
the two figures in 'The Tree of Forgiveness' has knowledge and
power, as well as refinement, and we should be at a loss to
mention another English artist who would have acquitted himself so honourably of such an attempt. Sir Frederick Leighton
deals more or less in the nude, but Sir Frederick Leighton's
drawing is more superficial than Mr. Burne-Jones's. In regard to
colour, the latter artist's pictures, it has usually seemed to us,
may be divided into the warm and the cool. 'The Tree of Forgiveness' is decidedly cool—cool with the coolness of a gray day in
summer. The mass of almond blossom introduces a great deal
of fresh and moist-looking white; the flesh-tones are wan and
bloodless, as befits the complexion of people whom we see
through the medium of a certain incredulity. It would never do
for Phyllis and Demophoön to present themselves with the
impudence of, say, Rubens's flesh and blood. Mr. Burne-Jones's
other large picture, which he has called, simply, we suppose, to
give it a label of some kind, 'At the Mill'[1], is in the opposite key.
It represents—but such a beginning is rash, for it would by no
means be easy to say what it represents. Suffice it that three
very pretty young women, in old Italian dresses, are slowly
dancing together in a little green garden, on the edge of a mill-
pond, on the further side of which several men, very diminutive
figures, are about to enter, or about to quit, the bath. To the
right, beneath a quaint loggia, a fourth young woman, the least
successful of the group, is making music for her sisters. The
colour is deep, rich, glowing, exceedingly harmonious, and both

[1] In the Victoria and Albert Museum, London.

in this respect and in its being, in feeling and expression, an echo of early Italianism, the picture has an extraordinary sweetness. It is very true that I have heard it called idiotic; but there is a sad want of good-humour in that. It is equally true that I have not the least idea who the young women are, nor what period of history, what time and place, the painter has had in his mind. His dancing maidens are exceedingly graceful, innocent, maidenly: they belong to the land of fancy, and to the hour of reverie! When one considers them, one really feels that there is a want of discretion and of taste in attempting to talk about Mr. Burne-Jones's pictures at all, much more in arguing and wrangling about them. They are there to care for if one will, and to leave to others if one cannot. The great charm of the work I have just mentioned is, perhaps, that to many persons it will seem impregnated with the love of Italy. If you have certain impressions, certain memories, of that inestimable land, you will find it full of entertainment. I speak with no intention of irreverence when I say that I think it delightfully amusing. It amuses me that it should be just as it is—just as pointless as a twilight reminiscence, as irresponsible as a happy smile. The quaintly-robed maidens, moving together in measure, and yet seeming to stand still on the grass; the young men taking a bath just near them, and yet the oddity being no oddity at all; the charming composition of the background, the picturesque feeling, the innocence, the art, the colour, the mixture of originality and imitation—all these things lift us out of the common. Sweet young girls of long ago—no one paints them like Mr. Burne-Jones. The only complaint I have to make of him is that one cannot express one's appreciation of him without seeming to talk in the air. For this reason I will pass on to Mr. Whistler, though on reflection I hardly know whether the case is bettered.

For Mr. Whistler, of course, is extremely peculiar; he is supposed to be the buffoon of the Grosvenor, the laughing-stock of the critics. He does the comic business once a year; he turns the somersault in the ring. The author of these hasty pages—exhibitions must be spoken of quickly, if they are to be spoken of at all—finds him, like Mr. Burne-Jones, extremely amusing; only the entertainment he yields is of a much broader quality. He is exceedingly unequal, but for Mr. Whistler this is rather a good year. He has no less than seven productions at the Grosvenor, but I can speak only of the two full-length sketches of female figures which he entitles, respectively, a 'Harmony in Flesh-Colour and Pink', and a 'Harmony in Black and Red'. It is a misfortune for Mr. Whistler that he once gave the measure of his talent, and a very high measure it was. The portrait of his mother, painted some years ago, and exhibited this year in New York, is so noble and admirable a picture, such a masterpiece of tone, of feeling, of the power to render life, that the fruits of his brush offered to the public more lately have seemed in comparison very crude. I know not whether the fine work I speak of was a harmony, a symphony, an arrangement, or a nocturne; to-day, at any rate, the artist takes the precaution of not calling his little sketches portraits. One of them, the 'Harmony in Black and Red', may or may not be a likeness of the lady who stood for it; but it bears a remarkable resemblance to another person. I conclude from this that it has the appearance of life, which is a good deal, by the way. It may have been painted in three hours; whereas I suppose it took Mr. Holman Hunt as many months to bring his garish 'Miss Flamborough' (also at the Grosvenor) to its extraordinary perfection of hideousness. The vague black shadow on Mr. Whistler's canvas lifts its head and poises itself and says something, and the huge, bloated doll, who, with an orange and a woolly lamb, appeals to one's interest in the misguided effort of the ex-Pre-Raphaelite, is equally inanimate and elaborate. Mr. Whistler is a votary of 'tone'; his manner of painting is to breathe upon the canvas. It is not too much to say that he has, to a certain point, the creative afflatus. His little black and red lady is charming; she looks like someone, as I have said, and if she is a shadow she is the shadow of a graceful personage. Her companion, in flesh-colour and pink, is a trifle less graceful, and her hat doesn't fit; I also contest her flesh-colour, which has a light gray tinge, not usually remarked in the human complexion. Still, she does very well on the wall—which is about all that one is obliged to claim for these light emanations.

If the contributors to the Grosvenor were mentioned in their order of distinction, I suppose that Mr. Millais, Mr. Watts, Mr. Alma Tadema, should be the principal names. These three artists are represented solely by portraits, except, indeed, that Mr. Tadema has a couple of very small subject-pieces. His main contribution, however, is his portrait of the German actor, Ludwig Barnay, who distinguished himself in London last year as the most brilliant member of the admirable company presided over by the Duke of Meiningen, which rendered *Julius Caesar* as *Julius Caesar* had not been rendered in England for many a year. Barnay is painted in the robes of Mark Antony, and of his handsome pagan-looking head Mr. Alma Tadema, so apt in such achievements, has had no difficulty in making a very actual and effective Roman. The artist's great hit this year is, however, the portrait he exhibits at the Academy, the admirable, masterly portrait of Mr. Whichcord, R.I.B.A.—whatever those mystic letters may mean. Mr. Whichcord, R.I.B.A., clad in simple black, but decorated with a brilliant but inscrutable badge, has had— whatever his other honours—the honour of inspiring the first portrait of the year. Such painting as Mr. Tadema's makes the painting of many of his fellows in England look like schoolboy work; his aim is so definite and so high, his taste so large, his art so much the art of knowledge. The present work, his only contribution to the Academy, has a subdued richness, a shaded glow, which reminds one of those few canvases of John Bellini which, in Venice, shed their quiet radiance from the depths of some sombre sacristy. There is nothing new to say of Mr. Millais, who this year contributes no less than nine pictures, all portraits, to the two exhibitions. He continues to be one of the most accomplished and most disappointing of painters. He has all the arts of success, but only some of the arts of perfection. No one who can do so well condescends at times to do so ill; and no one who does so ill gives you at times, in his grossest

aberrations, an equal impression of ability. His facility is unprecedented, and his fortune corresponds. He has no 'subject'
this year; he has indeed painted his annual fancy-piece, but it
constitutes the gem of a separate exhibition. None of his portraits
at the Academy or the Grosvenor are of great importance, but
some are much better than others, notably two or three representations of children, whom he often renders with great power.
There is a poor lady in light blue at the Grosvenor, planted
squarely before the public, with her arms akimbo, and looking
as if she were a good deal frightened at her position, which has
very much the style and weight of a chalk figure on a blackboard.
On the other hand, there are at least two brilliant renderings of
blooming little heroines of the nursery, painted in the large, free,
solid, confident way of which, at his best, Mr. Millais is an unsurpassed master. Of how nobly he can paint when he is in the
humour of it, a certain big silver bowl with a gilt interior, which
figures in one of these pictures, may remain as an example. Mr.
Millais paints the celebrities, his principal celebrity this year
being (at the Academy) that very holy man and very superior
model, Cardinal Newman. This was a great chance, but the
chance is sadly missed; the artist having made shipwreck, as it
seems to me, on the vast scarlet cape of his Eminence. This
exalted garment, of a very furious red, is painted with a crudity
which causes it to obliterate the face, without justifying itself.
It is violent, monotonous, superficial, uninteresting; it is nothing
but a cape, and yet it is not even a cape. I cannot speak of the
face; the face is not there—a grievous pity, for it is a very fine
one. The cardinals have had poor luck this year, Cardinal
Manning having been sacrificed simultaneously to Mr. Watts,
whose effort is less violent than that of Mr. Millais, but not more
successful. The best that can be said of his portrait of Cardinal
Manning is that it is not so bad as his portrait, at the Grosvenor,
of the Prince of Wales. A grateful recollection of some of the
former fruits of his once interesting talent—Mr. Watts has sometimes risen very high; he has had the great thing, he has had 'style'
—leads us to draw the curtain of silence over this ill-starred

performance, which, we should imagine, would expose its author to the penalties attached to that misdemeanour known to English law as 'threatening the Royal Family'. A painter of portraits who, on the other hand, every year reveals a more vigorous faculty is Mr. Frank Holl, one of whose present contributions to the Academy ranks in merit with Mr. Tadema's portrait of the ex-president of the R.I.B.A., from which in manner it widely differs. I refer to his singularly lifelike representation of the late Captain Alexander Mitchell Sim, 'painted for the board room of the Surrey Commercial Dock Company'. This is an ancient mariner in the evening of his days, and it is a really noble picture of tough and tranquil old age. I am not acquainted with the Surrey Commercial Dock board room, but I should say it was just the picture for the place. Mr. Frank Holl is rather wanting in style, and, I should suppose, in imagination; but he has qualities which, if a man of genius does not turn up, may make him the English portrait-painter of the future: a strong, comprehensive simplicity, a great appreciation of characters, a manly, resolute, general way of painting—an excellent power of summing up, as it were. The portrait of Captain Sim marks his highest point this year; but he has several other excellent things—noticeably, at the Grosvenor, a certain Mr. J. Jones Jenkins, M.P., a solid representation of a solid personage. It would be difficult to put before us more vividly the commercial, practical, political, successful Englishman—the 'City man' made perfect; difficult too, on the whole, to represent him more agreeably. This is the way he would paint himself if he knew how to paint; the picture is a good deal in the manner of a good speech in the House of Commons.

I cannot leave the Grosvenor without saying a word about Mr. W. B. Richmond's extraordinary portrait of Mr. Gladstone, in a crimson gown and in his most uplifted mood. He communes with the skies; he expounds the Scriptures, which appear to repose upon his knee. There has lately been more than one portrait of Mr. Gladstone from the theological point of view, but it was reserved for Mr. Richmond to depict him as of

African blood, of distracted intellect, and of the Methodist persuasion. I know not what may have been the success of Mr. Richmond's picture with the public, but it has a very interesting side. It is the last word of Philistinism—a character in which it must be confessed that it has many formidable competitors. Neither should I leave the Grosvenor Gallery without speaking of several American talents which are honourably exemplified there—Mr. Boughton, for instance (if Mr. Boughton is still an American), Mr. Julian Story, Mr. Sargent. Mr. Boughton is familiar to most of us; this year he has been to Holland, and contributes to the two exhibitions (mainly to the Academy) a series of Dutch subjects of combined landscape and figure, into which he has succeeded in infusing much of the low, cool tone of that delectable country. Mr. Julian Story, the younger son of the distinguished sculptor[1] who has lived and worked so long in Rome, is the author of the largest picture (but one) at the Grosvenor—an Entombment, of which the brilliant cleverness, the ready resource, the discreet, agreeable colour, the youthful energy, have, in the absence of some of the subtler qualities of feeling, attracted much attention. Mr. Julian Story is an executant—he has made a great hit. Mr. Sargent, whose only defect is a certain papery texture, contributes a charming little gray Venetian interior, with figures.

I have, after all, mixed up, if I may be allowed the phrase, the Grosvenor and the Academy, for which my excuse must be that most of the prominent artists represented in the one exhibition are represented in the other. The portraits, decidedly, are the best things of the year, and one of the best of these is Mr. Herkomer's remarkable picture of Mr. Archibald Forbes, the famous war correspondent of the *Daily News*, to-day well known in America. Two or three things are more delicate than this, but none are more living, more complete. The valiant journalist stands there almost at full length, in his professional blouse, face to face with his public, with a strong, good-humoured smile

---

[1] The subject of James's biography *William Wetmore Story and His Friends* (1903).

upon his energetic features. Mr. Herkomer has been much the fashion since he took the medal of honour for the English school at the last Paris exhibition; yet I have often found him, in spite of a great talent, rather heavy and coarse. With his portrait of Mr. Forbes, however, there is no fault to be found; there is no criticism to make of it. It is one of those fine pictures which, besides representing an individual, represent a type—raise the individual to the significance of a type. This is the roving Englishman, the man of energy and adventure, who has left his solid footprint in every corner of the globe, and has brought back from his furthest peregrinations a fund of good spirits and good stories. There is something equally masculine in the physiognomy of Mr. Herkomer's model and in the way the artist has rendered it. There is usually a so-called 'picture of the year' at the Academy, and I have been asking myself on what work of art, on this occasion, such a title may be bestowed. Is Sir Frederick Leighton's tall, long-legged, dun-coloured 'Phryne at Eleusis' the picture of the year? This is a study of the nude on a large scale: the beautiful Athenian, competing for the prize awarded to perfection of form, undrapes her loveliness before the admiring multitude. Her loveliness is considerable, for Sir Frederick Leighton has a great deal of elegance, a great sense of beauty; but neither in modelling nor in colour does her elongated person appear to justify this lavish exposure. The head is charming and charmingly placed, and the picture more freely painted than a number of other polished creations by the same artist, scattered through the neighbouring rooms. But the body strikes one as too monotonously yellow, too flat, too remodelled. The lady stands there in the atmosphere of Greece, and her beauty must have flashed more vividly, shone more splendidly, upon the eyes of Greeks. It is true that it is not with the eyes of Greeks that we look at her. This perhaps is what is needed to see deeper into the present manner of the accomplished president of the Academy. More than any English painter he devotes himself to the plastic, but his efforts remain strongly and brilliantly superficial. His texture is too often that of the glaze on the lid of a prune-box; his drawing too often that of the figures that smile at us from the covers of these receptacles. And yet, as I say, he has a great sense of beauty. I am reduced to believing that to-day there is no picture of the year; for neither Mr. Millais, nor Mr. Pettie, nor Mr. Orchardson, nor Mr. Marcus Stone, nor Mr. Long, nor Mr. Boughton, nor any other of the popular purveyors of pictorial anecdote has succeeded in providing it. Mr. Pettie has several clever things, but I know no painter possessing so many parts of the temperament of a painter in whom the total is less felicitous. He is a Scotchman by nativity, and his colouring has a Caledonian harshness, a kind of 'sandy' quality, which is fatal to the plastic idea. There could not be a better example of what I have called the Philistinism of English art than his exceedingly ugly picture of the young Duke of Monmouth kneeling in suppliance, with his hands tied, to the cowardly James II. The violation of taste here is quite bottomless. An artist whose success in England is, from the foreign point of view, absolutely inexplicable is Mr. Edwin Long, who paints *large* sentimental Eastern subjects, and who, the other day, sold one of these productions for six thousand pounds. Mr. Long, if I am not mistaken, would be regarded in France, in Germany, even in Italy, as dangerously weak. The Academy, which every year purchases out of a certain Chantrey fund a picture to call its own, has this year selected a very charming work by Mr. Marcus Stone: a love-scene in an old-fashioned garden, with a couple of figures and a great many very delicately treated accessories. The picture, which is not very solid, is yet the result of a great deal of talent, and though it is extremely English it is also extremely skilful. The increase and diffusion—signified on each wall of the exhibition—of the particular sort of skill which it reveals is perhaps the best thing to be noticed in English art to-day.

JOHN S. SARGENT

1893

I WAS on the point of beginning this sketch of the work of an
artist to whom distinction has come very early in life by saying,
in regard to the degree to which the subject of it enjoys the
attention of the public, that no American painter has hitherto
won himself such recognition from the expert; but I find myself
pausing at the start as on the edge of a possible solecism. Is Mr.
Sargent in very fact an American painter? The proper answer to
such a question is doubtless that we shall be well advised to
pretend it, and the reason of this is simply that we have an
excellent opportunity. Born in Europe, he has also spent his life
in Europe, but none the less the burden of proof would rest with
those who should undertake to show that he is a European.
Moreover he has even on the face of it this great symptom of an
American origin, that in the line of his art he might easily be
mistaken for a Frenchman. It sounds like a paradox, but it is a
very simple truth, that when to-day we look for 'American art'
we find it mainly in Paris. When we find it out of Paris, we at
least find a great deal of Paris in it. Mr. Sargent came up to the
irresistible city in his twentieth year, from Florence, where in
1856 he had been born of American parents and where his fortunate youth had been spent. He entered immediately the studio
of Carolus Duran, and revealed himself in 1877, at the age of
twenty-two, in the portrait of that master[1]—a fine model in more
than one sense of the word. He was already in possession of a
style; and if this style has gained both in finish and in assurance,
it has not otherwise varied. As he saw and 'rendered' ten years
ago, so he sees and renders to-day; and I may add that

[1] In the Clark Art Institute, Williamstown, Mass.

216

there is no present symptom of his passing into another manner.

Those who have appreciated his work most up to the present time articulate no wish for a change, so completely does that work seem to them, in its kind, the exact translation of his thought, the exact 'fit' of his artistic temperament. It is difficult to imagine a young painter less in the dark about his own ideal, more lucid and more responsible from the first about what he desires. In an altogether exceptional degree does he give us the sense that the intention and the art of carrying it out are for him one and the same thing. In the brilliant portrait of Carolus Duran, which he was speedily and strikingly to surpass, he gave almost the full measure of this admirable peculiarity, that perception with him is already by itself a kind of execution. It is likewise so, of course, with many another genuine painter; but in Sargent's case the process by which the object seen resolves itself into the object pictured is extraordinarily immediate. It is as if painting were pure tact of vision, a simple manner of feeling.

From the time of his first successes at the Salon he was hailed, I believe, as a recruit of high value to the camp of the Impressionists, and to-day he is for many people most conveniently pigeon-holed under that head.[1] It is not necessary to protest against the classification if this addition always be made to it, that Mr. Sargent's impressions happen to be worthy of record. This is by no means inveterately the case with those of the ingenuous artists who most rejoice in the title in question. To render the impression of an object may be a very fruitful effort, but it is not necessarily so; that will depend upon what, I won't say the object, but the impression, may have been. The talents engaged in this school lie, not unjustly, as it seems to me, under the suspicion of seeking the solution of their problem exclusively in simplification. If a painter works for other eyes as well as his own he courts a certain danger in this direction—that of being arrested by the cry of the spectator: 'Ah! but excuse me; I myself

[1] In this connection it is interesting to recall that Charles Waterlow, the American painter, in *The Reverberator* (1888) was 'a rising Impressionist.'

take more impressions than that.' We feel a synthesis not to be an injustice only when it is rich. Mr. Sargent simplifies, I think, but he simplifies with style, and his impression is the finest form of his energy.

His work has been almost exclusively in portraiture, and it has been his fortune to paint more women than men; therefore he has had but a limited opportunity to reproduce that generalized grand air with which his view of certain figures of gentlemen invests the model, which is conspicuous in the portrait of Carolus Duran, and of which his splendid 'Docteur Pozzi', the distinguished Paris surgeon (a work not sent to the Salon), is an admirable example. In each of these cases the model has been of a gallant pictorial type, one of the types which strike us as made for portraiture (which is by no means the way of all), as especially appears, for instance, in the handsome hands and frilled wrists of M. Carolus, whose cane rests in his fine fingers as if it were the hilt of a rapier. The most brilliant of all Mr. Sargent's productions is the portrait of a young lady, the magnificent picture which he exhibited in 1881;[1] and if it has mainly been his fortune since to commemorate the fair faces of women, there is no ground for surprise at this sort of success on the part of one who had given so signal a proof of possessing the secret of the particular aspect that the contemporary lady (of any period) likes to wear in the eyes of posterity. Painted when he was but four-and-twenty years of age, the picture by which Mr. Sargent was represented at the Salon of 1881 is a performance which may well have made any critic of imagination rather anxious about his future. In common with the superb group of the children of Mr. Edward Boit, exhibited two years later, it offers the slightly 'uncanny' spectacle of a talent which on the very threshold of its career has nothing more to learn. It is not simply precocity in the guise of maturity—a phenomenon we very often meet, which deceives us only for an hour; it is the freshness of youth combined with the artistic experience, really felt and assimilated,

[1] Portrait of Miss Burckhardt, now in the Metropolitan Museum, New York. It is dated 1882.

of generations. My admiration for this deeply distinguished work is such that I am perhaps in danger of overstating its merits; but it is worth taking into account that to-day, after several years' acquaintance with them, these merits seem to me more and more to justify enthusiasm. The picture has this sign of productions of the first order, that its style clearly would save it if everything else should change—our measure of its value of resemblance, its expression of character, the fashion of dress, the particular associations it evokes. It is not only a portrait, but a picture, and it arouses even in the profane spectator something of the painter's sense, the joy of engaging also, by sympathy, in the solution of the artistic problem. There are works of which it is sometimes said that they are painters' pictures (this description is apt to be intended invidiously), and the production of which I speak has the good-fortune at once to belong to this class and to give the 'plain man' the kind of pleasure that the plain man looks for.

The young lady, dressed in black satin, stands upright, with her right hand bent back, resting on her waist, while the other, with the arm somewhat extended, offers to view a single white flower. The dress, stretched at the hips over a sort of hoop, and ornamented in front, where it opens on a velvet petticoat with large satin bows, has an old-fashioned air, as if it had been worn by some demure princess who might have sat for Velasquez. The hair, of which the arrangement is odd and charming, is disposed in two or three large curls fastened at one side over the temple with a comb. Behind the figure is the vague faded sheen, exquisite in tone, of a silk curtain, light, undefined, and losing itself at the bottom. The face is young, candid and peculiar. Out of these few elements the artist has constructed a picture which it is impossible to forget, of which the most striking characteristic is its simplicity, and yet which overflows with perfection. Painted with extraordinary breadth and freedom, so that surface and texture are interpreted by the lightest hand, it glows with life, character and distinction, and strikes us as the most complete—with one exception perhaps—of the author's productions. I know not why this representation of a

young girl in black, engaged in the casual gesture of holding up
a flower, should make so ineffaceable an impression and tempt
one to become almost lyrical in its praise; but I remember that,
encountering the picture unexpectedly in New York a year or
two after it had been exhibited in Paris, it seemed to me to have
acquired an extraordinary general value, to stand for more
artistic truth than it would be easy to formulate. The language of
painting, the tongue in which, exclusively, Mr. Sargent expresses
himself, is a medium into which a considerable part of the public,
for the simple and excellent reason that they don't understand it,
will doubtless always be reluctant and unable to follow him.

Two years before he exhibited the young lady in black, in
1879, Mr. Sargent had spent several months in Spain, and here,
even more than he had already been, the great Velasquez became
the god of his idolatry. No scenes are more delightful to the
imagination than those in which we figure youth and genius confronted with great examples, and if such matters did not belong
to the domain of private life we might entertain ourselves with
reconstructing the episode of the first visit to the museum of
Madrid, the shrine of the painter of Philip IV, of a young Franco-
American worshipper of the highest artistic sensibility, expecting
a supreme revelation and prepared to fall on his knees. It is
evident that Mr. Sargent fell on his knees and that in this attitude
he passed a considerable part of his sojourn in Spain. He is
various and experimental; if I am not mistaken, he sees each work
that he produces in a light of its own, not turning off successive
portraits according to some well-tried receipt which has proved
useful in the case of their predecessors; nevertheless there is one
idea that pervades them all, in a different degree, and gives them
a family resemblance—the idea that it would be inspiring to
know just how Velasquez would have treated the theme. We
can fancy that on each occasion Mr. Sargent, as a solemn pre-
liminary, invokes him as a patron saint. This is not, in my
intention, tantamount to saying that the large canvas representing
the contortions of a dancer in the lamp-lit room of a *posada*,[1]

[1] In the Gardner Museum, Boston.

which he exhibited on his return from Spain, strikes me as having come into the world under the same star as those compositions of the great Spaniard which at Madrid alternate with his royal portraits. This singular work, which has found an appreciative home in Boston, has the stamp of an extraordinary energy and facility—of an actual scene, with its accidents and peculiarities caught, as distinguished from a composition where arrangement and invention have played their part. It looks like life, but it looks also, to my view, rather like a perversion of life, and has the quality of an enormous 'note' or memorandum, rather than of a representation. A woman in a voluminous white silk dress and a black mantilla pirouettes in the middle of a dusky room, to the accompaniment of her own castanets and that of a row of men and women who sit in straw chairs against the whitewashed wall and thrum upon guitar and tambourine or lift other castanets into the air. She appears almost colossal, and the twisted and inflated folds of her long dress increase her volume. She simpers, in profile, with a long chin, while she slants back at a dangerous angle, and the lamplight (it proceeds from below, as if she were on a big platform) makes a strange play in her large face. In the background the straight line of black-clad, black-hatted, white-shirted musicians projects shadows against the wall, on which placards, guitars, and dirty finger-marks display themselves. The merit of this production is that the air of reality is given in it with remarkable breadth and boldness; its defect it is difficult to express save by saying that it makes the spectator vaguely uneasy and even unhappy—an accident the more to be regretted as a lithe, inspired female figure, given up to the emotion of the dance, is not intrinsically a displeasing object. 'El Jaleo' sins, in my opinion, in the direction of ugliness, and, independently of the fact that the heroine is circling round incommoded by her petticoats, has a want of serenity.

This is not the defect of the charming, dusky, white-robed person who, in the Tangerine subject exhibited at the Salon of 1880 (the fruit of an excursion to the African coast at the time of the artist's visit to Spain), stands on a rug, under a great white Moorish arch, and from out of the shadows of the large drapery, raised pentwise by her hands, which covers her head, looks down, with painted eyes and brows showing above a bandaged mouth, at the fumes of a beautiful censer or chafing-dish placed on the carpet. I know not who this stately Ma-hometan may be, nor in what mysterious domestic or religious rite she may be engaged; but in her muffled contemplation and her pearl-coloured robes, under her plastered arcade, which shines in the Eastern light, she transports and torments us. The picture is exquisite, a radiant effect of white upon white, of similar but discriminated tones.

In dividing the honour that Mr. Sargent has won by his finest work between the portrait of the young lady of 1881 and the group of four little girls[1] which was painted in 1882 and exhibited with the success it deserved the following year, I must be careful to give the latter picture not too small a share. The artist has done nothing more felicitous and interesting than this view of a rich, dim, rather generalized French interior (the perspective of a hall with a shining floor, where screens and tall Japanese vases shimmer and loom), which encloses the life and seems to form the happy play-world of a family of charming children. The treatment is eminently unconventional, and there is none of the usual symmetrical balancing of the figures in the foreground. The place is regarded as a whole; it is a scene, a comprehensive impression; yet none the less do the little figures in their white pinafores (when was the pinafore ever painted with that power and made so poetic?) detach themselves and live with a personal life. Two of the sisters stand hand in hand at the back, in the delightful, the almost equal, company of a pair of immensely tall emblazoned jars, which overtop them and seem also to par-take of the life of the picture; the splendid porcelain and the aprons of the children shine together, while a mirror in the brown depth behind them catches the light. Another little girl presents herself, with abundant tresses and slim legs, her hands behind her, quite to the left; and the youngest, nearest to the spectator,

[1] 'The Daughters of Edward D. Boit', in the Museum of Fine Arts, Boston.

sits on the floor and plays with her doll. The naturalness of the composition, the loveliness of the complete effect, the light, free security of the execution, the sense it gives us as of assimilated secrets and of instinct and knowledge playing together—all this makes the picture as astonishing a work on the part of a young man of twenty-six as the portrait of 1881 was astonishing on the part of a young man of twenty-four.

It is these remarkable encounters that justify us in writing almost prematurely of a career which is not yet half unfolded. Mr. Sargent is sometimes accused of a want of 'finish', but if finish means the last word of expressiveness of touch, 'The Hall with the Four Children', as we may call it, may stand as a permanent reference on this point. If the picture of the Spanish dancer illustrates, as it seems to me to do, the latent dangers of the Impressionist practice, so this finer performance shows what victories it may achieve. And in relation to the latter I must repeat what I said about the young lady with the flower, that this is the sort of work which, when produced in youth, leads the attentive spectator to ask unanswerable questions. He finds himself murmuring, 'Yes, but what is left?' and even wondering whether it be an advantage to an artist to obtain early in life such possession of his means that the struggle with them, discipline, *tâtonnement*, cease to exist for him. May not this breed an irresponsibility of cleverness, a wantonness, an irreverence— what is vulgarly termed a 'larkiness'—on the part of the youthful genius who has, as it were, all his fortune in his pocket? Such are the possibly superfluous broodings of those who are critical even in their warmest admirations and who sometimes suspect that it may be better for an artist to have a certain part of his property invested in unsolved difficulties. When this is not the case, the question with regard to his future simplifies itself somewhat portentously. 'What will he do with it?' we ask, meaning by the pronoun the sharp, completely forged weapon. It becomes more purely a question of responsibility, and we hold him altogether to a higher account. This is the case with Mr. Sargent; he knows so much about the art of painting that he perhaps does not fear emergencies quite enough, and that having knowledge to spare he may be tempted to play with it and waste it. Various, curious, as we have called him, he occasionally tries experiments which seem to arise from the mere high spirits of his brush, and runs risks little courted by the votaries of the literal, who never expose their necks to escape from the common. For the literal and the common he has the smallest taste; when he renders an object into the language of painting his translation is a generous paraphrase.

As I have intimated, he has painted little but portraits; but he has painted very many of these, and I shall not attempt in so few pages to give a catalogue of his works. Every canvas that has come from his hands has not figured at the Salon; some of them have seen the light at other exhibitions in Paris; some of them in London (of which city Mr. Sargent is now an inhabitant), at the Royal Academy and the Grosvenor Gallery. If he has been mainly represented by portraits there are two or three little subject-pictures of which I retain a grateful memory. There stands out in particular, as a pure gem, a small picture exhibited at the Grosvenor, representing a small group of Venetian girls of the lower class, sitting in gossip together one summer's day in the big, dim hall of a shabby old palazzo. The shutters let in a clink of light; the scagliola pavement gleams faintly in it; the whole place is bathed in a kind of transparent shade. The girls are vaguely engaged in some very humble household work; they are counting turnips or stringing onions, and these small vegetables, enchantingly painted, look as valuable as magnified pearls. The figures are extraordinarily natural and vivid; wonderfully light and fine is the touch by which the painter evokes the small familiar Venetian realities (he has handled them with a vigour altogether peculiar in various other studies which I have not space to enumerate), and keeps the whole thing free from that element of humbug which has ever attended most attempts to reproduce the idiosyncrasies of Italy. I am, however, drawing to the end of my remarks without having mentioned a dozen of those brilliant triumphs in the field of portraiture with which

Mr. Sargent's name is preponderantly associated. I jumped from
his 'Carolus Duran' to the masterpiece of 1881 without speaking
of the charming 'Madame Pailleron' of 1879, or the picture of
this lady's children the following year. Many, or rather most, of
Mr. Sargent's sitters have been French, and he has studied the
physiognomy of this nation so attentively that a little of it perhaps remains in the brush with which to-day, more than in his
first years, he represents other types. I have alluded to his superb
'Docteur Pozzi', to whose very handsome, still youthful head and
slightly artificial posture he has given so fine a French cast that
he might be excused if he should, even on remoter pretexts, find
himself reverting to it. This gentleman stands up in his brilliant
red dressing-gown with the *prestance* of a princely Van Dyck. I
should like to commemorate the portrait of a lady of a certain
age and of an equally certain interest of appearance—a lady in
black, with black hair, a black hat and a vast feather, which was
displayed at that entertaining little annual exhibition of the
'Mirlitons', in the Place Vendôme. With the exquisite modelling
of its face (no one better than Mr. Sargent understands the beauty
that resides in exceeding fineness), this head remains in my mind
as a masterly rendering of the look of experience—such experience as may be attributed to a woman slightly faded and eminently distinguished. Subject and treatment in this valuable piece
are of an equal interest, and in the latter there is an element of
positive sympathy which is not always in a high degree the sign
of Mr. Sargent's work.

What shall I say of the remarkable canvas which, on the
occasion of the Salon of 1884, brought the critics about our
artist's ears, the already celebrated portrait of 'Madame G.'?[1] It
is an experiment of a highly original kind, and the painter has
had in the case, in regard to what Mr. Ruskin would call the
'rightness' of his attempt, the courage of his opinion. A con-
testable beauty, according to Parisian fame, the lady stands
upright beside a table on which her right arm rests, with her body
almost fronting the spectator and her face in complete profile.

---

[1] In the Metropolitan Museum, New York.

She wears an entirely sleeveless dress of black satin, against which her admirable left arm detaches itself; the line of her harmonious profile has a sharpness which Mr. Sargent does not always seek, and the crescent of Diana, an ornament in diamonds, rests on her singular head. This work had not the good-fortune to please the public at large, and I believe it even excited a kind of unreasoned scandal—an idea sufficiently amusing in the light of some of the manifestations of the plastic effort to which, each year, the Salon stands sponsor. This superb picture, noble in conception and masterly in line, gives to the figure represented something of the high relief of the profiled images on great friezes. It is a work to take or to leave, as the phrase is, and one in regard to which the question of liking or disliking comes promptly to be settled. The author has never gone further in being boldly and consistently himself.

Two of Mr. Sargent's recent productions have been portraits of American ladies whom it must have been a delight to paint; I allude to those of Lady Playfair and Mrs. Henry White,[1] both of which were seen in the Royal Academy of 1885, and the former subsequently in Boston, where it abides. These things possess, largely, the quality which makes Mr. Sargent so happy as a painter of women—a quality which can best be expressed by a reference to what it is not, to the curiously literal, prosaic, sexless treatment to which, in the commonplace work that looks down at us from the walls of almost all exhibitions, delicate feminine elements have evidently so often been sacrificed. Mr. Sargent handles these elements with a special feeling for them, and they borrow a kind of noble intensity from his brush. This intensity is not absent from the two portraits I just mentioned, that of Lady Playfair and that of Mrs. Henry White; it looks out at us from the erect head and frank animation of the one, and the silvery sheen and shimmer of white satin and white lace which form the setting of the slim tallness of the other. In the Royal Academy of 1886 Mr. Sargent was represented by three impor-

---

[1] The portrait of Lady Playfair is in the Museum of Fine Arts, Boston: that of Mrs. Henry White is in the Corcoran Gallery, Washington.

tant canvases, all of which reminded the spectator of how much the brilliant effect he produces in an English exhibition arises from a certain appearance that he has of looking down from a height, a height of cleverness, a sensible giddiness of facility, at the artistic problems of the given case. Sometimes there is even a slight impertinence in it; that, doubtless, was the impression of many of the people who passed, staring, with an ejaculation, before the triumphant group of the three Misses V.[1] These young ladies, seated in a row, with a room much foreshortened for a background, and treated with a certain familiarity of frankness, excited in London a chorus of murmurs not dissimilar to that which it had been the fortune of the portrait exhibited in 1884 to elicit in Paris, and had the further privilege of drawing forth some prodigies of purblind criticism. Works of this character are a genuine service; after the short-lived gibes of the profane have subsided, they are found to have cleared the air. They remind people that the faculty of taking a direct, independent, unborrowed impression is not altogether lost.

In this very rapid review I have accompanied Mr. Sargent to a very recent date. If I have said that observers encumbered with a nervous temperament may at any moment have been anxious about his future, I have it on my conscience to add that the day has not yet come for a complete extinction of this anxiety. Mr. Sargent is so young, in spite of the place allotted to him in these pages, so often a record of long careers and uncontested triumphs that, in spite also of the admirable works he has already produced, his future is the most valuable thing he has to show. We may still ask ourselves what he will do with it, while we indulge the hope that he will see fit to give successors to the two pictures which I have spoken of emphatically as his finest. There is no greater work of art than a great portrait—a truth to be constantly taken to heart by a painter holding in his hands the weapon that Mr. Sargent wields. The gift that he possesses he possesses completely—the immediate perception of the end and of the means. Putting aside the question of the subject (and to a

[1] In the Graves Art Gallery, Sheffield.

great portrait a common sitter will doubtless not always contribute), the highest result is achieved when to this element of quick perception a certain faculty of brooding reflection is added. I use this name for want of a better, and I mean the quality in the light of which the artist sees deep into his subject, undergoes it, absorbs it, discovers in it new things that were not on the surface, becomes patient with it, and almost reverent, and, in short, enlarges and humanizes the technical problem.

HONORÉ DAUMIER

1893

AS WE attempt, at the present day, to write the history of every-thing, it would be strange if we had happened to neglect the annals of caricature; for the very essence of the art of Cruikshank and Gavarni, of Daumier and Leech, is to be historical; and every one knows how addicted is this great science to discoursing about itself. Many industrious seekers, in England and France, have ascended the stream of time to the source of the modern movement of pictorial satire. The stream of time is in this case mainly the stream of journalism; for social and political cari-cature, as the present century has practised it, is only journalism made doubly vivid.

The subject indeed is a large one, if we reflect upon it, for many people would tell us that journalism is the greatest inven-tion of our age. If this rich affluent has shared the great fortune of the general torrent, so, on other sides, it touches the fine arts, touches manners, touches morals. All this helps to account for its inexhaustible life; journalism is the criticism of the moment *at* the moment, and caricature is that criticism at once simplified and intensified by a plastic form. We know the satiric image as periodical, and above all as punctual—the characteristics of the printed sheet with which custom has at last inveterately associated it.

This, by the way, makes us wonder considerably at the failure of caricature to achieve, as yet, a high destiny in America—a failure which might supply an occasion for much explanatory discourse, much searching of the relations of things. The news-paper has been taught to flourish among us as it flourishes no-where else, and to flourish moreover on a humorous and irreverent basis; yet it has never taken to itself this helpful concomitant of an unscrupulous spirit and a quick periodicity. The explanation is probably that it needs an old society to produce ripe caricature. The newspaper thrives in the United States, but journalism languishes; for the lively propagation of news is one thing and the large interpretation of it is another. A society has to be old before it becomes critical, and it has to become critical before it can take pleasure in the reproduction of its incongruities by an instrument as impertinent as the indefatigable crayon. Irony, scepticism, pessimism are, in any particular soil, plants of gradual growth, and it is in the art of caricature that they flower most aggressively. Furthermore they must be watered by education—I mean by the education of the eye and hand—all of which things take time. The soil must be rich too, the incongruities must swarm. It is open to doubt whether a pure democracy is very liable to make this particular satiric return upon itself; for which it would seem that certain social complications are indispensable. These complications are supplied from the moment a democracy becomes, as we may say, impure from its own point of view; from the moment variations and heresies, deviations or perhaps simple affirmations of taste and temper begin to multiply within it. Such things afford a *point d'appui;* for it is evidently of the essence of caricature to be reactionary. We hasten to add that its satiric force varies immensely in kind and in degree according to the race, or to the individual talent, that takes advantage of it.

I used just now the term pessimism; but that was doubtless in a great measure because I have been turning over a collection of the extraordinarily vivid drawings of Honoré Daumier. The same impression would remain with me, no doubt, if I had been consulting an equal quantity of the work of Gavarni, the wittiest, the most literary and most acutely profane of all chartered mockers with the pencil. The feeling of disrespect abides in all these things, the expression of the spirit for which humanity is definable primarily by its weaknesses. For Daumier these weaknesses are altogether ugly and grotesque, while for Gavarni they are either basely graceful or touchingly miserable; but the vision of them in both cases is close and direct. If, on the other hand, we look through a dozen volumes of the collection of *Punch* we get an equal impression of hilarity, but we by no means get an equal impression of irony. Certainly the pages of *Punch* do not reek with pessimism; their 'criticism of life' is gentle and forbearing. Leech is positively optimistic; there is at any rate nothing infinite in his irreverence; it touches bottom as soon as it approaches the pretty woman or the nice girl. It is such an apparition as this that really, in Gavarni, awakes the scoffer. Du Maurier is as graceful as Gavarni, but his sense of beauty conjures away almost everything save our minor vices. It is in the exploration of our major ones that Gavarni makes his principal discoveries of charm or of absurdity of attitude. None the less, of course, the general inspiration of both artists is the same; the desire to try the innumerable different ways in which the human subject may *not* be taken seriously.

If this view of that subject, in its plastic manifestations, makes history of a sort, it will not in general be of a kind to convert those persons who find history sad reading. The writer of the present lines remained unconverted, lately, on an occasion on which many cheerful influences were mingled with his impression. They were of a nature to which he usually does full justice, even overestimating perhaps their charm of suggestion; but, at the hour I speak of, the old Parisian quay, the belittered printshop, the pleasant afternoon, the glimpse of the great Louvre on the other side of the Seine, in the interstices of the sallow *estampes* suspended in window and doorway—all these elements of a rich actuality availed only to mitigate, without transmuting, that general vision of a high, cruel pillory which pieced itself together as I drew specimen after specimen from musty portfolios. I had been passing the shop when I noticed in a small *vitrine*, let into the embrasure of the doorway, half a dozen soiled, striking lithographs, which it took no more than a first glance to recognize as the work of Daumier. They were only old pages of the *Charivari*, torn away from the text and rescued from the injury of time; and they were accompanied with an inscription to the effect that many similar examples of the artist were to be seen within. To become aware of this circumstance was to enter the shop and to find myself promptly surrounded with bulging *cartons* and tattered relics. These relics—crumpled leaves of the old comic journals of the period from 1830 to 1855 —are neither rare nor expensive; but I happened to have lighted on a particularly copious collection, and I made the most of my small good-fortune, in order to transmute it, if possible, into a sort of compensation for my having missed unavoidably, a few months before, the curious exhibition 'de la Caricature Moderne' held for several weeks just at hand, in the École des Beaux-Arts. Daumier was said to have appeared there in considerable force; and it was a loss not to have had that particular opportunity of filling one's mind with him.

There was perhaps a perversity in having wished to do so, strange, indigestible stuff of contemplation as he might appear to be; but the perversity had had an honourable growth. Daumier's great days were in the reign of Louis-Philippe; but in the early years of the Second Empire he still plied his coarse and formidable pencil. I recalled, from a juvenile consciousness, the last failing strokes of it. They used to impress me in Paris, as a child, with their abnormal blackness as well as with their grotesque, magnifying movement, and there was something in them that rather scared a very immature admirer. This small personage, however, was able to perceive later, when he was unfortunately deprived of the chance of studying them, that there were various things in them besides the power to excite a vague alarm. Daumier was perhaps a great artist; at all events unsatisfied curiosity increased in proportion to that possibility.

The first complete satisfaction of it was really in the long hours that I spent in the little shop on the quay. There I filled my mind with him, and there too, at no great cost, I could make a big parcel of these cheap reproductions of his work. This work had been shown in the École des Beaux-Arts as it came from his hand; M. Champfleury, his biographer, his cataloguer and devotee, having poured forth the treasures of a precious collection, as I suppose they would be called in the case of an artist of higher flights. It was only as he was seen by the readers of the comic journals of his day that I could now see him; but I tried to make up for my want of privilege by prolonged immersion. I was not able to take home all the portfolios from the shop on the quay, but I took home what I could, and I went again to turn over the superannuated piles. I liked looking at them on the spot; I seemed still surrounded by the artist's vanished Paris and his extinct Parisians. Indeed no quarter of the delightful city probably shows, on the whole, fewer changes from the aspect it wore during the period of Louis-Philippe, the time when it will ever appear to many of its friends to have been most delightful. The long line of the quay is unaltered, and the rare charm of the river. People came and went in the shop: it is a wonder how many, in the course of an hour, may lift the latch even of an establishment that pretends to no great business. What was all this small, sociable, contentious life but the great Daumier's subject-matter? He was the painter of the Parisian bourgeois, and the voice of the bourgeois was in the air.

M. Champfleury has given a summary of Daumier's career in his smart little *Histoire de la Caricature Moderne*, a record not at all abundant in personal detail. The biographer has told his story better perhaps in his careful catalogue of the artist's productions, the first sketch of which is to be found in *L'Art* for 1878. This copious list is Daumier's real history; his life cannot have been a very different business from his work. I read in the interesting publication of M. Grand-Carteret (*Les Moeurs et la Caricature en France*, 1888) that our artist produced nearly 4,000 lithographs and a thousand drawings on wood, up to the time when failure of eyesight compelled him to rest. This is not the sort of activity that leaves a man much time for independent adventures, and Daumier was essentially of the type, common in France, of the specialist so immersed in his speciality that he can be painted in only one attitude—a general circumstance which perhaps helps to account for the paucity, in that country, of biography, in our English sense of the word, in proportion to the superabundance of criticism.

Honoré Daumier was born at Marseilles February 26th, 1808; he died on the 11th of the same month, 1879. His main activity, however, was confined to the earlier portion of a career of almost exactly seventy-one years, and I find it affirmed in Vapereau's *Dictionnaire des Contemporains* that he became completely blind between 1850 and 1860. He enjoyed a pension from the State of 2,400 francs; but what relief from misery could mitigate a quarter of a century of darkness for a man who had looked out at the world with such vivifying eyes? His father had followed the trade of a glazier, but was otherwise vocal than in the emission of the rich street-cry with which we used all to be familiar, and which has vanished with so many other friendly pedestrian notes. The elder Daumier wrought verses as well as window-panes, and M. Champfleury has disinterred a small volume published by him in 1823. The merit of his poetry is not striking; but he was able to transmit the artistic nature to his son, who, becoming promptly conscious of it, made the inevitable journey to Paris in search of fortune.

The young draughtsman appeared to have missed at first the way to this boon; inasmuch as in the year 1832 he found himself condemned to six months' imprisonment for a lithograph disrespectful to Louis-Philippe. This drawing had appeared in the *Caricature*, an organ of pictorial satire founded in those days by one Philipon, with the aid of a band of young mockers to whom he gave ideas and a direction, and several others, of whom Gavarni, Henry Monnier, Decamps, Grandville, were destined to make themselves a place. M. Eugène Montrosier, in a highly appreciative article on Daumier in *L'Art* for 1878, says that this same Philipon was *le journalisme fait homme*; which did not prevent him—rather in fact fostered such a result—from being perpetually in delicate relations with the government. He had had many horses killed under him, and had led a life of attacks, penalties, suppressions and resurrections. He subsequently established the *Charivari* and launched a publication entitled *L'Association*

Lithographique Mensuelle, which brought to light much of Daumier's early work. The artist passed rapidly from seeking his way to finding it, and from an ineffectual to a vigorous form.

In this limited compass and in the case of such a quantity of production it is almost impossible to specify—difficult to pick dozens of examples out of thousands. Daumier became more and more the political spirit of the *Charivari,* or at least the political pencil, for M. Philipon, the breath of whose nostrils was opposition—one perceives from here the little bilious, bristling, ingenious, insistent man—is to be credited with a suggestive share in any enterprise in which he had a hand. This pencil played over public life, over the sovereign, the ministers, the deputies, the peers, the judiciary, the men and the measures, the reputations and scandals of the moment, with a strange, ugly, extravagant, but none the less sane and manly vigour. Daumier's sign is strength above all, and in turning over his pages to-day there is no intensity of force that the careful observer will not concede to him. It is perhaps another matter to assent to the proposition, put forth by his greatest admirers among his countrymen, that he is the first of all caricaturists. To the writer of this imperfect sketch he remains considerably less interesting than Gavarni; and for a particular reason, which it is difficult to express otherwise than by saying that he is too simple. Simplicity was not Gavarni's fault, and indeed to a large degree it was Daumier's merit. The single grossly ridiculous or almost hauntingly characteristic thing which his figures represent is largely the reason why they still represent life and an unlucky reality years after the names attached to them have parted with a vivifying power. Such vagueness has overtaken them, for the most part, and to such a thin reverberation have they shrunk, the persons and the affairs which were then so intensely sketchable. Daumier handled them with a want of ceremony which would have been brutal were it not for the element of science in his work, making them immense and unmistakable in their drollery, or at least in their grotesqueness; for the term drollery suggests gaiety, and Daumier is anything but gay. *Un rude peintre de moeurs*, M. Champfleury calls him; and the phrase expresses his extreme breadth of treatment.

Of the victims of his 'rudeness' M. Thiers is almost the only one whom the present generation may recognize without a good deal of reminding, and indeed his hand is relatively light in delineating this personage of few inches and many episodes. M. Thiers must have been dear to the caricaturist, for he belonged to the type that was easy to 'do'; it being well known that these gentlemen appreciate public characters in direct proportion to their saliency of feature. When faces are reducible to a few telling strokes their wearers are overwhelmed with the honours of publicity; with which, on the other hand, nothing is more likely to interfere than the possession of a countenance neatly classical. Daumier had only to give M. Thiers the face of a clever owl, and the trick was played. Of course skill was needed to individualize the symbol, but that is what caricaturists propose to themselves. Of how well he succeeded the admirable plate of the lively little minister in a 'new dress'—tricked out in the uniform of a general of the First Republic—is a sufficient illustration. The bird of night is not an acute bird, but how the artist has presented the image of a selected specimen! And with what a life-giving pencil the whole figure is put on its feet, what intelligent drawing, what a rich, free stroke! The allusions conveyed in it are to such forgotten things that it is strange to think the personage was, only the other year, still contemporaneous; that he might have been met, on a fine day, taking a few firm steps in a quiet part of the Champs-Élysées, with his footman carrying a second overcoat and looking doubly tall behind him. In whatever attitude Daumier depicts him, planted as a tiny boxing-master at the feet of the virtuous colossus in a blouse (whose legs are apart, like those of the Rhodian), in whom the artist represents the People, to watch the match that is about to come off between Ratapoil and M. Berryer, or even in the act of lifting the 'parricidal' club of a new repressive law to deal a blow at the Press, an effulgent, diligent, sedentary muse (this picture, by the way, is a perfect specimen of the simple and telling in political caricature)—however, as I say, he takes M. Thiers, there is always a rough indulgence in his crayon, as if he were grateful to him for lending himself so well.

He invented Ratapoil as he appropriated Robert Macaire, and as a caricaturist he never fails to put into circulation, when he can, a character to whom he may attribute as many as possible of the affectations or the vices of the day. Robert Macaire, an imaginative, a romantic rascal, was the hero of a highly successful melodrama written for Frédérick Lemaître; but Daumier made him the type of the swindler at large in an age of feverish speculation—the projector of showy companies, the advertiser of worthless shares. There is a whole series of drawings descriptive of his exploits, a hundred masterly plates which, according to M. Champfleury, consecrated Daumier's reputation. The subject, the legend, was in most cases, still according to M. Champfleury, suggested by Philipon. Sometimes it was very witty; as for instance when Bertrand, the muddled acolyte or scraping second fiddle of the hero, objects, in relation to a brilliant scheme which he has just developed, with the part Bertrand is to play, that there are constables in the country, and he promptly replies, 'Constables? So much the better—they'll take the shares!' Ratapoil was an evocation of the same general character, but with a difference of *nuance*—the ragged political bully, or hand-to-mouth demagogue, with the smashed tall hat, cocked to one side, the absence of linen, the club half-way up his sleeve, the swagger and pose of being gallant for the people. Ratapoil abounds in the promiscuous drawings that I have looked over, and is always very strong and living, with a considerable element of the sinister, so often in Daumier an accompaniment of the comic. There is an admirable page—it brings the idea down to 1851—in which a sordid but astute peasant, twirling his thumbs on his stomach and looking askance, allows this political adviser to urge upon him in a whisper that there is not a minute to lose—to lose for action, of course—if he wishes to keep his wife, his house, his field, his heifer and his calf. The canny scepticism in the ugly, half-averted face of the typical rustic who considerably suspects his counsellor is indicated by a few masterly strokes.

This is what the student of Daumier recognizes as his science, or, if the word has a better grace, his art. It is what has kept life in his work so long after so many of the occasions of it have been swept into darkness. Indeed, there is no such commentary on renown as the 'back numbers' of a comic journal. They show us that at certain moments certain people were eminent, only to make us unsuccessfully try to remember what they were eminent *for*. And the comparative obscurity (comparative, I mean, to the talent of the caricaturist) overtakes even the most justly honoured names. M. Berryer was a splendid speaker and a public servant of real distinction and the highest utility; yet the fact that to-day his name is on few men's lips seems to be emphasized by this other fact that we continue to pore over Daumier, in whose plates we happen to come across him. It reminds one afresh how Art is an embalmer, a magician, whom we can never speak too fair. People duly impressed with this truth are sometimes laughed at for their superstitious tone, which is pronounced, according to the fancy of the critic, mawkish, maudlin or hysterical. But it is really difficult to see how any reiteration of the importance of art can overstate the plain facts. It prolongs, it preserves, it consecrates, it raises from the dead. It conciliates, charms, bribes posterity; and it murmurs to mortals, as the old French poet sang to his mistress, 'You will be fair only so far as I have said so.' When it whispers even to the great, 'You depend upon me, and I can do more for you, in the long-run, than any one else', it is scarcely too proud. It puts method and power and the strange, real, mingled air of things into Daumier's black sketchiness, so full of the technical *gras*, the 'fat' which French critics commend and which we have no word to express. It puts power above all, and the effect which he best achieves, that of a certain simplification of the attitude or the gesture to an almost symbolic generality. His persons represent only one thing, but they insist tremendously on that, and their expression of it abides with us, unaccompanied with timid detail. It may really be said that they represent only one class—the old and ugly; so that there is proof enough of a special faculty in his having played such a concert, lugubrious though it be, on a single chord. It has been made a reproach to him, says M. Grand-Carteret, that 'his work is lacking in two capital elements—*la jeunesse et la femme*'; and this commentator resents his being made to suffer for the deficiency—'as if an artist could be at the same time deep, comic, graceful and pretty; as if all those who have a real value had not created for themselves a form to which they remain confined and a type which they reproduce in all its variations, as soon as they have touched the aesthetic ideal that has been their dream. Assuredly, humanity, as this great painter saw it, could not be beautiful; one asks one's self what a maiden in her teens, a pretty face, would have done in the midst of these good, plain folk, stunted and elderly, with faces like wrinkled apples. A simple accessory most of the time, woman is for him merely a termagant or a blue-stocking who has turned the corner.'

When the eternal feminine, for Daumier, appears in neither of these forms he sees it in Madame Chaboulard or Madame Fribochon, the old snuff-taking, gossiping portress, in a nightcap and shuffling *savates*, relating or drinking in the wonderful and the intimate. One of his masterpieces represents three of these dames, lighted by a guttering candle, holding their heads together to discuss the fearful earthquake at Bordeaux, the consequence of the government's allowing the surface of the globe to be unduly dug out in California. The representation of confidential imbecility could not go further. When a man leaves out so much of life as Daumier—youth and beauty and the charm of woman and the loveliness of childhood and the manners of those social groups of whom it may most be said that they *have* manners—when he exhibits a deficiency on this scale it might seem that the question was not to be so easily disposed of as in the very non-apologetic words I have just quoted. All the same (and I confess it is singular), we may feel what Daumier omitted and yet not be in the least shocked by the claim of predominance made for him. It is impossible to spend a couple of hours over him without assenting to this claim, even though there, may be a weariness in such a panorama of ugliness and an inevitable reaction from it. This anomaly, and the challenge to explain it which appears to proceed from him, render him, to my sense, remarkably interesting. The artist whose idiosyncrasies, whose limitations, if you will, make us question and wonder, in the light of his fame, has an element of fascination not attaching to conciliatory talents. If M. Eugène Montrosier may say of him without scandalizing us that such and such of his drawings belong to the very highest art, it is interesting (and Daumier profits by the interest) to put one's finger on the reason we are not scandalized.

I think this reason is that, on the whole, he is so peculiarly serious. This may seem an odd ground of praise for a jocose draughtsman, and of course what I mean is that his comic force is serious—a very different thing from the absence of comedy. This essential sign of the caricaturist may surely be anything it will so long as it is there. Daumier's figures are almost always either foolish, fatuous politicians or frightened, mystified bourgeois; yet they help him to give us a strong sense of the nature of man. They are sometimes so serious that they are almost tragic; the look of the particular pretension, combined with inanity, is carried almost to madness. There is a magnificent drawing of the series of 'Le Public du Salon', old classicists looking up, horrified and scandalized, at the new romantic work of 1830, in which the faces have an appalling gloom of mystification and platitude. We feel that Daumier reproduces admirably the particular life that he sees, because it is the very medium in which he moves. He has no wide horizon; the absolute bourgeois hems him in, and he is a bourgeois himself, without poetic ironies, to whom a big cracked mirror has been given. His thick, strong, manly touch stands, in every way, for so much knowledge. He used to make little images, in clay and in wax (many of them still exist), of the persons he was in the habit of representing, so that they might constantly seem to be 'sitting' for him. The caricaturist of that day had not the help of the ubiquitous photograph. Daumier painted actively, as well, in his habitation, all dedicated to work, on the narrow island of St. Louis, where the Seine divides and where the monuments of old Paris stand thick, and the types that were to his purpose pressed close upon him. He had not far to go to encounter the worthy man, in the series of 'Les Papas', who is reading the evening paper at the café with so amiable and placid a credulity, while his unnatural little boy, opposite to him, finds sufficient entertainment in the much-satirized *Constitutionnel.* The bland absorption of the papa, the face of the man who believes everything he sees in the newspaper, is as near as Daumier often comes to positive gentleness of humour. Of the same family is the poor gentleman, in 'Actualités', seen, in profile, under a doorway where he has taken refuge from a torrent of rain, who looks down at his neat legs with a sort of speculative contrition and says, 'To think of my having just ordered two pairs of white trousers.' The *tout petit bourgeois* palpitates in both these sketches.

I must repeat that it is absurd to pick half a dozen at hazard, out of five thousand; yet a few selections are the only way to call attention to his strong drawing. This has a virtuosity of its own, for all its hit-or-miss appearance. Whatever he touches—the nude, in the swimming-baths on the Seine, the intimations of landscape, when his *petits rentiers* go into the suburbs for a Sunday—acquires relief and character. Docteur Véron, a celebrity of the reign of Louis-Philippe, a Maecenas of the hour, a director of the opera, author of the *Mémoires d'un Bourgeois de Paris*—this temporary 'illustration', who appears to have been almost indecently ugly, would not be vivid to us to-day had not Daumier, who was often effective at his expense, happened to have represented him, in some crisis of his career, as a sort of naked inconsolable Vitellius. He renders the human body with a cynical sense of its possible flabbiness and an intimate acquaintance with its structure. 'Une Promenade Conjugale', in the series of 'Tout ce qu'on voudra', portrays a hillside, on a summer afternoon, on which a man has thrown himself on his back to rest, with his arms locked under his head. His fat, full-bosomed, middle-aged wife, under her parasol, with a bunch of field-flowers in her hand, looks down at him patiently and seems to say, 'Come, my dear, get up.' There is surely no great point in this; the only point is life, the glimpse of the little snatch of poetry in prose. It is a matter of a few broad strokes of the crayon; yet the pleasant laziness of the man, the idleness of the day, the fragment of homely, familiar dialogue, the stretch of the field with a couple of trees merely suggested, have a communicative truth.

I perhaps exaggerate all this, and in insisting upon the merit of Daumier may appear to make light of the finer accomplishment of several more modern talents, in England and France, who have greater ingenuity and subtlety and have carried qualities of execution so much further. In looking at this complicated younger work, which has profited so by experience and comparison, it is inevitable that we should perceive it to be infinitely more cunning. On the other hand Daumier, moving in his contracted circle, has an impressive depth. It comes back to his strange seriousness. He is a draughtsman by race, and if he has not extracted the same brilliancy from training, or perhaps even from effort and experiment, as some of his successors, does not his richer satiric and sympathetic feeling more than make up the difference?

However this question may be answered, some of his drawings belong to the class of the unforgetable. It may be a perversity of prejudice, but even the little cut of the 'Connoisseurs', the group of gentlemen collected round a picture and criticizing it in various attitudes of sapience and sufficiency, appears to me to have the strength that abides. The criminal in the dock, the flat-headed murderer, bending over to speak to his advocate, who turns a whiskered, professional, anxious head to caution and remind him, tells a large, terrible story and awakes a recurrent shudder. We see the gray court-room, we feel the personal suspense and the immensity of justice. The 'Saltimbanques', reproduced in *L'Art* for 1878, is a page of tragedy, the finest of a cruel series. M. Eugène Montrosier says of it that 'The drawing is masterly, incomparably firm, the composition superb, the general impression quite of the first order'. It exhibits a pair of lean, hungry mountebanks, a clown and a harlequin beating the drum and trying a comic attitude to attract the crowd, at a fair, to a poor booth in front of which a painted canvas, offering to view a simpering fat woman, is suspended. But the crowd doesn't come, and the battered tumblers, with their furrowed cheeks, go through their pranks in the void. The whole thing is symbolic and full of grimness, imagination and pity. It is the sense that we shall find in him, mixed with his homelier extravagances, an element prolific in indications of this order that draws us back to Daumier.

THE NEW GALLERY

1897

I HAVE no difficulty in declaring that, for myself, I am far from liking the whole of Mr. Watts as well as I like the half or the third or even the quarter. The three full rooms of the New Gallery[1] are an extraordinary record of a painter's ups and downs, but even this reflection held me less than some others I was moved to make. Mr. Watts is 'Victorian'—that came home to me, more than ever, on the spot; but I mention it not as a discovery—only as a pretext for a friendlier appreciation. For if in the arts the epithet—or what we loosely understand by it— is almost necessarily invidious, Mr. Watts wears it with an interesting difference. He met his destiny in the terrible fifties, but she was luckily not the direst daughter of the decade. She reminds us of her fatal sisters, but she may pass for the flower of the family. She got him, at any rate, some very good orders— introduced him, I should say more nobly, to some very handsome models. For it is only, I make haste to mention, as a painter of portraits that I pretend to allude to Mr. Watts. His compositions, his allegories and fantasies are beyond me; they are mainly interesting, I think, as a fresh memento that nothing in a work of art can take the place of representation, nothing in a picture take the place of painting. Mr. Watt's imagination strikes me as productive just in proportion as his subject is concrete. There is nothing so concrete as a charming woman or a distinguished man; and these are just the cases in which, with the ground firm under his feet, he has indulged most happily in that

[1] The New Gallery at 121 Regent Street was opened in 1888 under the directorship of J. W. Comyns Carr and C. E. Hallé, who had been assistant directors of the Grosvenor Gallery until 1887. The New Gallery closed its doors in 1909.

pictorial emotion which has been his distinctive note—a passage
leading him straight to style. Style, for him, has resided in the
capacity to feel—and to feel as a poet or a woman feels, with
wonder and respect—the interesting individual. If women could
paint they would paint, I surmise, very like Mr. Watts. Sometimes he has felt a good deal more than he has painted, but when
the execution has kept pace he has risen very high. His later
work has not been, in general, his strongest; yet it was in 1891
that he produced his admirable portrait of Walter Crane, an
expression of both his gifts at their best and a supreme example
of his happy art of making, with a hundred refinements, a
mystery even of what he most seizes. This picture, a real triumph
of the sense within the sense and the craft within the craft, marks
the author's greatest day. Such a portrait—such a taking possession for taste and thought—has even a certain fine cruelty for
the sitter. It seems to do so much for him that it is a kind of
effacement of what he may have done or may wish to do for
himself. To be taken so seriously and set to such music is, in
short, possibly discouraging.

What, with the best-born of its companions, however, the
Walter Crane may well suggest is that all this experience on the
part of the painter, all this luxury of surrender to the claim, to
the possibilities, of another personality, is in itself a high form
of success. What came home to me at the New Gallery was that,
after all, the privilege of an artist of this temperament is perhaps
greater still than his work. It represents indeed an enviable
happiness. A spectator trying for a different form of representation (I mean in another craft) could wonder what it would
have been for himself—what it would have *not* been, rather—
to have felt and imagined, with that intensity, during so long a
career, so much definitely distinguished life. It could only have
been a great adventure, a sort of vicarious thrill. This gave the
spectator in question the desire for another look at that array of
a dozen celebrities lately presented by Mr. Watts to the National
Portrait Gallery, the great pictorial roll of the eminent English
which, after much dispersion and not a little dishonour, has

finally found a home in the low, swelling structure now pinned —a good deal as a 'bustle' is attached to a lady's waist—to the broad back of the gray museum of Trafalgar Square. But he suddenly remembered a reason to wait a little. The portrait of Coventry Patmore painted a couple of years since by John Sargent and just offered to the nation by the poet's widow is not yet in its place. Let us postpone our visit till we can by the same stroke renew acquaintance with that magnificent work.

LORD LEIGHTON AND
FORD MADOX BROWN
1897

IT IS NOT, as we meet them, so easy to say of what ages Lord Leighton and Ford Madox Brown were the product, though each offers us the aid of a copious exhibition, the former installed at Burlington House this month past, the other, within a day or two, affronting the new and somewhat fierce light of the elegant Grafton Galleries.[1] The honours are posthumous for both, but upon antecedents and, on the whole, with consequences so different, that the contrast has an interesting vividness. I am fully conscious that Lord Leighton incurs a kind of aesthetic grudge by the mere occupation, for so many weeks, of those admirable rooms of the Royal Academy which are usually, in winter, given up to older names and sturdier presences. When the light is mild, the days short, the sounds muffled and the spectators few, the Old Masters at Burlington House, gathered wondrously from English homes, diffuse, in the quiet halls, from year to year, an effect that is half of melancholy, half of cheer, and that, if the programme varies, one rather resentfully misses. I am not less reminiscent of the splendid obsequies, last spring, that at the time made us ask some of the questions of which the answer seems now to be coming in as ruefully as a shy child comes into a drawing-room. The day was suave and splendid, congruous, somehow, with the whole 'note' of Leighton's personality. The funeral, in the streets cleared of traffic and lined, for the long passage to St. Paul's, with the multitude, had the air of a national

[1] The Grafton Galleries, 8 Grafton Street, London, served as an art centre from 1893 until 1930.

demonstration, and under the dome of the great church, where all the England of 'culture' seemed gathered, the rites had the impressiveness of a universal mourning. They formed a suggestive hour, none the less, for a spectator not exempt from the morbid trick of reflection. They were for all the world so like some immense *committal* of the public spirit, that it was impossible not to wonder to what it was this spirit committed itself. Now that upwards of a year has come round, the reply would appear to be—simply to nothing at all.

The case bids fair—as far as we have got, at least—to offer promising material for at least one page of that history of the inconsequence of the mind of the multitude which has yet to be written, but for which, here and there, a possibly maniacal student will be found collecting illustrations. It always comes back, with the fluctuating fortune of artist, of author, of *any* victim of 'public attention', to the same, the eternal bewilderment: is the key to the enigma that there was too much noise yesterday, or that there is not enough of it to-day? Lord Leighton's beautiful house, almost immediately after his funeral, was offered as a memorial to the nation if the nation would subscribe to buy it. The nation, scarce up from its genuflections at St. Paul's, buttoned its pocket without so much as scratching its head. Since then his two sisters—one of them the accomplished Mrs. Sutherland Orr, friend and biographer of Browning —have generously made known that they will present the house as a museum for relics of their brother if the public, in its commemorative enthusiasm, will collect the relics and keep up the establishment. Nothing is more presumable than that the public will do nothing of the sort.[1] Small blame, however, to the persons who were misguided by the great show of homage and who must be now asking themselves what in the world it meant.

---

[1] In 1925 Mrs. Russell Barrington, the surviving trustee, 'offered the house and its contents to the Royal Borough of Kensington; this offer was gratefully received by the Borough Council to which body the property was transferred in 1926.' The Council subsequently purchased the freehold. The house is now 'maintained for the benefit of the public as a centre of art, music and literature.' (From a tablet in the vestibule of Leighton House.)

They will scarce find an obvious answer, I think, in the fine vacant chambers of the Academy. It may probably, however, be figured out there—in the presence of so much beauty and so little passion, so much seeking, and, on the whole, so little finding—that the late President of the institution was one of the happy celebrities who take it out, as the phrase is, in life.[1] Life was generous to him, as nature had been, and he drank deep of what it can give. The great demonstration last year was, like his peerage, simply a part of his success. It was not, as it were, of the residuum—it was still on the wrong side of the line.

I know not how to describe better the Madox Brown exhibition—the only complete one of this painter ever held, I believe, in London—than by saying that it is an opportunity for poetic justice rather tragically missed. Everything is there for it but justice herself: the revenge of time somehow stops half-way. The career of the artist was full of professional stumbles, and it is difficult not to see one more in this final miscarriage. Full of energy, passion and thought, he was, in his lifetime, appreciated neither by the public nor by the members of his own craft. The Academy rejected him, 'skied' him, by his own measure outraged him, and he laboured year after year in solitude and poverty. He 'met', as must have been said, 'no public want'. He would make no concessions and play no tricks, he was obstinate and rancorous, and he is so rare an example of popularity forfeited that, by every rule of the game, he should have appeared to-day in force only to confound the generations that misjudged him. He is, however, not quite up to his part. The sincerity that shines out in him lights up not only the vulgarity of his age, but too many of his own perversities and pedantries. A certain measure of redress he enjoys: his small but so interesting 'Christ washing

---

[1] See *The Notebooks of Henry James* edited by F. O. Matthiessen and Kenneth B. Murdock, entry dated 3 August 1891 in which James approaches his story 'The Private Life' and contemplates the character of Lord Mellefont, 'a personage suggested by F. L.' 'Lord Mellefont is the public *performer*—the man whose whole personality goes forth so in representation and aspect and sonority and phraseology and accomplishment and frontage that there is absolutely—but I *see* it: begin it—begin it! Don't talk *about* it only, and around it.'

the feet of Peter' is in the National Gallery, and the museum of the Louvre, which, I am told, coveted his still smaller, but so intensely queer and intensely charming, 'Romeo and Juliet', has accepted, as a legacy of the late Miss Mathilde Blind, a highly characteristic production. In the 'Romeo and Juliet', painted with a childlike *gaucherie*, the motion as of a rope-dancer balancing, the outstretched, level, stiff-fingered hand of the young man who, calling time, tearing himself away in the dovelike summer dawn, buries his face in his mistress's neck and throws his ill-shaped leg over her balcony—this little gesture of reason and passion is the very making of the picture. There are other things, like his 'Cordelia's Portion', which have a little of everything, including beauty, but which are so crammed with independent meanings as rather to be particoloured maps than pictures of his subject. Everything in Madox Brown is almost geographically side by side—his method is as lateral as the chalk on the blackboard. This gives him, with all his abundance, an air of extraordinary, of *invraisemblable* innocence. The moral of it all seems to be that, as regards the question of success, the best way to fail to please is to fail trying. Then the gods *may* come down. A case of poetic justice much more rounded was when, a fortnight ago, Mr. John Sargent was made an R.A. He may not indeed have tried too slavishly to please. On the other hand neither, at last, has he failed.

THE GUILDHALL AND
THE ROYAL ACADEMY
1897

IF A CERTAIN terror, for the nerves, attaches, each year, to the return of the May 'exhibitions', it may fortunately be said to conform to the general remedy for trepidation, the truth that, when looked well in the face, danger diminishes, shrinks even and shrivels. The exhibitions are in short only fearsome till you march straight up to them; by which I mean not so much that alarm is then changed to interest as that interest itself, dropping almost wholly out of the question, leaves a residuum as faint, for the most part, in relation to the mass, as the smell of burnt paper after a blaze. The problem this year, at any rate, if problem it be, is complicated by the recurrence, at the Guildhall, of one of the interesting loan exhibitions of which the promotion has lately become a graceful added attribute of the Lord Mayor. Of the three main shows open to the London *badaud* the Victorian array at the Guildhall—enhanced more or less, of course, by a Jubilee glamour—is on this occasion in the same degree as on others certainly the most beguiling. Its effect partly proceeds perhaps from its pleasant air, in the sordid strife of the City, of almost romantic unlikelihood. You travel to those parts to snatch, if you can, a precarious dividend—a return, for invested shillings, not of the aesthetic order. Your prize at the Guildhall is in fact the greater that the usual shilling is not, as I remember, demanded. The length of your pilgrimage is indeed a part of your amusement, and there is even a little thrill—at least for the artist in general—to be gathered from the implication, vaguely discernible, of the final irresistibility of art. Piccadilly and Bond

Street patronize it, but at the Guildhall, with the civic chambers for their *salon*, and the big policemen for their servants, the painters themselves are the patrons. On your way in, or your way out, you may turn moreover into the great gloomy central hall, which used to be thought so fine, the scene of heavy feasts and heavy speeches, with its immensity of roof, its rococo monuments, and its legendary Gog and Magog nestling in the dusk of its gallery like dolls forgotten in the window of a bankrupt toyshop: to feel in a peculiar degree, among the echoes of pompous old toasts, that if the ironic spirit has found a perch here it can only be because the ironic spirit has, after all then, to be propitiated. I hasten to admit that there are actually on view, under the Lord Mayor's rule, works that are not a little of a nature to stimulate it.

Old and forgotten things, on these occasions, come back to us, the so-called successes of past decades, the hits and the misses of faded or flourishing names; and what is really interesting, in almost any connection, is the ordeal and the proof of time. We seem to gaze through the glass of a great green aquarium, with a few inhabitants, a few 'objects', well at the top, half out of the water and catching the light, and a queer majority scattered, at different depths, in an increasing opacity of submersion. At the bottom several are prostrate, motionless among mosses and pebbles. There they lie in a posture so tragic as to make it indelicate to look at them. Of the painters who, if my image have any truth, still play on the surface Sir John Millais is, this year, all the more interesting to meet that his absence from Burlington House, where he reigned so long, has more to do perhaps than one would have dreamed in advance with the melancholy flatness of the Academy of 1897. It is surely with him as with Leighton, that he cast across the desert a bigger shadow than we knew. We might find him falling lower, but he gave, even in his fall, what schoolboys call a 'back' to the show. It climbed a little higher from his shoulders, long as his shoulders had ceased to be those of the painter of the 'Blind Girl', the 'Huguenots' and the 'Ferdinand and Ariel', the three pearls, to my sense, of the Guildhall. The liveliest impression really to be obtained there is the intensity of reflection suggested by these reminders of that strangest of careers. I can think, in this order of matters, of no mystery more impenetrable than the comparatively common maturity of the man who had risen so high in his youth. The difference of quality in the two periods is not to be explained, the explanation not to be imagined, the hiatus, in fine, not to be bridged. The case would have been a subject for Browning, a story for him to have dealt with or got behind, as we say, in some replete monologue that might have been a match for his study of the bold Filippo Lippi or his elucidation of the subdued Andrea. The 'Blind Girl' would need only to be in the National Gallery to become a national treasure; it has found a home, if I am not mistaken, in one of the provincial museums.[1] Masterly are the power and the beauty of the sealed, simple, blooming English face, framed in its red hair and its country shawl and offered, in its pretty, pathetic, plebeian smugness, as a sacrifice to the vividness of the summer and the glory of the rainbow. Rossetti is also present in some force, and Holman Hunt, and Frederick Walker, and two or three others before whom it would be no loss of a moment to pause; but I can only stop long enough to make amends to the name of Madox Brown for not having mentioned the other day, in speaking of his own exhibition, where it was conspicuous, his 'Farewell to England', valuable perhaps supremely as an example of his queer, hard, ugly, but rich and full sincerity. Husband and wife, in the dreariest dress of the fifties—the bonnet-strings of the lady an especial desolation, united by their open umbrella and by the passion that forms peculiarly the artist's subject, sit hand in hand on the deck of a departing vessel and, in a deadliness of bad weather, a wonderful verity of wind and rain and seasickening salt spray, watch, with a heartache that wells into their fixed eyes and brings tears into one's own, the shores of their country recede. It would take more time than I command to give an idea of the curious 'middle-class' poetry and prose of this work and say over all that it adds up, as it were, to hand you, on a

[1] Now in the Birmingham Museum and Art Gallery.

total made grimly distinct and without an attenuating flourish, as straight as an unpaid bill. The intensity is extraordinary; marvellous the truth, the flatness, the directness of the 'British' note, and the wealth of drama in the faces; the force, above all, of the discrimination between the emotion of the woman and the emotion of the man. These things and fifty others make the picture surely one of the most expressive in the world.[1]

Wide is the kingdom of art, in which the critic must turn from it to Sargent's ineffable 'Mrs. Hammersley', the very finest flower of a method all shimmering off into mystery, with the same small and stale apparatus of enjoyment and reflection. I should endeavour to escape by postponement from such a shock to the machine, were it not that, this year, the year—heaven save the mark!—of his full Academicianship, Mr. Sargent declines even more than usual to be relegated. If I fly for delay to the New Gallery he is the only thing I see, and if I hurry thence to Burlington House he is certainly the very first thing. If one wished to make a great point of it one might, I suppose, remark that with Mr. Sargent's 'Mrs. Carl Meyer and her children' and Mr. Abbey's 'Hamlet and Ophelia', to say nothing of Mr. Shannon's conspicuous and abundant work, the new Americans, in 1897, have it much their own way. But *is* a painter an American, and above all a new one, after he has become an R.A.; especially a painter born, like Mr. Sargent, beside the Arno and with forty years of Europe on his conscience? The portrait of Mrs. Meyer, at any rate, may render the visitor of whatever race the service of simplifying his despair. It is so far higher a triumph of painting than anything else in the place that, meeting it early in his course, the spectator turns from it with a grateful sense that the whole message of that art has on this occasion, so far as he is concerned, been uttered and that nothing can be added to it by anything else he may endeavour to get into relation with. It is a fashion as old, I believe, as the Academy to say, any year, that the Academy is deplorable; so far as that is the case there is little at the present crisis to contribute to a breaking of the spell.

[1] Now in the Birmingham Museum and Art Gallery.

Never, since I have known these demonstrations, has the 'line' been held by so many dogs-in-the-manger, painters who neither make a figure nor allow others room to make it. The first year of the reign of the new President is literally an *année terrible*, with honours unaccountable rendered to productions unmentionable, some of them indeed works imposed by a fatal membership, a heritage of woe, but others, in no small number, hung apparently on their merits. A part of the general triviality springs, no doubt, from our missing the note of style, the note in particular of knowledge, as it was struck by Leighton and Millais. There were things that, on occasion, we missed in *them;* but evidently, after all, they could ill be spared. Knowledge and style are not enthroned in the vacancy.

There came over me as never before at Burlington House that wanton fancy, engendered from time to time by a picture, a book, a play, of reading into the impression produced, not the qualities of the producer, but those of the public involved or implied, the public addressed and aimed at, wooed, whether won or not, and on theory at all events to be captured. This is an interesting little game when played in certain conditions; it consists, strictly, in trying to brush from the mind whatever image of the great absorbent multitude one's own experience may have deposited there and in constructing instead, from the evidence before one, the particular multitude depended upon, in the artist's thought, to admire and to buy. We arrive hereby, according as the thought in question has been fine or coarse, at evocations the most various and the most curious. Reading three days ago *L'Orme du Mail,* the last loose flower—as spicily sweet as a clove pink—of the genius of Anatole France, my interest in the author's talent and subject suddenly, and under mystic coercion, found itself merged in an interest still more persuasive in the special group of readers, large or limited, posited, so to speak, by the imagination, by the intention of the writer. My glimpse of this group drew me, for the moment, by an insidious charm, from the insidious charm of the book itself, making me literally murmur to myself as I read: 'Oh, the adorable people; the intelligent, exquisite, delicious people; oh, the people to commune with, to live with, to work for!' So great a glamour could settle on the particular public that such an appeal could in good faith take for granted. Does any public so particular exist?—is any such appeal to be conceived as being really met? The answer, it seems to me, concerns only M. Anatole France: he alone can take the measure of the response, the success encountered. The game, for our own part, is sufficiently played when we have dreamed that there *may*, in the weary world, be such good company—that, in short, it would be the best company possible if it did provably exist. Playing our game, then, at the Academy, we evoke the responsive populations on which, as it stands, the Academy exerts its blandishments. Do they, the populations, in the same way, really exist? Are they rightly to be taken for granted? It is for the Academy, as for M. Anatole France to determine; the Academy only can sound the abyss and appreciate the affinity. What touches ourselves is simply the reflection that their existence would be a heavy blow to civilization if established beyond a doubt. What would become of any individual who should directly charge the British public with the vulgarity and ignorance that it is the effect of so many of the acres of canvas in question to nail upon it with a positive frenzy of the hammer? Exhibitions, in truth, are more and more cruel, and are not more misleading in anything, doubtless, than just in making such an indictment appear so collective. Individual pieces make their finer appeal and seek their finer affinity: the misery is that they are lost in the general loudness and glare. One would like to pick them all out, to remove them, wounded and dying, from the choking battle smoke and carry them into the cool, dim hospital of isolation and independence.

All the more happy then the painter round whom, as round Mr. Sargent, the royal tent seems serenely to close. The artist who is most of a master is anywhere practically isolated. The subject of Mr. Sargent's principal picture wears a pale pink satin dress with wonderful gauzy accessories and, sitting on a Pompadour sofa, presents to incredulous view a pair of imperceptible feet. Her dark hair, powdered or, in spite of youth, faintly grey, is raised high over her forehead and dressed with a pale pink top-knot and small black plume, and, though her type is markedly Jewish, the tinting, ever so delicate, of the space between her upper lip and her nose is not an effect of the shadow of the latter feature. She has round her neck a string of pearls, ineffably painted, that hangs down to her shoes; and one of her hands, raised to rest as she turns, against the old faded, figured tapestry of her seat, holds the hand of one of her two children, boy and girl, who, with their dark heads together, show, over the back of the sofa, shy olive faces, Jewish to a quaint orientalism, faces quite to peep out of the lattice or the curtains of closed seraglio or palanquin. Of these elements Mr. Sargent has made a picture of a knock-down insolence of talent and truth of characterization, a wonderful rendering of life, of manners, of aspects, of types, of textures, of everything. It is the old story; he expresses himself as no one else scarce begins to do in the language of the art he practises. The complete acquisition of this language seems to so few, as it happens, a needful precaution! Beside him, at any rate, his competitors appear to stammer; and his accent is not to be caught, his process, thank heaven, not to be analysed.

THE GRAFTON GALLERIES

1897

LONDON reminds one of nothing so often as of the help she gives one to forget her. One of the forms actually taken by this happy habit is the ingenious little exhibition, at the Grafton Galleries, of so-called Dramatic and Musical Art. The name is rather a grand one, and the show has many gaps; but it profits, as such places, in London, so often profit, by the law that makes you so often care less what you get into than what you get out of. With its Hogarths and Zoffanys—none too many, I admit—its other last-century portraits and relics, its numerous ghosts of Garrick, its old play-bills and prints, its echoes of dead plaudits and its very thin attendance, it happens to be for the moment a quiet bower in the bear-garden. It is a 'scratch' company, but it is only—I can scarce say why—in the portion in which the portraits of the day prevail that the impression is vulgar. Even there indeed this impression receives a grand lift from Mr. Whistler's exquisite image of Henry Irving as the Philip of Tennyson's *Queen Mary*. To pause before such a work is in fact to be held to the spot by just the highest operation of the charm one has sought there—the charm of a certain degree of melancholy meditation.[1] Meditation indeed forgets Garrick and Hogarth and all the handsome heads of the Kembles in wonder reintensified at the attitude of a stupid generation toward an art and a taste so rare. Wonder is perhaps, after all, not the word to use, for how *should* a stupid generation, liking so much that it does like, and with a faculty trained to coarser motions, recognize in Mr. Whistler's work one of the finest of all distillations of the artistic intelligence? To turn from his picture to the rest of

[1] Now in the Metropolitan Museum, New York.

258

the show—which, of course, I admit, is not a collection of masterpieces—is to drop from the world of distinction, of perception, of beauty and mystery and perpetuity, into—well, a very ordinary place. And yet the effect of Whistler at his best is exactly to give to the place he hangs in—or perhaps I should say to the person he hangs for—something of the sense, of the illusion, of a great museum. He isolates himself in a manner all his own; his presence is in itself a sort of implication of a choice corner. Have we, in this, a faint foresight of the eventual turn of the wheel—of one of the nooks of honour, those innermost rooms of great collections, in which our posterity shall find him? Look at him, at any rate, on any occasion, but above all at his best, only long enough, and hallucination sets in. We are in the presence of one of the prizes marked with two stars in the guidebook; the polished floor is beneath us and the rococo roof above; the great names are ranged about, and the eye is aware of the near window, in its deep recess, that looks out on old gardens or on a celebrated *place*.

One of the curiosities in Grafton Street is Mr. Sargent's portrait of Ellen Terry as Lady Macbeth;[1] which reminds me that I some time ago, in this place, recorded a vow to the painter in question which I shall perhaps never have a better chance than the present to redeem. His wondrous portrait of Coventry Patmore is now admirably hung in the National Portrait Gallery —a better place still than Grafton Street, at this moment, for shaking off the incubus. The National Portrait Gallery, in the brightness—if brightness be the word—of its new and final home, deserves more commemoration than I find opportunity to give it. It is intrinsically so great a monument and so interesting a show that one hangs back a little from meeting the occasion it offers to deplore afresh the baleful influence, the pennywisdom—whatever it be to be called—that, for the most part, in London, blights such undertakings. Great and interesting and, at least—to avert a longer scandal, substantially if grudgingly housed, these treasures have been treated with the usual meagre-

[1] Now in the Tate Gallery.

ness and given a setting which, besides being already a tight fit, is guiltless of a single element of style. If they triumph, therefore, they triumph by their remarkable character. One reflection, of course, is prompt—the inevitable want of coincidence between character of subject and character of portrayal. The great painters—so far as they appear at all—have often painted the small celebrities, and the small painters the great ones. On the whole, however, nothing is more striking than the number of honoured persons who have been agreeably figured. If the biggest pictures are not the biggest people—for both the legal and the regal professions enjoy, I think, an undue acreage—there are many mementoes that, as well as being precious on any terms, are both modest and charming. A treasure of treasures is Hogarth's tiny portrait of himself at work in his perfect little dress of a green velvet coat and wine-coloured breeches, a masterpiece of pleasant tone and reduced life. Delightful is Joseph Severn's small John Keats, in queer pantaloons and flat-soled pumps, trying, near a window that opens upon Hampstead Heath, to make himself comfortable, over Shakespeare or Spenser, on two impossible chairs—on the bare back of one of them in particular, and on a tired elbow and a brow-supporting palm; above all on what we fancy a headache delicious to posterity. One of the greatest good fortunes perhaps—if not absolutely for posterity, at least for the original—is Sir Frederick Burton's admirable drawing of George Eliot, as fine an example as can be met of the 'sympathetic' control of elements that might well at first have appeared uncontrollable. Mr. Sargent's picture —the subject so rich in character as to be a prize for a painter— hangs in the company of the great array of canvases presented by Mr. Watts to the nation, his own series of heads of distinguished contemporaries. Never more sharply than here, I think, has Mr. Watts brought home to us the space that separates his custom and habit from his few highest flights. No painter, surely, was ever so much better or worse than another as this one is, on occasion, better or worse than himself. Much his finest thing, in Trafalgar Square, is his splendid William Morris.

Not a little of the rest is silence. On this odd phenomenon there would be more to say, were it not that every lesson fades, in the halls in question, in the light of the great moral phrased for us by the Tudor and Stuart groups. This moral, startling perhaps in its levity, is simply the glory of costume, the gospel of clothes. From the ages of costume to the ages of none the drop is more than pitiful, and distinction is shattered by the fall. If you are to be represented, if you are to be perpetuated, in short, it is nothing that you be great or good—it is everything that you be dressed.

NOTES AND ESSAYS ON THE VISUAL ARTS NOT
REPRINTED IN THIS VOLUME

"Art," *Atlantic Monthly* 29 (February 1872): 246–47 (unsigned). (Comment on paintings by Hunt, Gérôme, Zamaçois, and Vibert exhibited in Boston. The comments on Hunt and Gérôme are reprinted in this volume.)

"Art: Boston," *Atlantic Monthly* 29 (March 1872): 372–74 (unsigned). (Comment on paintings by Foxcroft Cole, Daubigny, and J. Appleton Brown exhibited in Boston.)

"Henri Regnault," *The Nation* 16 (2 January 1873): 13–15 (unsigned). (Review of *Correspondence de Henri Regnault,* ed. A. Duparc, 1872.)

"Art," *Atlantic Monthly* 35 (January 1875): 117–19 (unsigned). (Comment on paintings by Wilde, Boughton, J. Appleton Brown, Mrs. W. J. Stillman, and Egusquiza exhibited in Boston.)

Unsigned Note, *The Nation* 20 (3 June 1875): 376–77. (Comment on portraits by Duveneck exhibited in Boston.)

Unsigned Notes, *The Nation* 20 (17 June 1875): 410. (Comment on a newspaper correspondence between Charles H. Moore, Hunt, and others comparing the merits of Veronese's "St. Catherine" deposited in the Athenaeum, Boston, with pictures by Millet in the same institution.)

Unsigned Review, *The Nation* 21 (26 August 1875): 137–38. (Review of *A Christian Painter of the Nineteenth Century,* the biography of Hippolyte Flandrin.)

"Paris As It Is," *New York Tribune* 25 December 1875, 3:1–2. (Comment on sculpture by Barye and Carpeaux.)

"Parisian Topics," *New York Tribune* 19 February 1876, 3:1–2. (In addition to comment on Delacroix reprinted in this volume, the piece contains a notice of the life and work of Isadore Pils.)

"Parisian Topics," *New York Tribune* 1 April 1876, 3:1–2.

(Comment on Gérôme's "Chariot Race.")

"Art and Letters in Paris," *New York Tribune* 22 April 1876, 3:1–2.

(Comment on work of Decamps, Marilhat, Meissonier, Boldini, with brief references to Delacroix, Millet, Rousseau, Gérôme, Rosa Bonheur, and others.)

"Art in France," *New York Tribune* 27 May 1876, 3:1–2.

(Comment on the Salon of 1876.)

"Art in Paris," *New York Tribune* 5 June 1876, 2:1–2.

(Comment on the Salon of 1876: Gérôme, Cabanel, Bouguereau, Moreau, Vibert, and others.)

"Parisian Topics," *New York Tribune* 17 June 1876, 3:1–2.

(Brief comment on the Salon des Refusés.)

Unsigned Note, *The Nation* 22 (22 June 1876): 397–98.

(Comment on the Salon of 1876, particularly on the sculpture of Paul Dubois.)

Unsigned Note, *The Nation* 22 (29 June 1876): 415–16.

(Comment on Victor Cherbuliez' s article on the Salon of 1876, with particular mention of Puvis de Chavannes, Paul Dubois, and Moreau.)

Unsigned Note, *The Nation* 23 (26 October 1876): 258.

(Comment on the monument to Henri Regnault.)

Unsigned Note, *The Nation* 24 (15 March 1877): 164.

(Comment on the sculpture of John Gibson.)

Unsigned Note, *The Nation* 24 (26 April 1877): 250–51.

(Comment on the military paintings of Miss Elizabeth Thompson, later and better known as Lady Butler.)

"The Grosvenor Gallery and the Royal Academy," *The Nation* 24 (31 May 1877): 320–21 (unsigned).

(A more detailed review of these exhibitions was published in *The Galaxy,* 24 (August 1877): 149–61, and is reprinted in this volume.)

Unsigned Note, *The Nation* 27 (19 December 1878): 388–89.

(Review of *Memoirs of Anna Jameson* by Geraldine Macpherson. Brief comment on Mrs. Jameson's art books.)

"The Winter Exhibitions in London," *The Nation* 28 (13 February 1879): 115–16 (unsigned).

(Among the works praised are a Franz Hals, the Queen's col-

lection of Holbein portraits, and drawings by Michelangelo,
Leonardo, and Raphael. Elsewhere in the same number was
printed the note on Whistler which is reprinted in this volume.)
"Du Maurier and London Society," *Century Magazine* 26 (May
1883): 48–65.
(Revised and retitled "George Du Maurier" for *Partial Portraits*
[1888].)
Notes on a collection of drawings by George Du Maurier at the
Fine Art Society, 148 New Bond Street, 1884.
(Printed in the catalogue.)
"Edwin A. Abbey," *Harper's Weekly* 30 (4 December 1886): 786–
87.
(Revised for *Picture and Text,* 1893.)
"Our Artists in Europe," *Harper's New Monthly Magazine* 79 (June
1889): 50–66.
(Revised and retitled "Black and White" for *Picture and Text,*
1893.)
"Charles S. Reinhart," *Harper's Weekly* 34 (14 June 1890): 471–72.
(Revised for *Picture and Text,* 1893.)
Picture and Text. New York, 1893.
(A collection of essays, including one on Alfred Parsons, be-
sides those on Sargent and Daumier, reprinted in this volume,
and those on Abbey, Reinhart, and "Our Artists in Europe,"
mentioned above. All essays were revised for book publication.)
"London," *Harper's Weekly* 41 (20 February 1897): 183.
(In addition to comment on Lord Leighton and Ford Madox
Brown reprinted in this volume, these notes review *The Life
and Letters of Frederick Walker* by J. G. Marks.)
"George Du Maurier," *Harper's New Monthly Magazine* 95 (September 1897): 594–609.
(Another article with this title, discussing Du Maurier as a novelist, appeared in *Harper's Weekly* 38 (14 April 1894): 341–42. A
quotation from it appears in the introduction.)

Stories and Novels Concerning the Artist and
the Work of Art

"A Landscape Painter" (1866)
"The Story of a Masterpiece" (1868)
"Traveling Companions" (1870)
"The Madonna of the Future" (1873)
"The Sweetheart of M. Briseux" (1873)
Roderick Hudson (1875)
"The Liar" (1888)
The Reverberator (1888)
The Tragic Muse (1890)
"The Real Thing" (1892)
"The Tree of Knowledge" (1900)
"The Special Type" (1900)
"The Beldonald Holbein" (1901)
"Mora Montravers" (1909)
The Outcry (1911)
"Hugh Merrow" (unfinished, see
    Complete Notebooks [1987])

Travel Sketches with Comment on Art

Henry James's occasional comments on the works of art which he saw during his visits to the Continent appear in travel essays which were later revised and collected in *Transatlantic Sketches* (1875), *Portraits of Places* (1883), and *Italian Hours* (1909), particularly in those listed below.

"A European Summer. VI. From Chambery to Milan," *The Nation* 15 (21 November 1872): 332–34 (unsigned).

(Revised for *Transatlantic Sketches* and again for *Italian Hours.*)

"A European Summer. VII. From Venice to Strassburg," *The Nation* 16 (6 March 1873): 163–65 (unsigned).

(Revised and retitled "From Venice to Strasburg" for *Transatlantic Sketches* and revised and retitled "Venice: An Early Impression" for *Italian Hours.*)

"Roman Neighborhoods," *Atlantic Monthly* 32 (December 1873): 671–80.

(Revised for *Transatlantic Sketches* and again for *Italian Hours.*)

"The Autumn in Florence," *The Nation* 18 (1 January 1874): 6–7 (unsigned).

(Revised for *Transatlantic Sketches* and again for *Italian Hours.*)

"A Chain of Italian Cities," *Atlantic Monthly* 33 (February 1874): 158–64.

(Revised and retitled "A Chain of Cities" for *Transatlantic Sketches* and revised again for *Italian Hours.*)

"Florentine Notes," *The Independent* 21 May 1874: 1–2.

(Revised and retitled "Florentine Notes. III" for *Transatlantic Sketches* and revised again for *Italian Hours.*)

"Tuscan Cities," *The Nation* 18 (21 May 1874): 329–30 (unsigned).

(Revised for *Transatlantic Sketches* and again for *Italian Hours.*)

"Siena," *Atlantic Monthly* 33 (June 1874): 664–69.

(Revised for *Transatlantic Sketches* and revised and retitled "Siena Early and Late" for *Italian Hours.*)

"Old Italian Art," *The Independent* 11 June 1874: 2–3.
(Revised and retitled "Florentine Notes. IV" for *Transatlantic Sketches* and revised again for *Italian Hours.*)
"Ravenna," *The Nation* 19 (9 July 1874): 23–25 (unsigned).
(Revised for *Transatlantic Sketches* and again for *Italian Hours.*)
"A Northward Journey," *The Independent* 27 August 1874: 4.
(Revised and retitled "The Splügen. II" for *Transatlantic Sketches.*)
"In Holland," *The Nation* 19 (27 August 1874): 136–37 (unsigned).
(Revised for *Transatlantic Sketches.*)
"In Belgium," *The Nation* 19 (3 September 1874): 151–52 (unsigned).
(Revised for *Transatlantic Sketches.*)
"Italy Revisited," *Atlantic Monthly* 41 (April 1878): 437–44.
(Revised and retitled "Italy Revisited. I–III" for *Portraits of Places* and revised again for *Italian Hours.*)
"Recent Florence," *Atlantic Monthly* 41 (May 1878): 586–93.
(Revised and retitled "Italy Revisited. IV–VI" for *Portraits of Places* and revised again for *Italian Hours.*)
"Venice," *Century Magazine* 25 (November 1882): 3–23.
(Revised for *Portraits of Places* and again for *Italian Hours.*)
"The Grand Canal," *Scribner's Magazine* 12 (November 1892): 531–50.
(Revised for *Italian Hours.*)

GENERAL INDEX

INDEX OF PICTURES